MARJORIE Y. LIPSON

Teaching Reading

Beyond the Primary Grades

⬛SCHOLASTIC

New York • Toronto • London • Auckland • Sydney
Mexico City • New Delhi • Hong Kong • Buenos Aires

Dedications

This book is dedicated, like the others, to my friend, confidante, and husband, Michael, and my cherished children Nora and Theo. I could not do it, and would never have begun, without your support and understanding.

Credits

Page 31: Strickland Model for Flexible Grouping. Based on a model created by Dorothy Strickland. Used by permission of Dorothy Strickland.

Pages 91 and 143: From *A Long Way from Chicago* by Richard Peck. Copyright ©1998. Dial.

Page 110: From *Passage to Freedom: The Sugihara Story*. Text copyright ©1997 by Ken Mochizuki. Permission arranged with Lee & Low Books, Inc. New York, NY 10016.

Page 126: Portions of Chapter 5 are loosely based on an article that appeared in the *New England Reading Association Journal*. See M. Y. Lipson (2003). Used by permission of the New England Reading Association.

Page 144: From *Dogzilla* by Dav Pilkey. Copyright ©1993. Harcourt Brace.

Page 209: QIWK Short Form. Adapted from Palmer, E. (2004) and Schlagal, R. (in press). Used by permission of Robert Schlagal.

Page 233: QT: Quick Text Level Check-In. Adapted from Biggam, S. C., & Thompson, E. A. (2005).

Every effort has been made to find the authors and publishers of previously published material in this book and to obtain permission to print it.

Cover and interior design by Maria Lilja
Cover photos: Maria Lilja and Blend Images/Veer
Interior photos: Pam Chomsky-Higgins and Marjorie Y. Lipson
Acquiring Editor: Margery Rosnick
Development Editor: Raymond Coutu
Copy Editor: Carol Ghiglieri
ISBN 13: 978-0-439-76757-6
ISBN 10: 0-439-76757-1
Copyright © 2007 by Marjorie Y. Lipson

1 2 3 4 5 6 7 8 9 10 23 12 11 10 09 08 07

Contents

Acknowledgments

I am indebted to a great many people. First, I thank all the wonderfully talented and enormously committed teachers who have taught me so much over the years. Some of you were my colleagues when I was a public school teacher, and your expertise, knowledge, and humor helped me survive, and then thrive. Some are teachers with whom I collaborated on professional development efforts. Some are teachers I "studied" in one research project or another. I understand the impact of excellent teaching because I have seen your thoughtful and intelligent instruction. There are simply too many to name, but I hope you recognize yourself in the positive aspects of this book.

I am deeply indebted to my talented colleagues in the Vermont Reads Institute and especially the literacy experts of the Bridging Project: Sue Biggam and Ellen Thompson, who have been with it from the beginning, and to Pam Chomsky-Higgins, Kathleen Harrington, Mary Beth Monahan, Cathy White, and Nancy Woods. These women are gifted teachers and compassionate mentors who are deeply committed to school improvement. The children and teachers of Vermont are fortunate to have such incredible literacy expertise available to them. Thank you for thinking, laughing, and arguing with me over the years.

I thank also the teachers, administrators, parents, and students of our original six successful schools and, equally, the three schools who were less successful. Their willingness to open their doors to our research team provided invaluable insights. We learned so much.

Thanks to Bob Pequignot, principal at JFK school in Winooski, Vermont, who was the first to insist that we apply our research insights to a new and challenging setting. He and his teachers are an inspiration; their determined pursuit of excellence and very hard work have demonstrated that all schools can achieve high standards—even schools where many students live in poverty and speak languages other than English. Special thanks to Drew Blanchard, Lisa Goetz, and Glenn Willette and their students for sharing their work and their photos.

I also extend special thanks to Liz Fothergill, Andrea Murnane, Amber Profitt, Cathy Smith, and Melinda Tate, who agreed to share their great work. Thanks also to their students, who are justifiably proud of the work samples in this book.

Without Ray Coutu this book would not have been published. He is an editorial genius—an author's dream. I am grateful to him and you should be too, since the book is far better than it would have been without him. Anything that doesn't make sense is my own!

Finally, I thank my friends and colleagues Jim Mosenthal and Jane Mekkelsen. I could not possibly name all the debts I owe them—for the inspiration I receive, the ideas I steal, the motivation they provide, the thinking that they've stimulated, the fun I have with them. Only they know how inadequate this acknowledgment is.

Foreword

As a teacher, teacher educator, and researcher in literacy education, I know *Teaching Reading Beyond the Primary Grades* is an important book being published at a critical time. Over the past three decades, researchers have established a consistent, powerful base for practicing comprehension instruction with emergent readers, adult readers, and every reader in between. Yet, the national agenda and many publications in recent years have emphasized early intervention for very young children, without addressing the needs of older children. At the same time, national and state assessments reveal a troubling pattern of students who are able to say the words on the page, but who struggle to understand the content of what they are reading. Marge Lipson's book provides a clear, research-based framework for detailing what is needed to help our students in grades 3 through 8 become self-sufficient, engaged readers and writers.

At the heart of the book is Marge's extensive experience as a teacher, a clinician, a teacher educator, and a literacy researcher. She knows how important it is for students to be active members of a literacy community and, within this community, receive high-quality literacy instruction that emphasizes the importance of building background knowledge, word knowledge, and knowledge of how texts work. She knows how critical it is for teachers to be able to organize, create, and manage a literacy community. And, she knows that to meet the needs of individual students, teachers need a range of assessment and evaluation tools and practices. Each chapter in the book provides critical information that will be useful to teachers, whether they are new to the profession or have taught many grade levels and hundreds of students.

For the past five years, Marge has been working with a team of colleagues, including grades-3-to-6 classroom teachers, in the Bridging Project. Specifically, she has brought together a career's worth of experiences as those teachers seek to reform their literacy instruction by providing a bridge between learning-to-read in the primary grades and becoming fluent, proficient readers and writers in middle school. She has been able to codify a large body of research—her own and that of many others in the field—to create a practical, useful guide to high-quality instruction.

TEACHING READING BEYOND THE PRIMARY GRADES

The book begins with a chapter that addresses big-picture issues related to effective comprehension instruction. In Chapters 2 and 3, teachers are introduced to possible ways of organizing the classroom to meet their dual obligations (Raphael, Florio-Ruane, George, Hasty, & Highfield, 2004). That is, they learn how to provide contexts in which *all* students, regardless of reading level, have access to age-appropriate texts and are held accountable for thinking about, writing in response to, and discussing the ideas in those texts. At the same time, they learn how to provide contexts in which *each* student is able to participate in instruction with texts at their individual instructional levels. While we may hope that all our students are reading at levels that match their ages, that is not the reality, as Marge lays out so clearly in her first chapter.

The subsequent chapters provide specific ideas for developing knowledge; teaching comprehension, fluency, and word-identification strategies appropriate to students in grades 3 through 8; and using assessment approaches that lead to sensible decisions about curriculum and instruction. I especially like the descriptions of what recommended instruction looks like in practice. For example, the description of Eve Gordon's classroom gave me a picture of the flow of a morning in which students were engaged in meaningful, extended opportunities for sustained reading and writing. It helped me see what the Eve was doing to provide instruction in whole-group, small-group, and one-on-one contexts. The windows into Megan Johnson and Andrea Murnane's classrooms showed me how teachers adapt research-based practices to meet their own goals—and, of course, I loved seeing that one of those practices was Question Answer Relationships! I appreciated the many lists of books that support recommended practices, including books for genre-based and author-study thematic units, books for teaching strategies such as perspective-taking, and books that can be used as anchor texts for leveling classroom library materials.

In the final chapter, Marge details how teachers can work within the classroom contexts discussed in the opening chapters to differentiate instruction for individual students, using the ideas for instruction and assessment presented in Chapters 4 to 7.

In short, Marge has written a wonderful contribution to the field, one that will be useful to a wide range of literacy educators and that is destined to improve the literacy lives of our intermediate and middle school students.

—Taffy E. Raphael

Raphael, T. E., Florio-Ruane, S., George, M., Hasty, N. L., & Highfield, K. (2004). *Book Club Plus! A literacy framework for the primary grades*. Littleton, MA: Small Planet Communications, Inc.

CHAPTER 1

Literacy in Grades 3 to 6:

Where Do We Stand?

For some years now educators and policy makers alike have focused attention on early literacy and early intervention. In many places, their efforts have paid off. More young children are reading better than ever before (Forgione, 1998; Vermont Department of Education, 2006; National Assessment of Educational Progress (NAEP), 2005). This is cause for celebration. However, an early investment in education alone cannot address the challenges of achievement in the United States, as recent findings prove. Unfortunately, getting off to a good start is not enough (RAND Reading Study Group, 2002).

Charlie

When I met Charlie, he was an active and talkative fifth grader from an upper-middle-class family. He loved to talk about the many places he had been with his family, especially Disney World in Florida. Books were another matter, however. He could not name a single book that he had enjoyed, and his list of things he liked to read was very short.

Charlie had glided through the primary grades as a bit of a clown. The skills-based reading program in his school focused on and rewarded accurate word identification, and Charlie had accomplished this quickly. He had been considered a good reader, one who could read easily and well.

Now, however, he was in fifth grade and struggling. His teacher reported that he read well but did not complete his work and was often "off task." The situation was so dire that she asked me to conduct an assessment.

I used a variety of (mostly informal) tools to examine Charlie's reading, and my assessment confirmed some of what his teacher had reported. Notably, his oral reading accuracy was excellent. He was able to handle sixth- and even seventh-grade material with ease. In addition, his rate of reading was good. At the same time, however, Charlie's comprehension seemed almost nonexistent. It was startling to listen to him read words so well and then find that he could not answer even the easiest questions about the text's content. Of course, he was even less successful in answering more complex questions and/or summarizing what he had read. It is not surprising that Charlie did not like to read, since he was getting so little out of the experience.

Almost every recent report and summary review of literacy achievement in the U.S. suggests that Charlie is not alone. The inescapable conclusion is that children beyond grade 3 are not performing as well as we would like. Reports by E. D. Hirsch (2003) and others have dramatically labeled this long-standing phenomenon the "fourth-grade slump."

The National Assessment of Educational Progress (NAEP) is one of the major methods of tracking students' literacy achievement across the country. Since its beginnings in 1969, it has been administered periodically to fourth- and eighth-grade students. The most recent results, published in 2005, indicate that there was no significant change in reading performance between 1992 and 2005.

Overall, only 64 percent of fourth-grade students and 73 percent of eighth-grade students were at or above the Basic level in reading.

It is important to understand how widespread the problem is. This matter of slowing student progress is not limited to struggling students, minority youth, or poor communities. As the table below demonstrates, fewer than a third of all fourth- and eighth-grade students are considered Proficient readers and, most seriously, many students (between one-fourth and one-third) are Below Basic.

In addition, students from various demographic groups do not perform equally well. Although students who receive free or reduced-cost lunch did perform better in 2005 than they had in 1998, these differences were not significant. Similarly, African American and Hispanic students scored better in 2005, but the differences were small.

Percentage of Fourth- and Eighth-Grade Students at Each Reading Achievement Level

Grade	Below Basic	Basic	Proficient	Advanced
4	36%	33%	23%	8%
8	27%	42%	26–28%	3%

Troubling patterns are also evident along gender lines. In reading on the 2005 NAEP at grade four, 78 percent of females were at or above Basic, but only 68 percent of males were. At eighth grade, 67 percent of females versus 61 percent of males were at or above Basic. Although this problem is pervasive across communities, it is much more serious among high-poverty and minority students. In 2002, the RAND Reading Study Group was charged with reviewing all available research on comprehension—both how people comprehend and what types of instruction might improve it. In their report, these researchers concluded, "The achievement gap between children of different demographic groups persists" and that student achievement in literacy in the U.S. has "stagnated."

These patterns appear to be the result of several factors, including the fact that the demand for literacy skills in society is much more widespread than it used to be. At one time, young adults in the United States could expect to make a good living even if they did not possess high literacy levels. This is no longer the case. Most well-paid jobs today demand high levels of reading and writing ability. Old standards of achievement need to be reconsidered. We need citizens who can not only read and write basic texts, but also think with print, solve complex problems using texts, and communicate with others in sophisticated ways.

To make matters worse, while the demands for literacy have accelerated, reading comprehension instruction in many schools is often minimal or ineffective (RAND Reading Study Group, 2002). In part this reflects the erroneous belief that accurate word recognition automatically leads to good comprehension (M. Y. Lipson, 2003). Thus educators and policy makers have traditionally focused attention on the word-level aspects of literacy, believing that accurate and automatic word identification would take care of any reading problems. Further, teachers beyond grade 2 often feel that they should not be concerned about reading instruction—that the primary grade teachers are responsible for this work. Unfortunately, even when students acquire high levels of word-level proficiency, they may not develop the other knowledge and skills needed to become highly literate adults (RAND, 2002).

Despite clear evidence that well-articulated literacy instruction is needed in grades 3 to 6, little attention has been focused on teaching and learning during this period. Too often, intermediate students are on their own as they negotiate the move from the primary grades, where they received daily guided reading instruction, to middle school, where they are expected to be able to read with comprehension in a variety of genres in order to accomplish a variety of tasks. What is needed is a bridge between good primary-level instruction and solid instruction for adolescents. This book is intended to lay the foundation for that bridge.

What Does Research Say About Reading in Grades 3 to 6?

It is becoming clear that students in grades 3 to 6 do not necessarily need "more of the same"—that is, a continuation of the modes of instruction they've received so far. To become more capable readers and writers, they need materials, tasks, and contexts different from those they received in the primary grades. "As content demands increase, literacy demands also increase: students are expected to read and write across a wide variety of disciplines, genres, and materials with increasing skill, flexibility, and insight" (Snow & Biancarosa, 2003, p. 6). Instruction for both on-level and struggling readers must respond to these changing demands. Reading in grades 3 to 6 can be viewed through two lenses: word-level concerns and text-level concerns.

Word-Level Concerns

Word-level concerns in grades 3 to 6 relate to both decoding and meaning. Most reading experts use the term "word recognition" or "word identification" to signal the ability to decode words and "vocabulary" to indicate word meanings. Therefore, when I discuss phonics or syllabication, I'll be talking about word recognition; whenever I am addressing the development of word meanings, I'll be talking about vocabulary.

Often young readers encounter words that are difficult to recognize, but familiar in meaning. Thus, while reading *Too Many Tamales* by Gary Soto, words like *cousins, bright, underneath*, or *stomachs* may be difficult for primary-grade students to decode. The meanings of these words, however, are not at all challenging. On the other hand, while reading *The View from Saturday* by E. L. Konigsburg, words like *claim, emerge, vigor*, or *hybrid* may be reasonably easy to decode, but their meanings may be unknown even to capable fourth- or fifth-grade readers.

Instruction in the intermediate grades must emphasize the meaning of vocabulary because researchers conclude that students who enter fourth grade with limited vocabulary are likely to experience significant reading comprehension difficulties, even if they have good decoding skills (RAND Reading Study Group, 2002). The problem is compounded by the fact that, as Andrew Biemiller points out, "current school practices typically have little effect on oral language development during the primary years. Because the level of language used is often limited to what the children can read and write, there are few opportunities for language development in the primary grades" (2003, p. 2). Even students who have relatively good vocabulary development can struggle because during grades 3 to 6 there is a dramatic increase in vocabulary difficulty.

At the same time, of course, word identification does get more difficult—even for students who have mastered phonics. In E. L. Konigsburg's *The View from Saturday*, the first chapter includes words like *electronic, commissioner, volunteered, counterclockwise, unaccompanied*, and *signifying*. These words are exactly the sort of "long words" that absolutely terrify many intermediate-grade students. Even though these students probably do know (or could infer) the meanings and might be able to decode them, they often panic—saying the first word that comes into their heads and moving on with a shrug. Applying decoding skills to multisyllabic words is difficult for many students in grades 3 to 6. To make matters worse, there are also many words that are *both* hard to decode and unfamiliar in terms of meaning, such as *benevolently, calligraphy*, and *domicile*.

In later chapters, I explain these word-level concerns in more detail and also provide ideas for how to improve both word recognition (Chapter 6) and vocabulary development (Chapter 4).

Text-Level Concerns

There is a good research base regarding effective comprehension instruction (Block & Pressley, 2001; Dole, Duffy, Roehler, & Pearson, 1991). Yet few schools have strong programs in this area, for several reasons. First, of course, many teachers simply have not been well prepared to teach children to comprehend text. For years we believed that comprehension would occur naturally as a by-product of accurate word recognition. The idea was that if we taught children to decode and recognize words, comprehension would take care of itself. We now know otherwise. The overwhelming weight of evidence suggests that comprehension requires more than good reading accuracy (Kamil, Mosenthal, Pearson, & Barr, 2000; National Reading Panel, 2000).

The limited focus on comprehension is a problem for students at all grade levels, especially children at grades 3 to 6, since the nature of reading changes so dramatically during these years. Students need stamina and motivation to stick with much longer and more complex texts. As well, they must develop the strategies for comprehending many diverse texts for a variety of purposes, "all the while developing their identities not only as readers but as members of particular social and cultural groups" (Snow & Biancarosa, 2003, p. 7).

In the primary grades, students generally do not encounter a balanced diet of texts. Nell Duke's important research demonstrated that young children read hardly any informational material (Duke, 2000). Fewer than 10 percent of the classroom books in primary classrooms are informational and less than four minutes a day are spent reading informational text! Clearly, in these early grades, students have limited exposure to varied types of texts. As students move into grades 3 to 6, they encounter many more nonfiction textbooks, newsmagazines, and other informational materials, all of which they are likely to find interesting, but also difficult.

Finally, the tasks that students encounter in these upper grades are also more challenging. Students are expected to answer higher-level questions, respond both critically and personally, find evidence to support their answers, make inferences about complex ideas, and connect ideas across multiple texts and contexts. Not only have they never carried out many of these tasks, they've probably never received instruction in how to go about them.

Teaching Reading in Grades 3 to 6: Taking the Steps to Improve Instruction

This worrying convergence of results has sometimes led to the conclusion that there is little that can be done for students in grades 3 to 6, especially for high-poverty students with few opportunities to read books and develop sophisticated oral language. Jeff Howard has rejected this type of thinking with his provocative assertion that "smart is not something you *are*; smart is something you *get*" (1995, p. 90). He argues that schools should be less concerned with how smart children are at the moment they arrive and a great deal more about how to help them "get smart" through powerful instruction and excellent, demanding learning experiences. I share his view.

This book is designed to help you acquire the knowledge and skill necessary to help students get smart. It summarizes what we know about effective literacy instruction beyond the primary grades, describing the types of classroom organization and practices needed to ensure that students achieve high levels of comprehension and sophisticated abilities to think with print.

I tell stories and share lessons from my own work and from the work of many educators and researchers. For more than three decades, I have been teaching reading and studying literacy. That work has taken place in urban, suburban, and rural schools and at universities. Many of the experiences I have had and the people with whom I have worked appear in one way or another in this book, so you deserve to know a little background about them.

I read my way to an excellent education from modest roots and I want the students with whom I work to have the same opportunity. I began teaching in a bilingual (Spanish-English) community in Milwaukee, Wisconsin, and then later taught in inner-city Washington, D.C. I always taught in grades 4 to 6. I love intermediate students' energy and emerging thinking. I like the books they read, the content they study, and their sense of humor and their willingness to take risks. Teaching them can be a joy.

I currently teach graduate and undergraduate courses and have conducted research on many aspects of literacy. For years I directed the reading clinics at two different universities. Ten years ago my colleagues and I (see M. Y. Lipson, Mosenthal, Mekkelsen, & Russ, 2004; Mosenthal, Lipson, Torncello, Russ, & Mekkelsen, 2004) began a study of unusually successful schools. In our research, we studied schools from all socioeconomic situations and added an examination of less successful schools, to be sure we could see how the two groups were alike and different. Although, affluent schools are more likely to be successful, many schools that serve high-poverty populations are successful, too. (See M. Y. Lipson et al., 2004.) We spent two years in these schools, examining all aspects of their classroom and school-based programming, trying to identify key factors that distinguished successful from unsuccessful schools. Throughout the book I share those findings.

Most recently, I have been collaborating with a talented team of literacy experts to apply the lessons we learned in our study to schools that are struggling. We are working with teachers in grades 3 to 6 in an effort we call the Bridging Project.

This work, and the work of many other researchers, has shown us that there are a number of challenges facing teachers in grades 3 to 6. Organizing and managing a complex classroom that responds to the enormous diversity and range of abilities of students is one such challenge. Dealing with comprehension problems is another. Too many intermediate students are inexperienced thinkers—they cannot comprehend multiple genres and complete challenging tasks. Other students lack the prior knowledge and vocabulary to read the content area texts; this is true across all socioeconomic levels. And, of course, some students are still struggling with decoding or fluency. They find reading too difficult at the word level. Lack of motivation and engagement is a common problem among many students in these grades.

To complicate matters further, assessment tools and strategies that were effective and efficient for primary-grade teachers are often not appropriate for intermediate students. In addition, there is often much more mandated testing occurring at these grade levels so that teachers feel they cannot or should not do more. Thus, teachers may not have the type of assessment data that would truly help them to differentiate instruction.

Some Background on the Bridging Project

The Bridging Project is designed to promote interest and expertise in teaching reading in grades 3 to 6. In these grades, children must "bridge" from emergent literacy in the primary grades to fluent reading in middle school, where they are expected to read with comprehension in a variety of genres to accomplish diverse tasks. Despite its critical importance, little attention has been directed to teaching and learning in this period. The project is designed to investigate the special challenges of teaching and learning in the "bridge years" and also to develop specific approaches and materials to increase students' literacy achievement in grades 3 to 6.

Drawing on Research and Practice for This Book

Over the years, my colleagues and I have learned as much as we've taught. Our own research and that of others indicates that a program designed to help students "get smart" needs a number of elements. Instead of arguing about whether children should be immersed in literature or whether they should receive direct instruction, we need to accept the fact that children need both. Further, the program needs at least four relatively distinct but interacting components:

1. Engagement and discussion of text within a community of learners

2. A focus on conceptual development and higher-order thinking

3. Instruction designed to teach comprehension and build independence

4. Appropriate approaches to develop word identification, vocabulary, and fluency

These components are important for all students but they only come to fruition against the background of effective classroom organization, effective assessment, and a plan for differentiation.

Each of the following chapters in this book is designed to address one or more of the major challenges we have encountered in our work. (See Figure 1.1.) I start with organization and end with differentiation. In between, I address ways to engage students in discussion, help students comprehend both narrative and informational texts, promote students' development of concepts and vocabulary, identify and select texts and tasks designed to help students become better thinkers, and explain how to assess reading in grades 3 to 6.

Each chapter is organized more or less the same way. In the first section, I summarize lessons from research and practice and provide both background information and instructional tools for the specific strategy being discussed in that chapter. Each chapter also includes a section entitled "Into the Classroom," in which I provide advice and examples related to classroom implementation.

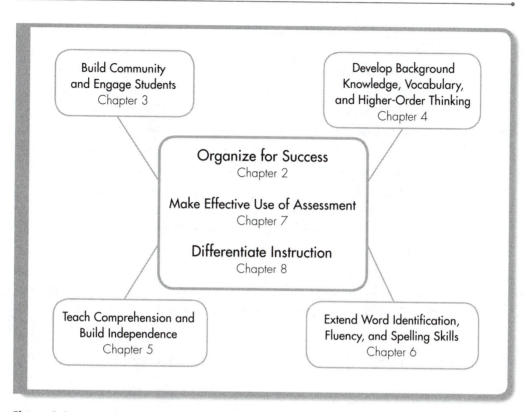

Figure 1.1 A comprehensive approach to literacy instruction for grades 3 to 6

Throughout, you will find descriptions of real classrooms, examples of student work, and practical suggestions for teaching students in grades 3 to 6. Finally, each chapter closes with three brief sections: "Concluding Thoughts," which summarizes the chapter; "Discussion and Reflection," which contains ideas that you can use alone or with colleagues; and "Digging Deeper," which lists resources for further information on the chapter's topic.

Concluding Thoughts

Despite the dismal picture of performance, there has never been a better time to be teaching in grades 3 to 6. For the first time, experts from many fields are looking closely at these students, and more and better resources and supports are available to those of us who think we can make a difference.

There is still too little research, but what research there is points to the intersection of excellent work on early literacy and adolescent literacy. Drawing from that research, as well as reflecting on our own practice, we can create a reading program that makes sense for our students. And there are lots of materials available to help. There are now more informational texts for students than ever before. A wide selection of novels and short stories can motivate students and keep them engaged with fiction. And more professional resources are available to help us learn how to teach with these wide-ranging materials. In the chapters that follow I will bring new ideas and tried-and-true practices together.

Discussion and Reflection

- What do the test data say about student performance in your school/district?

- What, if any, initiatives have already been started?

- What are your greatest challenges in teaching grades 3, 4, 5, or 6?

- What do you feel is your greatest strength in teaching reading in these intermediate grades?

Digging Deeper

If you are interested in exploring the issues in this first chapter more fully, check out these resources:

- "Building Knowledge and Fashioning Success One School at a Time" by Marjorie Lipson, James Mosenthal, Jane Mekkelsen, and Barbara Russ. *The Reading Teacher.* Vol. 57, pp. 534–542.

- *Reading to Learn: Lessons from Exemplary Fourth-Grade Classrooms* by Richard Allington and Peter Johnston. New York: Guilford Press, 2002.

- *Successful School Change: Creating Settings to Improve Teaching and Learning* by Claude Goldenberg. New York: Teachers College Press, 2004.

- *Teaching Reading: Effective Schools, Accomplished Teachers* edited by Barbara M. Taylor and P. David Pearson. Mahwah, NJ: Erlbaum, 2002.

CHAPTER 2

Organize for Success:

Block Scheduling, Flexible Grouping, Curriculum Planning, and Other Baseline Essentials

Highly sophisticated management and organization is a common feature of successful schools. Teachers in these schools do not just have orderly classrooms with few behavior problems; they have achieved something much more than that. In fact, if the idea of sophisticated organization and management conjured up a vision of a quiet classroom with desks in rows and a teacher up in front talking while everyone else listens, then you actually pictured a room more typical of our *less* successful schools!

John Burgess, multi-age teacher

John Burgess teaches a class of third and fourth graders in one of our "successful" schools. (See Mosenthal et al., 2004). More than 80 percent of the students in his school meet or exceed state standards in literacy. John's school does not serve an affluent population, but neither is it high poverty. His is a small-town school that falls exactly in the middle of incomes for his state. About 35 percent of the students are eligible for free or reduced-cost lunch, and class sizes are smaller than most urban schools.

John organizes his literacy instruction in a block of time that lasts from 10:15–11:35 on most days. During this block, several things are going on at once. Generally, the first half hour is devoted to language arts, which includes word work, spelling, and writing workshop, with mini-lessons interspersed as needed. Then, the balance of the block is devoted to reading.

John's typical schedule for the literacy block is shown below. His 24 students complete work sheets, engage in process writing and silent reading, and participate in discussion of a novel. Students work independently, in small groups, and as a whole class. John and his students (including one student with Down's syndrome and two others in Individual Education Programs [IEPs] for learning difficulties) squeeze a great deal of learning into the block. They do not waste time. John and his colleagues have worked hard to limit the number of interruptions during this time; no intercom announcements are permitted and no "specials" may be scheduled. His room is a terrific place to be because students are reading and writing interesting things and talking about their work.

Literacy Block: 10:15–11:35
Monday, February 1

TIME	ACTIVITY
10:15–10:25	John is meeting with a small group (the "Monday group" about their previous week's "Binder Work." All the rest of the students are engaged in some phase of writers' workshop; some were illustrating the setting and characters of stories they have written, while several tell me they are working on the "problem" of their stories.

10:25–10:30   John circulates and then begins very quick writing conferences with children who are creating stories. The focus of these conferences is generally on the content—what makes sense? Mechanical errors that affected meaning are also addressed at this time.

10:30–10:40   John does a mini-lesson on the use of quotations, something he had observed was posing problems for several students.

10:40–10:55   John pulls the whole group together on the floor in a circle. He conducts a "state of the classroom" check of all the students—asking what book they are reading and what page they are on. He notes this information on a chart. The instructional focus of the meeting is comprehension. The students are asked to compare and contrast the setting and details from *Little House on the Prairie* with those of their own stories (using "Ingalls's House" and "My House" as categories). John asks children to refer to the text to support their responses as they complete a group chart. He also asks them to think about setting in the other books they are reading.

10:55–11:25   John begins a reading group with six children; one child with special needs is with an instructor's assistant (IA), and everyone else is spread out around the room, reading silently. All children are reading from trade books during this time. The books vary in difficulty and appear to be self-selected.

With his small group, John begins with a read-aloud, and then students read with partners, stopping periodically to discuss. They are all reading the same book. The student with the IA is engaged in a guided reading activity with a different book. All are engaged in the *same type* of activity, adjusted for difficulty and length.

11:25–11:35   Whole-group debriefing. Everyone returns to the meeting area and considers the evidence from today's reading that relates to setting and details. This is an open-ended discussion, and John doesn't do a "lesson." Instead, he makes sure everyone is staying on topic and he looks for ways to move the conversation toward more complex ideas.

Lessons from Research and Practice: What We Know About Organizing for Success

Over the years, a steady trickle of research has been conducted on successful schools and effective teachers. One of the factors that has emerged consistently is that successful schools require skillful classroom management involving effective use of instructional time (Brookover & Lezotte, 1979; Edmonds, 1979; Mosenthal et al., 2004; Taylor, Pearson, Clark, & Walpole, 2000; Weber, 1971).

Observations and interviews in thriving schools all over the country suggest that these are complex places where multiple activities are often occurring simultaneously (M. Y. Lipson et al., 2004; Mosenthal et al., 2004; Taylor et al., 2000; Taylor, Pearson, Peterson, & Rodriguez, 2003). John's classroom is typical. A number of characteristics are shared by successful schools, many of them evident in John's classroom:

- Opportunities for large amounts of reading and writing
- Block scheduling
- Flexible grouping
- Purposeful focus on productive work
- A combination of independent and guided work
- Collaborative discussions
- Yearlong and weekly planning

Opportunities for Large Amounts of Reading and Writing

Students in high-achieving schools have significant opportunity to read and write, regardless of their socioeconomic status. Opportunity is created in several concrete ways. First, these schools have large numbers of books in the classroom. The classroom book collections are not only larger, they are more *accessible to students*. Books are displayed by genre or author in individual book cubbies, or they are part of attractive centers—both library corners and content displays.

Second, students in these classrooms spend extensive amounts of time on sustained reading practice as part of a planned instructional program. We found that primary-grade children engaged in continuous-text reading for 20 to 30 min-

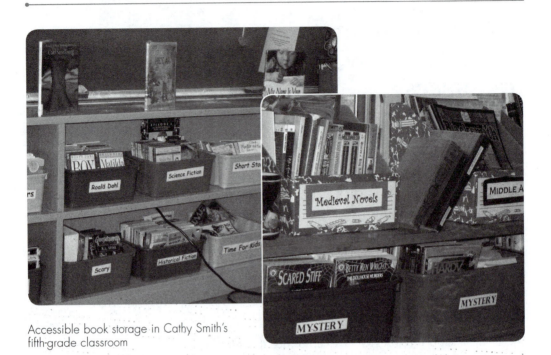

Accessible book storage in Cathy Smith's
fifth-grade classroom

utes each day, while intermediate-grade children read as much as an hour a day.
(See M. Y. Lipson et al., 2004; Taylor et al., 2000.) In schools where achievement
was lower, the amount of text reading time was significantly less.

Reading time allows students to practice skills and strategies, which both
our own common sense and decades of research tells us is crucial when learning to read. As Joseph Torgesen (2002) has noted, "Once the solid foundations
for reading growth are established in the early primary grades, further reading
growth is dependent almost entirely on the breadth and depth of the child's
reading experience and practice" (p. 24).

The amount of time children spend reading books is strongly linked to reading comprehension and overall reading achievement gains (Anderson, Wilson,
& Fielding, 1988; Taylor, Frye, & Maruyama, 1990). What may not be quite so
evident is how important reading practice is to developing both the ability to
comprehend and general cognitive competence. As Keith Stanovich (1992)
has argued, "Reading does make people smarter" (p. 226). In part, this conclusion comes from the fact that wide reading promotes vocabulary development.
Research summaries by two recent commissions concluded that both overall
exposure to print and independent reading promote and develop vocabulary and
comprehension (National Reading Panel, 2000; Snow, Burns, & Griffin, 1998).

Block Scheduling

Ideally, you and your students would have 90 minutes of uninterrupted time for literacy, which sets the stage for three significant accomplishments: (1) establishing a commitment to and a seriousness about the kind of productive work that is expected in literacy; (2) creating genuine opportunity to read and write for extended periods; and (3) reducing the frequency of transitions and, therefore, making the most of your time.

Of course, simply creating a 90-minute block does not ensure high-quality literacy instruction. Quantity is important, but the quality of the time spent is even more crucial. However, having continuous time does allow for some types of activities and certain interactions that are not possible in short spurts with frequent transitions. In addition, blocks provide flexibility. We can decide to spend a bit more time for reading today because we want students to write extended responses or to create genre models tomorrow. Block scheduling is not easy. The schools in our projects have sometimes required more than a year to fully transition to this more open schedule. Administrators must often take an active role since such large blocks of time may require juggling the schedules of specialist teachers—and even adjusting the start of the school day or the timing of lunch! In our experience, however, it *is* possible—at least four days a week, especially if not everyone insists on teaching reading/writing in the morning. Several of our original successful schools allocate the afternoon to intermediate literacy instruction so that they can make effective use of para-educators and/or special educators and Title I teachers.

The types of activity taking place during this block vary from school to school, and even from classroom to classroom. Throughout this book, I offer suggestions for instructional activities and events that can be used in these blocks. For now, let's consider two different, but general, models. Figure 2.1, for example, shows a comprehensive literacy framework that includes reading—both comprehension and word work—and writing. It starts with a reading-writing workshop but provides for word work and grade-level content development. Many teachers find this type of block schedule to be effective. The specific components within each part of the block may vary, especially if literacy is integrated with content in other parts of the day. For example, instruction and application to extend and reinforce strategies, skills, vocabulary, and grade-appropriate text content may happen during social studies, math, and/or science periods.

Sample Literacy Block for Daily Instruction

READING WORKSHOP: 30–50 minutes daily

1. Mini-lesson for whole class on needed skill/strategy (topic determined from work during all aspects of reading instruction)

2. Independent reading to practice skills and strategies taught in mini-lesson; use leveled texts at independent or instructional levels to extend the reading skills and strategies taught through the grade-level text as follow-up and as part of reading workshop

3. Simultaneously occurring:
   - strategy groups
   - guided reading groups
   - conferences with individuals

4. Focused whole-class sharing that connects back to the mini-lesson

WRITING WORKSHOP: At least three times a week for 30–45 minutes

Mini-Lesson: 10–15 minutes
Writing: 30–40 minutes
- guided writing
- conferring and coaching
- strategy lesson
- partnerships
Share Time: 5–10 minutes

WORD WORK: 10–20 minutes daily

Focus on Decoding
- Structural analysis
- Phonics (if needed)
Spelling
Vocabulary Development

ACCESS TO GRADE-LEVEL TEXT: 20–40 minutes daily

Core Commercial Program Anthology and/or Read-Aloud

- Instructional read-aloud to introduce the strategies, skills, vocabulary, and grade-level text accessible to all children (grades 3 to 6)

- Grade-level text accessible to all children in one of these ways: audio CD, guided reading, or independent reading to extend and practice the skills and strategies taught in the whole-group lesson

- Whole-class discussion

Figure 2.1 Sample 90- to 120-minute block schedule

You may prefer an approach that allows for different types of activities to occur on different days and with different groups. In Figure 2.2 you can see a blueprint that rests firmly on a traditional core-program approach (a literature-based basal program, for example) but includes differentiation and provides a great deal of opportunity for flexibility. Depending on the type of core text you're using, you may meet with one group for a long block while others read independently. On another day, some students may be working on a written response while others are still completing the reading.

Opportunity means more than time spent reading—or even the availability and accessibility of varied and appropriate texts. To be successful, we must transform a classroom full of books and a schedule that allocates time into a busy and productive place with complex teaching and learning going on. Of course, this cannot happen unless students are developing some degree of independence. The balance of this chapter explains ways to help them do that.

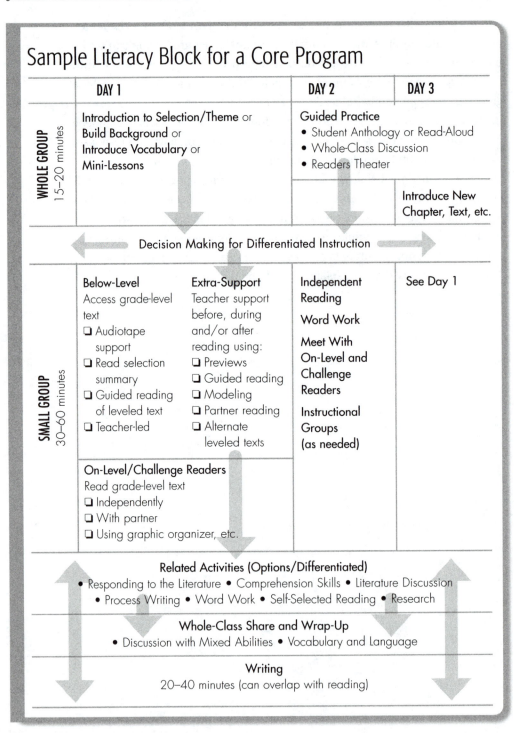

Sample Literacy Block for a Core Program

	DAY 1		DAY 2	DAY 3
WHOLE GROUP 15–20 minutes	Introduction to Selection/Theme or Build Background or Introduce Vocabulary or Mini-Lessons		**Guided Practice** • Student Anthology or Read-Aloud • Whole-Class Discussion • Readers Theater	
				Introduce New Chapter, Text, etc.

Decision Making for Differentiated Instruction

| **SMALL GROUP** 30–60 minutes | Below-Level
Access grade-level text
❑ Audiotape support
❑ Read selection summary
❑ Guided reading of leveled text
❑ Teacher-led | Extra-Support
Teacher support before, during and/or after reading using:
❑ Previews
❑ Guided reading
❑ Modeling
❑ Partner reading
❑ Alternate leveled texts | Independent Reading

Word Work

Meet With On-Level and Challenge Readers

Instructional Groups (as needed) | See Day 1 |
| | On-Level/Challenge Readers
Read grade-level text
❑ Independently
❑ With partner
❑ Using graphic organizer, etc. | | | |

Related Activities (Options/Differentiated)
• Responding to the Literature • Comprehension Skills • Literature Discussion
• Process Writing • Word Work • Self-Selected Reading • Research

Whole-Class Share and Wrap-Up
• Discussion with Mixed Abilities • Vocabulary and Language

Writing
20–40 minutes (can overlap with reading)

Figure 2.2 Sample literacy block for a core program

Flexible Grouping

The prevailing mode of literacy instruction in the United States, especially in intermediate- and middle-grade classrooms, is whole-group instruction (McIntosh, Vaughn, Schumm, Haager, & Lee, 1993; Zigmond & Baker, 1990). Yet whole-class instruction has consistently been shown to be less effective than small-group instruction for both students with and without learning difficulties (Lou et al., 1996; Vaughn, Hughes, Moody, & Elbaum, 2001). Barbara Taylor, David Pearson, and their colleagues, for example, studied more than 40 teachers in 14 high-poverty schools and found that accomplished teachers in effective schools use more small-group instruction than less successful ones. (See Figure 2.3.)

	Time Spent in Whole-Group Instruction	Time Spent in Small-Group Instruction
MOST ACCOMPLISHED TEACHERS	25 minutes/day	48 minutes/day
MODERATELY ACCOMPLISHED TEACHERS	29 minutes/day	39 minutes/day
LEAST ACCOMPLISHED TEACHERS	48 minutes/day	25 minutes/day

Source: Taylor, B. M., Pearson, P. D., Clark, K., & Walpole, S. (2000).

Figure 2.3 Grouping patterns and teacher effectiveness

Although the study conducted by Taylor et al. involved primary-grade teachers, the implications from both research and practice are clear: Students benefit from small-group instruction (National Reading Panel, 2000; Paratore & Indrisano, 2003).

One reason that small groups are so effective is that student engagement is typically higher and research shows that engagement is an essential factor in academic achievement. (See Chapter 3 for other ways to promote engagement.) Nevertheless, the success of small-group instruction depends on the quality of the instruction that takes place once the groups have been established. For example, Don Lou and his colleagues found that small-group instruction is especially effective when teachers match materials and instruction to students' needs (Lou et al., 1996).

Even though small-group instruction is clearly linked to improved achievement, many teachers in grades 3 to 6 do not practice it. Our conversations and interviews with teachers suggest several reasons why this is so. First, many teachers know that they should be doing more small-group instruction, but they cannot see how to do it with so many students possessing such varied abilities. Often they aren't sure how to provide effective instruction to the rest of the class while they are working with small groups. In Chapter 3, I describe ways to build routines so that everyone is productively engaged, allowing you to conduct small-group instruction.

Many teachers equate small-group instruction with ability grouping and are (justifiably) concerned about such groups' well-documented negative effects (see Hiebert, 1983; Juel, 1988; Optiz, 1999). The unintended consequences of small, permanent ability groups is especially worrisome. For example, research suggests that students in low-ability groups spend less time overall reading text, spend more time in round-robin oral reading, receive more lower-level skills instruction, and have only a limited experience with comprehension and higher-order thinking.

Flexible grouping, an effective alternative to ability grouping, "involves allowing students to work in differently mixed groups *depending on the goal* of the learning task at hand" (Optiz, 1999, p. 4). Once the goal has been achieved, the group is disbanded (and others are created). This definition highlights the importance of teacher decision making and also the wide variability in groups that might be formed in the classroom. Note that "ability groups" are not prohibited under this definition. Rather, they are formed for a specific purpose—such as providing students with practice in relatively easy text in order to build fluency and/or accuracy—and then eliminated once the purpose is met. (See Chapter 8 for more on differentiating instruction.)

Managing groups within the schedule is a particularly challenging part of teaching. One of the most sensible models for grouping has been articulated by Dorothy Strickland. It includes both focused homogenous grouping and heterogeneous grouping—an organized approach to flexible grouping. (See Figure 2.4.) The critical point is that during the week students participate in *more than one* group and that, at least some of the time, they are engaged in groups with varied abilities, interests, and experiences. Small groups can and should be used for a variety of purposes, including explicit instruction, guided reading, and peer support and discussion.

	GROUP 1	GROUP 2	GROUP 3	GROUP 4
	1 Tyler	2 Matt	3 Andy	4 Annie
	5 Susan	6 Daniel	7 Joann	8 Katie
	9 Marta	10 Jennie	11 Kamil	12 Kyle
	13 Sarah	14 Angela	15 Cathy	16 Brian
	17 Scott	18 Vladic	19 Amy	20 Brianna
	21 Elizabeth	22 Hannah	23 Jamie	24 Kyla
	25 Justin	26 Myra	27 Mark	

Multiple Homogeneous Groupings for Different Purposes:

■ Reading same book

▨ Instruction in skill or strategy, etc.

STUDENTS

Figure 2.4 Strickland Model for Flexible Grouping

Figure 2.4 shows a classroom with 27 students. One way to group them is into three or four mixed-ability groups along these lines:

Group 1: Tyler, Susan, Marta, Sarah, Scott, Elizabeth, Justin

Group 2: Matt, Daniel, Jennie, Angela, Vladic, Hannah, Myra

Group 3: Andy, Joann, Kamil, Cathy, Amy, Jamie, Mark

Group 4: Annie, Katie, Kyle, Brian, Brianna, Kyla

Another way to group these students is by the book they're reading or by the type of skill or strategy instruction they require. In this case, students 5–12 are all reading the same book, whereas students 17–24 are all in the same skills group.

Mixed-ability groups meet for any number of purposes, including these:

- Discussion of teacher read-alouds
- Discussion of jointly read texts (e.g., *Time for Kids* or common novels)
- Problem solving and projects

At other times, students might be pulled for different purposes and meet in different groups. Let's follow student 18, "Jennie." Jennie belongs to the mixed-ability group 2. Whenever her teacher wants students to discuss something in mixed-ability groups, Jennie gathers with the other students in group 2. But, Jennie belongs to other groups throughout the week as well. During the literacy block on Monday, for example, all of the students meet in discussion groups to discuss the articles they'd read in *Time for Kids* (a version of *Time* magazine written for intermediate-grade students); Jennie joins her mixed ability group for that. Then, she and her book group meet with the teacher to discuss and set goals. On Tuesday, she and her book group continue that goal-setting work. The teacher works with a group of students who need practice in fluency, but that group does not include Jennie. She continues her reading. (See Figure 2.5; note that bulleted items indicate with which group the teacher is meeting.)

MONDAY:	Meet in discussion group 2 for read and discuss *Time for Kids*
	• Meet in book group to discuss and set goals for the novel Jennie is reading with students 9, 11, 12 (all at about the same overall reading ability)
TUESDAY:	Meet in book group to discuss and set goals for the novel Jennie is reading with students 9, 11, 12
	• Meet in flexible group to practice fluency with students 1, 15, 20
WEDNESDAY:	Book group joins another book group to discuss how their novels (by the same author) are similar and different (Jennie and students 9, 11, 12 join with students 17, 18, 19, 20)
	Meet in discussion group 2 to discuss current events topic
THURSDAY:	• Teacher-led book group
	• Meet in flexible group to practice fluency with students 1, 15, 20
	Work with self-selected interest group on project
FRIDAY:	Peer conference (choice) in writing
	• Meet in flexible group to work on spelling with students 1, 15, 20, 24
	Work with self-selected interest group on project

Figure 2.5 Flexible group membership for "Jennie"

Purposeful Focus on Productive Work

Teaching really is a complicated matter—at least when it is most effective. Across many disciplines and over many years, researchers and practitioners have concluded that the most effective teaching and the deepest learning occurs in complex, active, and engaged classrooms (Corno & Mandinach, 1983; Guthrie & Anderson, 1998; Langer, 2001). Without a doubt, effective teachers ensure that students are appropriately engaged in instruction for as much of the available time as possible. Time is important, but time alone is not enough. The nature of classroom work is an important factor in our success with students.

Effective teachers make the most of their time by providing challenging and authentic tasks and by expecting their students to accomplish them. Most of us are well aware of the research that shows how high (or low) expectations can have an impact on student achievement. The earliest research in this area is decades old (Brophy & Good, 1970; Rosenthal & Jacobson, 1968), but recent research summarized by both Jere Brophy (1998) and Rhona Weinstein (2002) confirms the earlier findings.

"By expecting high performance from students, by setting high but achievable goals, and by positively reinforcing students, high-level learning can be achieved and performance recognized. One thing is for certain, if teachers don't expect much from their students, their students will not disappoint them. Low expectations are deadly for student performance." (Gore, 2002)

More recently, researchers have been finding that students of all background and abilities benefit when the standards are high (Au, Hirata, & Raphael, 2004; Snow, Griffin, & Burns, 2005).

In order for students to engage in productive, meaningful work, they need more than high expectations, however. They require classroom tasks that are challenging, cooperative, and hands-on and much less emphasis on rote memorization and teacher lecture. Students need knowledge-centered work that challenges their cognitive abilities and builds their understanding.

Fred Newmann and his colleagues have been studying the relationship between student success and challenging tasks for many years (Newmann & Associates, 1996). They study the work that students do in the classroom, looking to see how much actual constructive thinking is required, whether the task requires any elaboration, and how authentic it is. For example, a task may be difficult but not intellectually challenging (requiring only the memorization of many facts). Similarly, a task may be fun but not very authentic, because it has so little value outside the classroom—such as writing letters to the main characters

Student engagement and learning improve when assignments are challenging.

in a book. There may be value in memorizing facts and in writing letters to fictional characters, but without more-substantive assignments student achievement will not likely improve.

Some of Newmann and his colleagues' most provocative studies on productive work have been carried out in the Chicago public schools, in grades 3 to 8. Initially, they found that almost all of the work assigned to students in these schools was fairly rote—filling in the blanks, completing work sheets, and so on. But they also discovered something interesting. Although most classrooms did not contain much challenging activity, a few did. And in those classrooms, student performance was considerably higher. "Although giving challenging assignments does not automatically raise student achievement, it provides the necessary opportunity for students to demonstrate higher levels of performance, whereas low-quality assignments offer no such opportunity" (Newmann, Lopez, & Bryk, 1998, p. 1). In subsequent studies, they have shown that challenging, authentic tasks (as opposed to more conventional skills work) actually lead to much higher levels of achievement on standardized tests (Bryk, Nagaoka, & Newmann, 2001). According to their framework, authentic intellectual work has several key characteristics:

1. **Construction of knowledge.** The assignment asks students to analyze, synthesize, or evaluate information.

2. **Disciplined inquiry.** Students must draw conclusions, make generalizations, or support arguments through extended reading or writing.

3. **Connection to students' lives.** The results involve discourse, products, or presentations that have meaning beyond success in school.

Tasks that meet these criteria do not have to be elaborate or extraordinarily time-consuming; examples might include persuasive essays on self-selected topics, student-generated literature logs for guiding reading responses, or peer discussion about a mutually enjoyable book.

A Combination of Independent and Guided Work

The most effective literacy classrooms are ones in which there is a variety of activity. Students not only participate in teacher-supported, small-group work, but they also spend more time independently engaged in reading and writing (Taylor et al., 2000). Researchers have consistently found that successful teachers are much more likely to provide explicit instruction in how to read or write (Paris, Lipson, & Wixson, 1983) and, at the same time, guide students in understanding the relationships between and among ideas and concepts. Judith Langer found this to be so in her study of middle school classrooms:

In the most successful classrooms we are studying, teachers constantly make connections between the content and skills taught and used not merely within lessons, but also across lessons, topics, and time. Content that is studied at one point in time is always connected to something the students already know or have previously studied, and the connections are overt, so that students are aware of the links they are making (Langer, 1998).

Although successful classrooms tend to include much more teacher-supported and small-group work, they also include instruction that helps students manage their own learning to some extent. As I noted, students are more likely to be reading and writing independently for extended periods in high-achieving classrooms. This independence is important because students need it to become powerful readers and learners, and also because it helps teachers manage their classroom. In order to form small groups and use small-group instruction effectively, for example, students must be able to work independently over sustained periods on significant reading and writing (versus "busywork"). However, careful and continuous monitoring of students is necessary to make sure that they are using their time to their advantage. In addition, teachers must instruct students in the skills needed to sustain independent engagement, such as how to choose an appropriate book, how to manage writing projects, how to confer with a peer, and how to write a response to reading. Throughout this book, I will provide examples of how to do this in actual classrooms.

Collaborative Discussions

Judith Langer and her associates (2001) note that schools and teachers who "beat the odds" tend to have classrooms in which students work together. Successful teachers were much more likely to organize their classrooms so that learning was treated as a "social activity" involving interaction with peers about substantial content. Langer's data are as compelling as the results reported by Taylor et al. (2000)—in a somewhat different way. Among teachers in higher-performing schools, more than 90 percent engaged their students in challenging and interactive discussion. Among teachers in *less*-successful schools, fully 90 percent organized their instruction so that students did *not* work together. In fact, most of those teachers expected their students to engage in individual thinking without collaboration.

Reading comprehension and engagement improve when students participate in discussion. The quality of student thinking also changes—with students generating more inferences and using text evidence to support opinions (Gambrell & Almasi, 1993). Facilitating and sustaining discussion can be challenging at times. For example, I was helping three struggling readers attempt their first literature discussion with the book *A Taste of Blackberries* (Smith, 1973). Despite my best efforts, these three were having a difficult time listening to each other—they seemed to view their job as asserting their own opinions ("*I* thought the best part was . . ."; "No, that's not right"). Jake, in particular, had been argumentative; his demeanor suggested he thought this whole activity was a waste of time. Trying to help them dig deeper, I asked a fortuitous question:

MARJORIE: So, did anything surprise you in this book?

DANIELLE: Yes, that he died.

RACHEL [*who had been completely silent*]**:** Wait! *Who* died?

DANIELLE: Jamie—you know, his friend.

RACHEL: No, he didn't?!

JAKE and DANIELLE: Yes, he did!

[*Danielle grabs a book and begins to try to find the place.*]

RACHEL: How did he die?

JAKE: He's a lot like me. He gets in trouble a lot and he was in the wrong place at the wrong time.

This sophisticated connection to the text took me completely by surprise. Indeed, I don't think that Jake had been aware of his response until he began to discuss it with others. All of a sudden, everyone in the group was more interested. Certainly Rachel was—since she had previously failed to understand a major episode in the story. But both Danielle and Jake became more animated, too, because they now had a more personal frame of reference.

Into the Classroom

Despite the competing demands, we must find ways to devote large blocks of uninterrupted time to teaching literacy. The need for extended periods is actually greater in grades 3 to 6, since students are typically reading and writing much longer texts and having deeper conversations requiring more, not less, time.

A Typical Morning in an Effective Reading Classroom

Some years ago, as part of a research project, I spent a lot of time in Eve Gordon's fourth- and fifth-grade classroom. There is much to learn by taking a closer look.

As Eve Gordon's students enter her classroom, they greet Eve and chat with their friends, hand in their homework, and post current events articles clipped from the paper on the News Wall. By 8:15, with no visible signal from Eve, almost everyone has pulled out a book and has begun to read. Eve quietly gets the stragglers to commit to their reading and she conducts the early business of the day.

Whole-Group Mini-Lesson: 8:30–8:50

By 8:30 Eve is ready and everyone gathers around for morning meeting. Although everyone is relaxed and there is a bit of informal greeting and laughter, the focus is

Guidelines for Getting Started With Small-Group Instruction

- Establish a routine and stick to it.

- Teach the routines and the skills students need to be successful.

- Provide significant opportunities for sustained reading for all students.

- Plan so that there is some whole-class, small-group, and one-on-one instruction each day.

- For struggling readers, meet at least 20 minutes three times a week to provide extra "doses" of instruction.

- Make sure small groups meet every week to discuss texts.

- Monitor student performance frequently.

clearly on instruction. Eve wastes little time in introducing the mini-lesson that will focus students' reading for the day. She reads just the first page or so from three books that have intriguing leads (which she will discuss again during writers' workshop): *Anastasia Krupnik* (Lowry, 1979), *Yang the Youngest and His Terrible Ear* (Namioka, 1992), and *A Long Way From Chicago* (Peck, 1998). These diverse texts start quickly with vivid descriptions of setting and introductions to the families of the main characters. Eve explains that the settings of stories are often important to understanding the characters and events. She helps the students quickly identify the settings and time period of these three books (which are being used in various guided reading groups in her class) and models how she thinks the setting of *Yang the Youngest* might influence how Yang (the main character) reacts in this story. She tells students their response journal writing today should identify the setting and its influence on their character.

Flexible Group 1: 8:50–9:05

Before the students leave their team meeting, Eve reminds them that she will be meeting with two guided reading groups today and also with one group of students who have asked for help in writing responses to their reading. Eve tells students that she will meet first with the group reading *Yang the Youngest*. Everyone else starts on his or her guided reading book, does independent reading, works on written response from yesterday, or (in a few cases) works on extended writing pieces from writers' workshop.

Yang the Youngest is the easiest book that is being read at the moment; the reading group contains three struggling readers, one student who is a very good decoder but who struggles with inferential thinking, and two students who find the book easy to comprehend but who can benefit from the fluency practice and group discussion. Eve meets with this group first because they sometimes struggle to get started during reading workshop. She picks up the discussion where she left off during group meeting. Although the students were well into this book, Eve feels that they need to revisit the beginning of the text to really understand what Yang's motivations are later on. She uses the mini-lesson on setting to focus this rereading and renews the discussion. After some discussion and selected reading aloud, Eve asks the students to continue reading right there in the group (she plans to return to them a bit later). They begin reading.

Monitoring: 9:05–9:10

Eve circulates among the rest of the students to make sure everyone is on task. She answers a question or two and laughs with two students about an event in *Anastasia Krupnik*. She counsels one student to leave his writing and begin reading.

Flexible Group 2: 9:10–9:25

Eve meets with the students who are reading *A Long Way from Chicago*. This is a group of capable readers, but the setting (1929) and the dated language (e.g., "concrete overshoes" and "privy") are challenging their comprehension. The group has only just begun the book, so Eve wants to make sure they get off to a good start. She uses the mini-lesson on setting with this group, noting how the time period controls the story. She also makes reference to "historical fiction" and asks the students to begin a chart of the words and phrases that the author uses to establish a rural small-town setting in the 1920s. This also allows the students to clarify vocabulary and concepts. Once she is sure that the students are oriented, she encourages them to return to their seats to read the next chapter and reflect on the type of stories that are being told in this book.

Check-In With Group 1: 9:25–9:35

Eve rejoins the first guided reading group to see how they're doing. The advantage to staying in the group is that the struggling readers can ask one another for help with challenging words. As well, it tends to keep them all reading. Eve checks to see whether students have been able to use the earlier conversation to focus their reading. She asks several specific questions and then directs them to return to their seats to begin writing their response to the day's reading.

Flexible Group 3: 9:35–9:50

Eve meets next with a small group of students who have indicated that they want more information about how to write good responses. (Eve has also asked two other students to join the three who asked for help.) Eve has pulled several examples of good responses from other students' journals (with students' permission). She uses them to discuss specific criteria for a good response and to show how their responses meet the criteria. Then, Eve asks the students to look at a recent response in their own journals and to see if they can identify one dimension that needs work. Students read aloud and comment on each other's responses. Each leaves with a specific area to work on: length, better use of evidence, or good mechanics.

Whole-Group Meeting: 9:50–10:00

Eve calls all the students together and they return to the issue of settings and families within settings. Eve asks students who have not met with her today to tell the group what they noticed about setting in their own independent reading. Other students make connections to their books, and the whole class is reminded that attention to setting can enhance comprehension.

What Are Other Students Doing (When They Aren't With the Teacher)?

Because Eve and her students spent a great deal of time in the beginning of the year working on routines for independence, all but a few of her students can sustain themselves with print for long periods of time. So, most of the students are engaged with reading in one way or another. Here's what they're doing:

- Reading independently from books they have self-selected

- Reading from their guided reading book (either in preparation for a meeting with the teacher or as a result of an assignment from her)

- Reading with a partner

- Discussing the text

- Listening to the text on tape or reading with another adult (parent volunteer, special educator, etc.)

When students are not reading, they are writing in their response journals, working on their own writing, or working on word-work packets that Eve has prepared. Although Eve does not have centers, other teachers I have worked with do. These centers may have word-level activities (see Chapter 6), comprehension guides (see Chapter 5), or book group materials for sharing projects.

Yearlong and Weekly Planning

There are many competing demands for time and focus in the intermediate grades; districts and states routinely mandate specific expectations for literacy and content areas. Planning isn't just a good idea—it's a necessity.

Yearlong Planning

Creating ample opportunity for reading and writing and developing a purposeful focus on productive work requires a firm grip on the big picture of what must be done. We need an idea of what will be taught across the year, how the content areas inform each other, and what projects we would love to undertake with our students. In addition, state and local curriculum expectations and standards require us to plan carefully so that both literacy outcomes and content knowledge and skill are addressed. My colleagues and I have found it useful to create a yearlong plan that cycles through the year by alternating, for example, reading novels and units of informational text with more focused sessions involving lots of guided reading and shorter texts that can be used for explicit instruction. Using guidance from thoughtful educators like Heidi Jacobs (1997) and Grant Wiggins (Wiggins & McTighe, 1998), we do Curriculum Mapping. In Figure 2.6, you can see the sort of planning that we use to get a broad overview.

Yearlong plans are valuable planning tools that help us begin with the end in mind and create a road map for the year. They are organized by month and provide an overview of:

- The essential understandings and goals for the period
- The standards or grade-level expectations to be addressed
- The type of assessment that is relevant (e.g., major writing assignments, projects, performances)

Figure 2.6 shows the kind of plan my colleagues and I have used. Yours will, of course, reflect your own local context, goals, and standards. Within each unit, additional planning is needed for specific units, daily plans, and mini-lessons.

Yearlong Planning

SEPTEMBER	OCTOBER	NOVEMBER	DECEMBER	JANUARY
Literacy Strand: Building Community • Choosing your own book • Learning more about narrative stories • How to have a book discussion • Building stamina for reading • Selecting topics for writing	**Literacy Strand: Building Stamina and Making Connections in Reading and Writing** • Learning to stick with text • Making connections in reading: text-self; text-world; text-text • Using reading to model writing and vice versa (realistic fiction) • Refining book talk during discussion	**Literacy Strand: Using Text to Read and Think** • Introduction to nonfiction/informational text structure • Reading for new purposes • Using evidence to support responses • A focus on technical vocabulary	**Literacy Strand: Continue Nonfiction Focus** • Strategy: summarization • Strategy: monitoring • Using evidence	**Literacy Strand: Exploring New Genre** • Introduce new genre/text type (e.g., fantasy or historical fiction) • Strategy focus: making inferences, synthesizing, and/or visualizing • Author's craft: setting and imagery
Curriculum Link • Community (depending on social studies curriculum—local, state or global focus) • Environment or interrelationships (depending on science curriculum)	**Curriculum Link** • Any content can be used during this period	**Curriculum Link** • Any content can be used • Select informational text that is within students' instructional range	**Curriculum Link** • Continue nonfiction work	**Curriculum Link** • (Historical fiction connection to social studies unit, for example) • Using multiple sources of information • Influence of setting from a historical and literary viewpoint

Figure 2.6 Sample ten-month planning calendar

FEBRUARY	MARCH	APRIL	APRIL–MAY	MAY–JUNE
Literacy Strand: Special Genre and/or Author Study (Poetry, Folklore, Mystery, etc.) • Comparing genre characteristics • Authors' craft (depending on genre) • Strategy: questioning • Author study • Sources of ideas	Literacy Strand: Thematic Studies • Identifying theme • Addressing essential questions[1] • Using multiple sources—fiction and nonfiction—to consider major ideas • Strategy: evaluating • Vocabulary: a focus on Tier 2 words[2]	(2 WEEKS) Literacy Strand: Continue theme work	(4 WEEKS) Literacy Strand: Character Studies • How an author teaches readers about characters • Identifying character traits and using examples from text for support • Reading/learning about narrative fiction and nonfiction (biography)	Literacy Strand: Book Club • Self-selected literature • Individualized projects • Coordinating strategies • Rereading for fluency and enjoyment
Curriculum Link	Curriculum Link • Identifying theme and addressing essential questions • Viewing major ideas from multiple perspectives • Identify theme vocabulary	Curriculum Link • Continue theme work	Curriculum Link • Writing—characterization • Important people in history; biography reports in social studies	Curriculum Link • Selecting and revising writing pieces • Science topics (separated from literary work for this period) using literacy skills

[1] See Chapter 4 regarding themes and essential questions.

[2] See Chapter 4 for a discussion of vocabulary.

Weekly Planning

Weekly planning is an essential ingredient in the management and organization of successful classrooms. Because I am advocating a type of teaching and an overall approach that is multifaceted, it is important to use frameworks that have some flexibility. This is a delicate dance. If we plan our weeks too rigidly, there is often no opportunity to capitalize on important teaching moments. Too little planning, and nothing much happens. I like to start with big blocks of time—to make sure that there are places for extended reading, writing, and/or discussion. Smaller tasks, like spelling or fluency work, can be incorporated into workstations (see Chapter 8) or during flexible group time.

Intermediate-grade students are capable of adjusting to changing daily/weekly schedules. Every week does not need to be identical to the one before. Realistically, of course, it's not practical or even desirable to change too frequently. As children move toward greater proficiency, they do not need to meet every single day with the teacher. Indeed, too much guided reading can undermine students' independence and stamina. In Figure 2.7 you'll see two of the types of schedule we use. Of course, these are only examples. You may have fewer groups and/or the specific needs of your students may vary. As well, you may want to have groups like these only four days a week, preserving the fifth day for other types of literary activities or projects.

Sample Weekly Schedule A

Over a five-day period (90 minutes daily)

Whole Group (WG): Mini-Lesson and Group Share

Group A: Fluency development

Groups B and C: Guided reading of ability-level texts

Groups D and E: Comprehension and vocabulary development

MONDAY	TUESDAY	WEDNESDAY	THURSDAY	FRIDAY
WG: 30 min. Read-Aloud and Mini-Lesson	**WG:** 20 min.	**WG:** 30 min. Read-Aloud and Mini-Lesson	**WG:** 10 min.	**WG:** 10 min.
	C: 15 min.		**A:** 10 min.	**B:** 10 min.
A: 10 min.	**D:** 15 min.	**D:** 25 min.	**B:** 20 min.	**D:** 15 min.
B: 15 min.	**E:** 20 min.	**E:** 25 min.	**C:** 20 min.	**E:** 15 min.
D: 20 min.	**WG:** 10 min. Community Share	**WG:** 10 min. Community Share	**WG:** 10 min. Community Share	**WG:** 10 min. Community Share
WG: 10 min. Community Share				

15–30 minutes of self-regulated independent reading

→

Students who are not meeting with the teacher are reading or writing
with independently chosen and/or assigned texts.

Figure 2.7a

Sample Weekly Schedule B

Over a five-day period (90 minutes daily)

Whole Group (WG): Mini-Lesson and Group Share

Group A: Fluency development

Groups B, C, and D: Guided reading of ability-level texts

Group E: Vocabulary and/or English-language development
                      (may include members from groups B, C, D)

Group F: Phonics development and word work (includes members
                      from groups B, C, D)

MONDAY	TUESDAY	WEDNESDAY	THURSDAY	FRIDAY
WG: 30 min. Read-Aloud and Genre Lesson Guided Reading Group: 15 min. Guided Reading Group: 20 min. E: 15 min. WG: 10 min. Community Share	WG: 15 min. Guided Reading Group: 20 min Guided Reading Group: 20 min F: 20 min. WG: 10 min. Community Share	WG: 15 min. A: 15 min. E: 20 min. Mixed-Ability Discussion Groups: 25 min. WG: 10 min. Community Share	WG: 10 min. Guided Reading Group: 20 min. Guided Reading Group: 20 min. F: 20 min. WG: 10 min. Community Share	WG: 10 min. E: 15 min. Mixed-Ability Discussion Groups: 35 min. E: 20 min. WG: 10 min. Community Share

15–30 minutes of self-regulated independent reading

→

Students who are not meeting with the teacher are reading or writing
with independently chosen and/or assigned texts.

Figure 2.7b

TEACHING READING BEYOND THE PRIMARY GRADES

Once these big frameworks are in place, we can plan for instructional groups. Because I use flexible groups, these instructional plans must be easy to use. On page 48, you'll find a reproducible version of the plan we use for guided reading groups. (See Chapter 4 for further discussion of guided reading.) Of course, more detailed planning is necessary for longer-term projects such as units or author studies. (See Chapters 4 and 5 for examples of this type of unit.)

Concluding Thoughts

Teaching students in grades 3 to 6 is challenging work. Very little else will matter if classroom focus, management, and organization are not in place. I have worked with very bright, very interesting, very caring teachers who were not as effective as they might have been because they were not able to organize for success. At the same time, I frequently work with teachers who still have a lot to learn about teaching reading who are quite effective because they have put the basic building blocks in place. When we organize so that every day includes literacy teaching, student reading, small-group instruction, and a focus on productive work, good things happen. It is not necessary to do everything all at once. Begin by organizing to do something new, and little by little it's possible to add new things. It's always possible to change your structures and plans once the students are more adept and you feel more comfortable (in fact it's inevitable). I tell people to just *start*.

Discussion and Reflection

- Which elements of effective classroom organization discussed here do you practice? Are there areas where you feel that you would like to make changes? Try something new?

- Discuss flexible grouping. How is it related to your own grouping practices?

- Take another look at the description of Eve Gordon's class. What elements of this classroom stood out for you? Discuss your reactions with a colleague.

- Work with your colleagues to develop a schedule that is the most productive, given your school.

Guided Reading Planning Guide

Week _____ Group _____

Instructional Focus/Objectives _____

MONDAY	TUESDAY	WEDNESDAY	THURSDAY	FRIDAY
Focus/objective _____	Focus/objective _____	Focus/objective _____	Focus/objective _____	Focus/objective _____
Text _____	Text _____	Text _____	Text _____	Text _____
Vocabulary	Vocabulary	Vocabulary	Vocabulary	Vocabulary
Before Reading	Before Reading	Before Reading	Before Reading	Before Reading
During Reading	During Reading	During Reading	During Reading	During Reading
After Reading	After Reading	After Reading	After Reading	After Reading

Digging Deeper

If you are interested in reading more about classroom organization and management check out these references:

- *Flexible Grouping in Reading* by Michael Opitz. New York: Scholastic, 1999.

- *Modifying the Four Blocks for Upper Grades: Matching Strategies to Students' Needs* by Cheryl Sigmon. Greenboro, NC: Carson-Dellosa, 2002.

- *Practice with Purpose: Literacy Work Stations for Grades 3-5* by Debbie Diller. Portland, ME: Stenhouse, 2005.

- *Seeking Diversity: Language Arts with Adolescents* by Linda Rief. Portsmouth, NH: Heinemann, 1992.

CHAPTER 3

Build Community and Engage Students

Every educator knows that literacy is not accomplished in schools alone. Many children participate in social groups devoted to story time or reading and writing in settings such as day care, preschool, clubs, and church groups. These social contexts "shape the purposes, conditions, constraints, audiences, standards, and motivation to engage in reading and writing activities" (M. Y. Lipson & Wixson, 2003). They influence how students think about reading and writing and whether they come to school with anticipation or with dread. Students live in complex worlds that involve home,

Terrell

I met Terrell many years ago, when I began teaching in Washington, D.C. He was in my fourth-grade class and could not read at all. The only word I was sure that he could read was his own nickname, Tuno. Tuno fought with everyone, refused to go to any reading group, and could not read any of the available texts. In desperation, I borrowed a technique from the primary grades called "experience charts." Daily, I posted three- or four-sentence stories about what I had seen Tuno doing on the playground or things I knew he liked. I changed these stories each day by simply flipping the page and writing a new one, but I did not call the class's attention to them. Nevertheless, they created quite a stir in the classroom, and Tuno was always eager to have a classmate read the stories to him. Within a week, Tuno asked why *he* never got to have a reading group! I told him I thought we could probably work it into the schedule. Within a month, Tuno had begun to dictate his own stories, which he could reread comfortably. At about the time that Tuno started losing interest in the technique, his mother appeared in my classroom with no warning. She was an imposing woman with a reputation for criminal activity; all of my students fell silent when they saw her. She introduced herself to me and then—loudly enough for everyone to hear—announced that she had heard that I was teaching Tuno to read. I said we were working on it. She said that I should know that Tuno wanted a bike as a Christmas present, and she would be checking in with me to see whether he was working hard enough to earn it. What a gift for *me*: periodic contact with Tuno's mother for the rest of the year! By the end of the year, Tuno was reading. Not as well as his peers, but he was reading.

community, and school. These various communities are not always compatible, and we are not always lucky enough to have a mother like Terrell's, profiled in the box above, as an ally.

We cannot change these external conditions. We can, however, make the most of the social community that is our school and classroom. It is easy to forget why we teach children how to read and what we want them to learn. Everyone who really loves to read knows that teaching skills and strategies, as important as they are, is not enough. To cultivate thoughtful, even passionate, readers requires that we help students learn how to interact with text and with each other.

In this chapter, I will discuss the role of motivation and engagement in learning to read, describing elements that improve students' desire and interest. I'll present specific ideas for promoting students' response and discussion. In addition, I will describe how techniques like reading aloud and thinking aloud can both create a sense of community and increase students' knowledge and motivation.

Lessons From Research and Practice: What We Know About Building Community and Engaging Students

In recent years, researchers and educators have begun to recognize that school communities have a culture, just as other communities do, meaning they have beliefs, customs, practices, and social behaviors that define them. It is becoming increasingly clear how important community can be to the success of a school's literacy program. In this section I explore that idea.

Building Community

Despite variations in teaching practice and experience, the teachers in successful schools believe that everyone in their building has the common good in mind and is responsible for student outcomes. These teachers have a shared vision of where they are headed. They frequently talk about how everyone is responsible for *all* students. They believe that children can succeed and have a mutual respect for each other. The school culture matters, and building a collaborative community with high expectations and a climate of commitment is critical to success. In our studies, success is the result of the intelligent and committed actions of the professionals in the school.

Community-building doesn't end at the schoolhouse door. Research shows that when members of a school community reach out to members of the larger community, students' performance improves (Goldenberg, 1993; Moll, 1992). Especially in diverse communities, the relationships between school and the larger local community are important to student achievement (Reyes, Scribner, & Scribner, 1999). Over and over in our work and in the work of others, we see that one size does *not* fit all. Across the U.S., children live in communities where the adults have varying expectations, aspirations, and abilities to be supportive. In the same way that particular instructional approaches must be adapted for specific students, schools needs to adapt to the needs of the student body and local community. I will talk about the need to appreciate and respond to specific cultural differences in Chapter 8.

Changing the culture of a school can be extremely time-consuming, but it's time well spent. While that is happening, we can create classrooms that increase student engagement and deepen their thinking. Dick Allington, Peter Johnston, and Jeni Day studied 30 exemplary fourth-grade teachers from five different states (New York, Texas, California, New Jersey, and New Hampshire) and remarked on the striking nature of classroom talk. First, they noticed how *much* these teachers and their students talked. And, then, they noticed the quality of the talk:

> Talk between teacher and student was personalized and personal. Even the instructional talk was often conversational; with teachers engaging students in discussions of their understandings, responses, and puzzlements. Teachers encouraged students to engage each other's ideas; authority was more distributed than centralized. (2002, p. 463)

Research repeatedly suggests that learning communities in which teachers and students engage in productive, lively, meaningful dialogue are the hallmark of successful classrooms.

Engaging Students

One of the things that we worry about most in grades 3 to 6 is students' motivation—or lack of it. Without a positive "disposition" toward reading, students cannot become mature readers. As Susan Villaume and Edna Brabham (2002) have noted, negative dispositions can actually interfere with thoughtful reading. They describe students whose "sullen expression, silent apathy, defiant remarks, or distracting and outlandish responses" are significant barriers to reading and learning (p. 673). They also describe students who are "disenfranchised"— students who are simply "doing school reading assignments" without any real expectation of meaning or success. These students appear to mistake compliance for engagement, and of course, teachers can make the same mistake.

Some years ago in our university reading clinic, we had a sixth-grade student named Andrew. Although he had been with us for six months, Andrew was not making progress at school. In fact, he was falling further behind. In an effort to get a better idea about what was happening for Andrew, we had him read a brief portion of text and then tell us about the experience:

TEACHER:	What were you doing and thinking as you read that part?
ANDREW:	Not much.
TEACHER:	Did that part make sense?
ANDREW:	Not really.
TEACHER:	Is there anything you could do that might help you understand it better?
ANDREW:	I don't know. You tell me—you're the teacher.

Andrew was prepared to read and even reread the passage; he was *compliant*, but he was not inclined to apply strategies or get involved in the reading.

John Guthrie and Alan Wigfield (2000) have studied motivation and engagement for many years. In a comprehensive review of the research, they concluded that although instructional techniques and methods are important, they do not appear to affect students' performance or achievement directly. Instead, changes in student outcomes appear to occur in relation to the level of student engagement, including its sustainability over time. This means that we must take into account the degree to which students engage (or disengage) over time in a learning task.

I realized this when I was teaching grades 5 and 6 in the inner core of Washington, D.C. My students were all from high-poverty homes and most were struggling academically. Colleagues and I formed a multi-age team and worked with them to improve their reading. After two years, most of our students were reading on or above grade level, at least as measured on standardized tests. However, although they *could* read, most of them chose not to. Very few carried books home from the library and none engaged in book talk voluntarily. As a result, their literary development was neither broad nor deep. They were not reading enough to become really good readers. More than explicit instruction was needed to turn this picture around.

Years later, Scott Paris, Karen Wixson, and I concluded that if students are to become accomplished readers, they need both intellectual and cognitive "skill" and affective "will" (Paris, Lipson, & Wixson, 1983). It is not enough to know what to do and how to do it, one also must want to do it. Unfortunately, all of the available research suggests that students' interest in and motivation for reading decline in the intermediate grades (Guthrie & Wigfield, 2000). By middle school, the problem reaches a critical level. The research also suggests that it does not have to be that way.

Techniques for Building Community and Engaging Students

John Guthrie's research on student engagement led him to argue that "instructional context fosters engagement processes and reading outcomes [and that] students who participate in a 'community of learners' are more likely to be intrinsically motivated readers" (Guthrie, 2001, Motivation research section, para. 4).

Like others, Guthrie concluded that students' learning and motivation improve in classrooms that promote collaboration and community. Lessons from research and practice point to an array of socially based instructional techniques. Specifically, students need opportunities to do the following:

- Practice sustained reading and writing
- Choose reading materials
- Respond to reading in a variety of ways
- Discuss diverse texts
- Hear texts read aloud and teachers think aloud

As I discuss these elements in this chapter, I point out how they promote motivation and engagement. Creating a sense of community is not just a good idea for students in grades 3 to 6, it is an essential task because it increases students' interest in and commitment to learning.

Opportunities to Practice Sustained Reading and Writing

Both research and our own common sense tell us that students must have many opportunities to practice in order to become proficient in any skill. With complicated and complex abilities like reading and writing, this practice needs to take many forms over many years. Keith Stanovich has studied many aspects of reading and has concluded that more is better:

> All things being equal, more reading leads to more rapid growth in vocabulary and other knowledge bases. However, other things are not equal. Better readers read more. The greater reading volume then leads to precisely the things— more differentiated vocabulary, language awareness and knowledge—that serve to make subsequent reading easier and thus more enjoyable, thereby leading to even higher

levels of print exposure which in turn, etc. etc. etc. . . . Reading does make people smarter. (1992, p. 226)

Sustained Silent Reading (SSR)

During the pivotal grades 3 to 6, students should engage in significant amounts of reading practice. SSR, which is sometimes called DEAR (Drop Everything and Read) or SQUIRT (Sustained Quiet Reading Time), has come under fire in recent years; there is mixed evidence about its impact. (See NRP, 2000.) Although the impact on fluency or decoding may be unclear, there is very solid research that SSR increases vocabulary and comprehension, as well as interest in, and motivation for, reading (Nagy, Herman, & Anderson, 1985; Ozburn, 1995; Sadowski, 1980; Valeri-Gold, 1995).

Further, when students are permitted to read from materials of their own choosing, when the classroom library provides access to a wide range of literature, and when teachers model silent reading themselves, the benefits are considerable. One of the benefits is increased stamina, or the ability to stick with a text. Since many intermediate grade students find it difficult to read longer books, this sustained practice is critical.

In Janice Pilgreen's helpful book, *The SSR Handbook: How to Organize and Manage a Sustained Silent Reading Program* (2000), she argues that students need 15- to 45-minute periods at least twice a week to develop the reading habit. This is similar to the time periods we see allotted in successful schools, where

students generally have between 25 and 50 minutes of sustained reading three times a week in grades 4 to 6. This sustained reading may occur during daily reading workshop or it may occur during a set-aside period.

The value of sustained reading is enhanced when students have an opportunity to discuss their reading in "community share time" (Raphael, Kehus, & Damphousse, 2001). Even when children are all reading different texts, some

Students engaged in sustained silent reading

TEACHING READING BEYOND THE PRIMARY GRADES

common elements can be discussed. For example, one week everyone in the class may focus on "character," while another week students will look for vivid language or common themes. Simply sharing a particularly moving part of a story can be a powerful motivator for students. Literary discussions like these not only improve reading proficiency but also build classroom community.

Opportunities to Choose Reading Materials

It is important to allot time every week for students to read texts of their own choosing. However, students also need to be able to sustain themselves when reading assigned material. So, I and the teachers I work with often apply a "1/3 rule":

- 1/3 of the time, students are reading self-selected, free-choice texts.

- 1/3 of the time, students are reading texts assigned by the teacher to be used for instruction.

- 1/3 of the time students are reading texts that have been "negotiated"—students choose from within a certain parameter established by the teacher (e.g., everyone will read realistic fiction, but students may choose specific texts).

Opportunities to Respond to Reading in a Variety of Ways

Student response develops critical-thinking skills and enhances comprehension. Taffy Raphael and her colleagues describe three different categories of response to literature (Raphael et al., 2001):

Personal response: sharing personal perspective (related texts, class experiences, family experiences, personal experiences) and feelings

Critical response: analyzing literary elements, author's message, effectiveness of the author's message

Creative response: engaging creatively with text—imagining self in situation, altering text event ("What if . . ."), extending the text

Like many students in his fourth-grade classroom, 10-year-old Trevor read a great deal of provocative literature and responded to it in many ways. Perhaps because he is African American himself, he responded personally and poignantly to Virginia Hamilton's *Many Thousand Gone* (1993). His journal entries show him grappling with difficult ideas. (See Figure 3.1.)

Summary: *Many Thousand Gone* by Virginia Hamilton is a well-written and exciting series of vignettes about the struggle of the many hundreds of thousands of slaves who escaped, or attempted to escape, to freedom in the northern U.S. and Canada. One vignette, for example, tells the story of Henry "Box" Brown, who had a sympathetic carpenter nail him into a box and mail him north. Factual detail, short, lively chapters, and beautiful illustrations make this a great book for skilled and reluctant readers alike.

Trevor's Entry

4/7: Why would the slave owners not want the slaves after they ran away and then were found? I think it is very interesting that the population of slaves was so high!!! Why did they choose to make black people slaves insted of other kind of people? Was there any time of day besides the night that the slaves could rest?

Why would free blacks even think about turning running-away slaves to slave owners.

4/13: I think that it would be scary to come over from Africa and not know anything about what was happening. Why would you want a slave who didn't speak English? Or, even having a slave? I'm glad that the Civil War took place for slavery and other things. Because if the North hadn't won the Civil War I would/might be a slave (good chance because I was born in Florida).

His Teacher's Remarks

Good issue for discussion!

Good point . . . some people respond to differences instead of spending time finding similarities.

Trevor – I'm very glad, also. Somehow I think you would have been one of the people who made a difference!

Figure 3.1 Trevor's journal entries

Response Journals

Response journals are notebooks in which students record their thoughts and reactions to the reading they are doing. Students can make connections, ask questions, and reflect personally, critically, or creatively. Response journals can help teachers assess students' critical thinking and are an excellent way to track students' reactions to a text or to promote a particular stance on the book by asking students to respond to specific prompts. In the example in Figure 3.1, Trevor's teacher, Melinda Tate, reacts to the content of his response in these journal entries because it is so personal. At other times, she moves his thinking toward more critical responses:

- After a response to *A Question of Trust* by Marion Bauer (1994), she writes, "Do the parents have the same reason for not paying attention? Please explain using examples."

- After a response to *Henry and the Clubhouse* by Beverly Cleary (1962), she writes, "What makes Henry such a believable character?"

- After a response to *Matilda* by Roald Dahl (1998), she writes, "Give some examples to prove your statement that the Trunchbull is not a good person!"

Prompts like these are designed to support students as they explore new and challenging ideas or tasks.

Written responses can take the form of formal projects such as book reports, essays, and research reports. We want to teach these formats to our students because they will need them in the middle school grades, where reports and essays are commonly used for assessment purposes. Middle school teachers often judge students' comprehension and reading ability based on their ability to write coherent and focused responses using evidence from the text. However, there are many other, less formal ways to respond.

Quickwrites and Dialogue Journals

One type of informal response is a "quickwrite," an activity in which students write continuously for about five minutes in response to a reading. Quickwrites can prepare students for more formal writing, but they generally serve other functions as well. For example, quickwrites can be used to give you a sense of whether students are comprehending the material or to help generate ideas for discussion. Prompts like these can be used to jump-start writers:

- List as many things as you can about this character that make you like her.

- What surprised you about the events that you read today?

- What other character(s) does this character remind you of ?

- How is the time period important to this story?

Informal letters are a variation on quickwrites. In Figure 3.2, 12-year-old Erin has written an "update" to her teacher about the book she is reading.

Dialogue journals are another example of informal response. These are written conversations between a student and teacher that take place over the course of the school year. Students write as much as they choose and the teacher writes back regularly, responding to students' questions and comments and probing their thinking. Andrea Murnane sets the stage for dialogue journals early in the year

November 8th

Dear Ms. Murnane,

I'm currently reading Code Talker, by Joseph Bruchac. It is about the Navajo Marines o[f] War Two. The Main Chara[cter] Ned Begay, wants to become a Marine. since he is a Na[vajo] he gets trained as a code[talker] Someone (a Navajo) who sends in code that the enemy c[an't] understand, because noone un[derstands]

In the begining of the [book] Navajo language is beaten ou[t] by the bilagáanaa, the Wh[ite] They say that it is worth le[ss] noone is allowd to speak i[t] it is very ironic that t[he] language that they tried t[o stop] them from using, helped the[m win] the war, and saved hundre[ds of] lives.

I haven't finished the [book] yet, but I look forward to [reading] it because this a great s[tory] aMazing contribution to his[torical] fiction.

④

Sincerely,
Erin ⊕

Figure 3.2 (top) Erin's letter about Joseph Bruchac

Dear ___Amanda___   09.26

This year, you and I will write letters to each other about books, reading, writers, and writing. Our letters will help us learn together. The letters will help you learn more about reading.

When you write letters in your reading journal, do your best work and share your best thinking. For example, you might:

*Tell what you <u>like</u> or <u>dislike</u> about a book and why
*Tell about the parts of your book that <u>puzzled you</u> or made you ask questions
*Tell what you noticed about the <u>characters</u>, such as what made them act as they did or how they changed.
*Write about something in the book that <u>surprised you</u> or that you found interesting
*Write your <u>predictions</u> and about whether your predictions were correct
*Ask for help in figuring out the <u>meaning</u> of your book
*Tell about the <u>connections</u> that you made while reading. Tell how it reminds you of yourself, of people you know, or of something that happened in your life. It might remind you of other books, especially the characters, the events or the setting
*Write about the <u>author's style</u> and how it makes you feel
*Write about the <u>language</u> the author used and why you think the author wrote it this way
*Write about the <u>author's craft</u> - what was effective about the way the author wrote

Write a letter to me once each week. The completed letter is due on the day indicated on the journal list. Use a letter form and include the title and author of your book. It is important that your letters are neat and easy to read so I can understand what you are thinking. Read through your letter to make sure it says all you want it to say before you place it in the basket.

When I read your journal, I will learn from you, and we will learn together about books. How cool it will be to learn <u>together</u>!

Yours truly,

☮ Ms. Murnane

Ms. Murnane

Figure 3.3 (right) Andrea's beginning-of-the-year letter to students

by detailing the types of letters she would like from her students. (See Figure 3.3.) She gives each of her sixth-grade students a notebook. (She uses *Reader's Notebooks* by Irene Fountas and Gay Su Pinnell.) In these notebooks, students write weekly letters, but they also keep track of the reading they do and maintain a list of books they would like to read.

A glance at Whitney's journal (see Figure 3.4) shows a reader with eclectic tastes who has found an author she likes—she's read three books by Jerry Spinelli. By mid-April, when Whitney's list was collected, she had read 23 books, whereas another student, Sadie, had read 46. No student had read fewer than 18 books. Having all this information in one place is useful for Andrea when she responds to students' letters.

All students write something and Andrea responds—sometimes supporting, sometimes pushing, and many times simply enjoying the exchange. Her response in Figure 3.5 shows how much reflection can be generated by good dialogue journals.

In another response (see Figure 3.6), Andrea asks a series of questions which she knows this student needs to address if she is going to write more. Notice also that she is recommending a much less challenging book because she knows it will be appropriate and also because it is early in the year and she wants to motivate the student to read more. Students in this room talk about books and they know that Andrea will be interested in their recommendations. They are willing to take chances because she does.

Reading List

Select a book to read. Enter the title and author on your reading list. When you have completed it, write the genre and the date. If you have abandoned it, write an (A) and the date you abandoned it in the date column. Note whether the book was easy (E), just right (JR), or a challenging (C) book for you.

#	Title	Author	Genre Code	Date Completed	E, JR, C
1	Loser	Jerry Spenelli	R.F.	9/10	JR
2	Star Girl	↓	R.F.	9/16	JR
3	Invisible Lisa	Natalie Honeycutt	R.F	9/21	JR
4	The secret life of Amanda K.	Ann cameron	RF	9/30	JR
5	Power of the Witch Woods	Laurie Cabot	N.A	9/23	JR
6	Artamis Fowl	Eion Colfer	F.	10/17	C
7	Surviveing the Applewhites	Stephanie S Tolan,	RF	10/24	JR
8	Kalpana's Dream	Judith			
DcF 9.	On Pointe	Laurie			
DcF 10	Lizzie Bright Buck Mirster boy	Gary S			
DcF 11.	Here Today	Ann M			
12	The Library Card	Jerry			
13.	The Rope Trick	Lloyd			
14.	Espeganza Rising	Pam R			
15	Steal Away	Jennife			

© 2002 by I.C. Fountas and G. S. Pinnell, Reader's Notebook, NH: Heinemann

you go Whitney!
Ms.M

Dear Erin, NOV. 14

☺ Hey now! That was an excellent letter! It was a pleasure to read. It was well-written, I had a good summary and excellent reflection on your part.

The author, Joseph Bruchac writes mostly about Native Americans. I enjoy his style very much. I bought the book, Code Talkers because it reminded me very much of my experiences teaching the Navajo in New Mexico.

The bilagaana (white people) didn't treat the Navajo well. Did you ever read about their "Long Walk"? It's a sad but good story. Many Navajo were forced to go to boarding school where they were not allowed to wear their native clothes or speak their native tongue. Many Navajo still resent it. You the language ge we s a large where I beautiful M

Dear Peachy ☺, aka Jenna

September 20

Hey now... thanks for the letter. How do you like your book so far? I read that one over the summer and really enjoyed it. I found parts to be somber and sad but also inspiring and comforting. I really envy Martha for getting to spend time with her grandma. I miss hanging out with mine.

How do you like the book so far? In your letter you told me about the part you were reading and gave me a summary. I would also like you to tell me a little bit about how it made you feel or what do you think will happen next. Can you relate to Martha, why or why not?

I have read several other books by that author, Kevin Henkes. They were all picture books. I'm going to lend you one to read during free reading time. The title is Chrysanthemum you're going to love it.

Thanks for being you.

Ⓐ ms. murnane

Figure 3.4 (top left) Whitney's book log

Figure 3.5 (top right) Andrea's response to Erin, and reflections on Bruchac's book

Figure 3.6 (bottom) Andrea's response to Jenna (a.k.a. "Peachy")

Literature response journals can be hard to keep up with, so most teachers rotate the reading, dividing the class into thirds, for example, and reading a third of the journals on Monday, another on Tuesday, and so on, or even rotating a week on and a week off.

Opportunities to Discuss Diverse Texts

Research on comprehension and on school effectiveness has consistently shown that students' achievement is improved when they have opportunities to discuss a variety of texts with teachers and peers. (See Dubin, 2003, and Fall, Webb, & Chudowsky, 2000, for excellent reviews of discussion.) When students engage in discussion, they do the following:

- Improve their comprehension and deepen their understanding of the text
- Confirm or disconfirm predictions
- Correct misconceptions and expand partial understandings
- Make connections between texts and their prior knowledge and experience
- Consider a different point of view
- Challenge each other's ideas
- Elaborate on others' ideas
- Become more motivated to read

What is discussion? Donna Alvermann and her colleagues, who have studied student and teacher discussions for many years, describe how discussions differ from a traditional lesson: "Discussants should put forth multiple points of view and stand ready to change their minds about the matter under discussion; students should interact with one another as well as with the teacher; and the interaction should exceed the typical two or three word phrase units common to recitation lessons" (Alvermann, Dillon, & O'Brien, 1987, p. 7).

Annemarie Palincsar (1986) and Claude Goldenberg (1993) note that discussion is an interesting, engaging conversation that deals with an idea or a concept that is meaningful and relevant to students. "There is a high level of participation without domination by any one person (including the teacher), and teachers and students are responsive to what others say, so each statement builds on, challenges, or extends a previous one. Teachers or discussion leaders question, prod, challenge, coax, or remain silent. They are skilled at 'weaving individual participants' comments into a larger tapestry of meaning'" (Goldenberg, 1993, p. 318).

Figure 3.7 provides research-based guidelines for managing productive discussions.

In many classrooms (including my own some years ago) what passes for discussion, however, is a pattern of a teacher-initiated question, a student response, and a teacher acknowledgement and evaluation. This pattern has been dubbed IRE (initiate, respond, evaluate), and it is pervasive. According to Courtney Cazden, IRE is the most common pattern of classroom discourse at all grade levels. Discussion is different from IRE in both its purpose and its results. It is not just a "nicer" way to ask questions and check whether students have read the book. While IRE can be an efficient way to communicate directions or information, it does not promote higher-order thinking or a sense of community. Discussion is a better choice when teachers want to raise important issues, evaluate students' comprehension, or identify and clarify students' misconceptions. It also actually stimulates and aids learning. In his article "Talking into Literacy," Roy Corden (1998) writes that "spoken language is not used simply to express thoughts, it is used in the creation of them" (p. 27).

In their wonderful book *Building Literacy Through Classroom Discussion* (2005), Mary Adler and Eija Rougle describe how talk creates a different class-

Guidelines for Discussion

- Maintain a focus and a direction. Identify a theme or an idea to serve as a starting point for focusing the discussion and try to anticipate how the conversation might unfold; then keep students on track.

- Activate and use relevant prior knowledge. Before the discussion begins, remind students that they already know something about the topic and direct their attention to the aspects of their prior knowledge that would be useful for the discussion.

- Support substantive student contributions. Strive for a "responsive" attitude toward the conversation. While attending to the overall focus, elicit and support student responses at the idea level (versus asking for one-word, discrete responses).

- Link student ideas to new information. Try to view the discussion or conversation as a set of interactive, connected turns and help students build upon and extend previous students' responses.

- Challenge students. Ask fewer known-answer questions and, instead, respond to a comment by saying "Tell more about that" or "What makes you think that?"

- Provide constructive feedback. Help students improve their responses by asking for expansion ("Tell me more") or by modeling ("I think you are absolutely right about . . . , but I was wondering . . .").

Figure 3.7 Research-based guidelines for managing productive discussion. Adapted from Palincsar, A. (1986) and Goldenberg, C. (1993).

room culture: "In these classrooms, the teacher sees students not as receivers of transmitted information but as thinkers and producers of ideas. Diverse voices are valued, so these classrooms tend to be more academically equitable" (p. 29). Not surprisingly, then, there is strong evidence that true discussion is a more productive instructional approach for many students, including students with limited English proficiency.

Choosing Books for Discussion

The most important thing to keep in mind when planning for discussion is to choose material that is worth discussing. Some texts are enjoyable, but there is simply not much to say about them. Texts with some amount of controversy or ones that invite different points of view are especially good for discussion. At left I list texts that have provoked excellent discussion with students in grades 3 to 6. Organizing the whole classroom around a specific theme, genre, or author can help promote community. That way, students of various abilities can all be discussing similar ideas even though their texts are at different levels of difficulty. (See Chapter 8 for more on differentiating instruction.)

Although we usually think of discussion as related to literary texts, I want to emphasize how useful discussion groups can be with informational texts as well. As Donna Ogle and Camille Blachowicz (2002) point out, it is important to reflect critically on the information presented in nonfiction materials, and since these texts are often more diffi-

Good Books for Discussion

GRADE 3: *Stories Julian Tells* by Ann Cameron
This book of vignettes is relatively easy to read but not so easy to understand. There is much to discuss in these stories about family dynamics.

GRADE 4: *The City of Ember* by Jeanne DuPrau
This book is set in a bleak future in an underground city where resources are running out. The creative problem solving of two young people saves the city. Easier to access than Lois Lowry's *The Giver,* but with similar themes.

GRADE 5: *The View From Saturday* by E. L. Konigsburg
This book is challenging and excellent for discussion since the complex characters and events can become confusing. Most students will find at least one character with whom they can connect.

GRADE 6: *Bud Not Buddy* by Christopher Paul Curtis
This book's historical context (it's set during the Depression in the 1930s) and its sometimes harsh conditions (homelessness, intolerance) make it appropriate for sixth-grade discussion. The characters are memorable but many students will benefit from guided support as they construct the challenging theme.

cult for students to comprehend, collaborative discussion can improve everyone's comprehension.

Carrying Out Discussion

One of the major challenges facing teachers in grades 3 to 6 is how to carry out discussion in the classroom. Most students need instruction if they are going to participate productively. Yet even after modeling, some students still cannot engage in collaborative conversation (Villaume, Worden, Williams, Hopkins, & Rosenblatt, 1994). We can do two things to help students engage in more productive discussion: The first is to help them know how to get ready for discussion. And the second is to teach them what to do when they are in a group.

Getting Ready for Discussion

We should remind students that the idea of discussion is not to ask questions they already know the answers to. Instead, they should identify aspects of the text that they really want to discuss. Here are some good suggestions we can make to students:

1. **If you are reading fiction, think about the story.** Stop at various points and ask yourself what you are thinking about the characters and events. Identify specific examples from the text that support your assessment. Ask yourself the following questions:
   - As I read, are there clues in the story that give me an idea of what will happen next? What were they?
   - Do I think the main character and I could be friends? Explain?
   - What advice do I have for the main character?

2. **If you are reading nonfiction, think about how the ideas are organized.** Stop at various points and ask yourself what the author is trying to say. Here are some ideas to consider:
   - How are the ideas organized? How do they relate to each other?
   - Generate questions about the text; what are you wondering?
   - Try to combine the information in this text with other information you have about the topic.

3. **Mark the text.** If you have questions or want to know what others think about some part of the text, put a sticky note on the page with a note to yourself. If the text can be written on (e.g., a weekly newsmagazine), you can do that instead.

4. **Use your journal.** Ask questions and/or write down interesting words and phrases. That way, when you meet with your group you will not only have something to share, you will be better prepared to defend you ideas.

5. **Make something visual.**
   - Draw a response showing how you see this book.
   - Map the characters. (See Chapter 5 for character-mapping activities.)
   - Map the story, including information about the characters, setting, problem, main events, and resolution.
   - Map the setting.

Sometimes teachers prefer to use reading logs to help their students get ready for discussion. In Figure 3.8, you can see a daily log for literature circles that is used by fifth- and sixth-grade teachers Cathy Smith and Andrea Murname. The log reflects the considerable work they have done throughout the year. Students may not complete the entire form every day but they do keep track

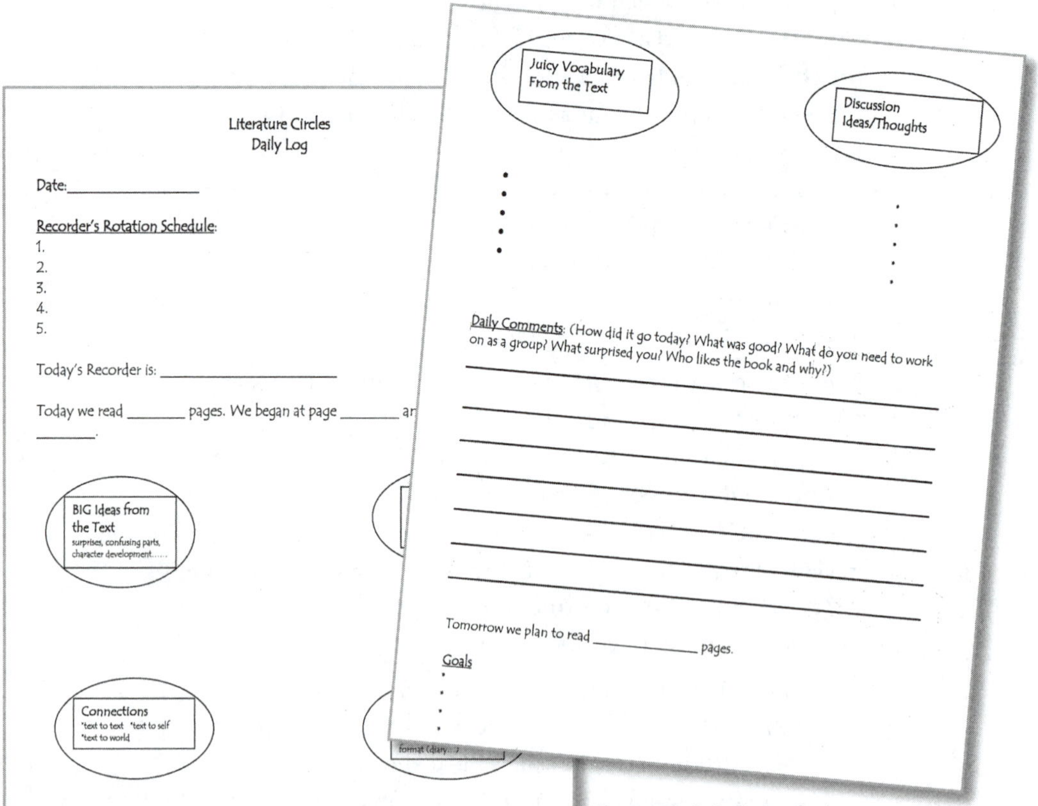
Literature Circles
Daily Log

Date:________

Recorder's Rotation Schedule:
1.
2.
3.
4.
5.

Today's Recorder is: ________

Today we read ______ pages. We began at page ______ ar
______.

BIG Ideas from the Text
surprises, confusing parts, character development.....

Connections
*text to text *text to self
*text to world

format (diary...)

Juicy Vocabulary From the Text

Discussion Ideas/Thoughts

Daily Comments: (How did it go today? What was good? What do you need to work on as a group? What surprised you? Who likes the book and why?)

Tomorrow we plan to read ________ pages.

Goals

Figure 3.8 Daily log for literature circles

of these elements as they are reading so that they are ready when they do meet for literature circles.

Students' discussion can be supported by creating a range of responses. Some students have an easier time discussing after open-ended written responses (Figure 3.1, page 58), while others feel on safer ground with the reading logs Cathy and Andrea use.

Preparing to discuss nonfiction material can be especially challenging for students. Because she wants her students to feel comfortable with nonfiction and because she knows they must learn to use evidence to support their ideas, Cathy takes time to teach the skills her students need. For example, before they read an issue of *Time for Kids*, Cathy previews three interesting stories with the class by introducing some vocabulary. Then she asks them to choose one article to read and gives each student several sticky notes to write on. Students are told to (1) generate an opinion about the topic and (2) select information from the text that led them to this opinion. They are to write both of these on the sticky note. Then, students post their notes on a sheet of chart paper, beneath the appropriate title. (See photos on the next page.) Not surprisingly, the discussion that follows is vigorous and substantial because students voice varied opinions and are able to point directly to the text as a way to resolve or clarify opinions.

Amber Profitt teaches students who struggle with reading. She chooses sources of high-interest nonfiction, such as *Muse* magazine, to teach key strategies like locating details in text. *Muse* is a science magazine with a twist. It features articles about such things as giant squids, Neanderthals, undersea adventures, and the physics of roller coasters. She uses the graphic organizer in Figure 3.9 to support students as they read "Mystery Spot," an article by Robin Meadows that appeared in *Muse* in 2003.

Retelling Graphic Organizer

Topic- 1 or 2 words telling what the article is about.

Mystery Spot

Main Idea- A sentence telling about the whole article. What it is about?

Do you want to here about the Mystery Spot.

Key Point 1: When you go to the mystery spot weird stuff happens.
Details: They are sideways and taller.

Key Point 2:
Details:

Key Point 3:
Details: Everything in the mystery spot isn't upside down.

Key Point 4:
Details:

Conclusion: It is scary.

Figure 3.9 Graphic organizer supporting comprehension of a nonfiction article on optical illusions

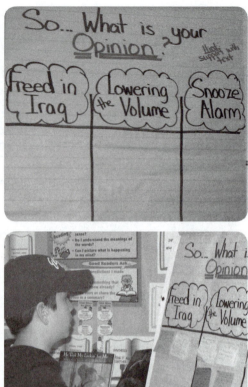

Clockwise from top left:

Highlighting text increases engagement and comprehension.

Cathy's preview of three articles helps students organize their reading and response.

Students post their opinions about interesting news articles.

Cathy uses students' notes and opinions to fuel discussion and highlight strategies for reading nonfiction.

Teaching Students How to Interact With Peers

Student-led, mixed-ability discussion groups result in greater engagement and more talk time than teacher-led groups. But students need explicit instruction in how to conduct themselves in discussion groups. A set of ground rules, timely feedback, and ongoing monitoring are essential. Taffy Raphael and her colleagues even conduct formal evaluations of the *groups* as they discuss. Below are some guidelines students should follow:

- Come prepared.
- Listen to others.
- Only one person talks at a time.
- Allow time to think and refer to the book.
- Try to connect what you are saying to what others have said.
- Stay on topic.
- Disagree agreeably.

Because research indicates that students in peer-led discussion groups actually generate better comprehension of text than teacher-led groups, it is important to take the time necessary to develop these discussion skills (Almasi, 1995; Villaume & Hopkins, 1995).

Debriefing After the Discussion

When students are just learning to discuss, it is helpful to debrief during community share time. Use specific examples from observations to make comments like the following:

> "I notice that Sarah made a good connection today between her ideas and Jessie's. That really helped the whole group."

Solicit student input to engage in problem solving:

> "Some groups are still having a hard time really listening to each other. Your idea is important but it's important to think about what others are saying also. What can we do about that?"

In addition, it is important to post the rules you've set for discussion and review them regularly throughout the year.

Opportunities to Hear Texts Read Aloud and Teachers Think Aloud

Young readers have much to learn. Since thinking and comprehending occur inside the head, it is often difficult to teach people how to get better at these tasks. According to Scott Paris and his colleagues, students need us *to make thinking public*, to bring our strategic moves and connections out into the open (Paris, 1985; Paris et al., 1983).

> The more that teachers understand about their own thinking, the better they can model for students [and] make thinking public and visible. Thinking—strategic, independent, and inquisitive—then becomes a topic of classroom discussion and an explicit goal of education. (Paris & Winograd, 1999, p. 1)

This type of public conversation not only boosts reading skills but also builds community.

Read-alouds and think-alouds help make thinking public—especially if they are treated as opportunities to provide different levels of support. Students learn through the modeling that happens around them. In fact, many of the most important aspects of high-powered literacy cannot be taught explicitly—they must be modeled, observed, experienced, and supported. Things like connecting one part of a text to another, challenging the meaning of an article, or wondering whether a story is true are habits of mind that develop over time and with the encouragement of others. Lev Vygotsky's notion of scaffolded instruction is at the heart of this type of teaching and learning (1978). He believed that instruction is most effective when the tasks or material is just beyond the reach of the learner, when it is challenging but not impossible. Students need some assistance and guidance from others who already know how to perform at these higher levels; students need a scaffold.

Scaffolded instruction has several key attributes:

- It allows students to perform tasks, solve problems, or achieve goals that could not be accomplished without support.

- It is temporary, lasting only until the student can perform the tasks on her own.

- It is socially mediated, involving an interaction between teacher and learner.

Scaffolded instruction is central to the development of independent learning because it involves the gradual release of responsibility from teacher to student

(Wilkinson & Silliman, 2000; Wood, Bruner, & Ross, 1976). In other words, as we engage in scaffolded instruction, we support students in challenging tasks, but we also have a plan for enabling them to perform these tasks on their own. Read-alouds clearly offer a high level of support, whereas think-alouds require students to take on some of the responsibility.

Read-Alouds

Virtually every primary teacher understands how important it is to read aloud to students. Teachers in grades 3 to 6, on the other hand, may not. A national survey of almost two thousand elementary teachers indicates that intermediate-grade teachers read aloud to their students much less often (Jacobs, Morrison, & Swinyard, 2000). In addition, they frequently use read-alouds to "settle students" before or after lunch or specials, and occasionally use them as an enjoyable break in routine. These are not bad reasons to read aloud, but they marginalize the practice, making it easier to drop it from the schedule when other "more important" matters arise.

The benefits of read-alouds are many. During a read-aloud we have one of our best opportunities to model how *we* construct meaning as we read. With a bit of planning, read-alouds can be used to model complex thinking and promote deep discussion. For example, I might stop as I read the first chapter of Cynthia Kadohata's wonderful Newbery Medal–winning book, *Kira-Kira* (2004). In that chapter, the extraordinary relationship between two sisters is laid out. Katie and her sister Lynn each relate the same vivid story about how a wild dog grabbed hold of Katie with its teeth. I might stop during the reading and say something like:

> I was really scared for the girls as I read this. I think the author
> is telling us these events as a way to introduce what will happen
> later. It makes me a little worried about what's going to happen.
> But I really love the way she describes these girls and how they
> feel about each other.

Of course, read-alouds expose students to complex syntax and sophisticated vocabulary that they might not encounter in their own independent reading. In this brief excerpt from the first chapter of *Kira-Kira*, you can see how embedded clauses and varied language patterns create interest but also challenge the reader. Words like *unruffled* and even *mild* introduce students to new usage for known words:

> It was hard to see how my father and Uncle Katsuhisa could be
> related. My father was mild, like the sea on a windless day, with
> an unruffled surface and little variation. He was as hard as the
> wall in our bedroom. (p. 11)

Guidelines for Teacher Read-Alouds

All Kinds of Read-Alouds

- Choose books or articles that you enjoy and/or find interesting.
- Choose books with specific purposes in mind.
- Practice reading the book or article before you share it with the class.
- Read fluently and with appropriate expression.
- Decide in advance where you will stop so that you can build suspense or resolve an issue.
- Feel free to abandon a book if it doesn't seem like a good choice. (It's a great way to model this skill.)
- Where appropriate, pause for genuine discussion but do not feel that you must ask many questions.

Read-Alouds for Engagement, Discussion, and Community-Building

- Choose books that (1) will fuel students' existing interests or tastes or (2) will expand their tastes and introduce them to a new, enjoyable genre or author.
- Have fun with the reading. Ham it up if you feel comfortable doing so.
- Do not provide definitions of all difficult or unknown words. Let the students ask about them, or assume that they will get the gist.
- Provide opportunities for conversation as a whole group or in small groups or pairs.
- Express your enjoyment of reading and discuss how you feel about the book(s) you read.
- Read books that students may not be able to decode or comprehend without the support of a read-aloud.
- Limit the amount of casual recreational reading aloud and extend the amount of sustained silent reading.

Instructional Read-Alouds

- Select books for specific teaching purpose(s), such as highlighting characterization, discussing setting, or teaching inference.
- Choose books that are well-written and engaging.
- Select books that challenge students' thinking and encourage high-level reflection.
- Read a wide range of texts that represent different cultures and settings, genres and text types, and authors.

(See Chapter 4 for more on instructional read-alouds.)

Read-alouds build community by providing a forum for listening to diverse ideas and opinions within a group or social context. These exchanges help students develop positive social interactions in their own classroom and, not surprisingly, promote positive attitudes toward reading and toward school.

According to Kate Walsh (2003), teachers should read aloud from texts that are approximately two levels above the students' grade level in order to build background knowledge and vocabulary. "Moreover, significant chunks of time—say 20 minutes daily—should be devoted to discussion after each read-aloud" (p. 25). The ideas described in the box on page 72 provide further guidance for making the most of read-alouds

Think-Alouds

The ultimate way to make thinking public is to think out loud. In a think-aloud, teachers or students talk about *what* they are thinking and *how* they are doing that. In a think-aloud, readers stop at various points during their reading and explain the processes and strategies they are using. Teachers often use think-alouds for instructional purposes to model their own cognitive activity. In fact, think-alouds were originally used as a research tool to help researchers gain a better understanding of what people do as they read. Since think-alouds reveal internal thinking processes, they are excellent for assessment. (See Chapter 7 for more on assessment.) The following surprising exchange between me and a seventh-grade student, for example, happened during a think-aloud:

MARJORIE: What were you doing and thinking as you read that part?

JUANITA: Oh, I don't usually think while I read!

Juanita's declaration provides us with an insight about her approach to reading that would not be available otherwise and also points to the fact that Juanita needs help in acquiring a meaning-oriented approach to reading.

One of the good things about think-alouds is that the technique also slows down the reading process, making students reflect on their own cognitive activity. As a result, it can be used very effectively in comprehension instruction (Lipson & Wickizer, 1989). In Figure 3.10, 9-year-old Shawn is reading *Yang the Youngest and His Terrible Ear* (Namioka, 1992). After summarizing the story on his teacher's request, Shawn thinks aloud as he reads, stopping as needed.

Shawn, age 9

Shawn has read to page 117 in *Yang the Youngest and His Terrible Ear*. Here, he reflects on what he's read thus far and thinks aloud as he continues to read.

SHAWN: Well, Yang is a kid that has a really bad ear, so when he tries to play the violin he always gets these screechy sounds. He made this friend, Matt, and Matt loves music, and Yang loves baseball—now, because they taught it to each other. And Matt's parents don't want him to play music until he improves on his baseball. Yang's folks don't want him playing baseball until he improves on his music. So . . . when Yang's family had their recital, [the boys] had, like, you could call it a "violin-synch" [instead of a lip-synch] because they put up a screen. So what happened was, Yang was just pretending to play but he kept his bow really close to his chest while Matthew was behind the curtain actually playing the violin, second part. Then, the screen fell over at the end of the recital when Third Sister got up to bow. And now Matthew and Yang are in trouble.

TEACHER: What do you think is going to happen now?

SHAWN: I think that maybe Yang's father will let him play baseball and Matthew will play the second part and then . . . they'll have a good life.

SHAWN [*begins to read aloud and stops spontaneously to comment*]: Well that sort of tells you that the parents, the Conners—Matthew's parents—don't know that it wasn't intended to happen. They thought he was going to stay home, but they didn't know he was going to be behind there. Everyone thought it was just a part of the recital.

SHAWN [*continues reading*]: "I bet the two of them cooked up the scheme between them."

"Scheme" must be a kind of Chinese food.

SHAWN [*continues reading*]: "I think what Mr. Conner means is that Third Sister and I planned everything together." Oh, when they said, "cooked up," I thought they meant like on a stove, but "they cooked up" must have meant that they thought it up and they used it. A scheme, like a plot, sort of.

Shawn demonstrates a sophisticated ability to summarize across lengthy text by selecting central themes and supporting details. He appropriately identifies the problem, the attempt, and the resulting consequence(s).

Shawn picks up on the clever analogy used by the author, paraphrasing with "violin synch."

Shawn shows that he is aware of the conflicting goals of the main characters and also the irony in the situation. On the other hand, his final prediction is too generic to be useful, given there is still a way to go in the book.

Shawn seems to be attempting to clarify the ideas of the various characters and resolve a bit of a misconception that he had as he read earlier.

Shawn delightfully reveals the type of thinking about word meanings that good readers do as they read. This starts him thinking about the next portion of text.

Shawn is monitoring his reading comprehension and using text to correct erroneous ideas. He uses the text language to extend his meaning revision. This is an excellent example of how thinking aloud can both reveal and promote problem solving.

Figure 3.10 Shawn reflects on and thinks aloud about *Yang the Youngest and His Terrible Ear.*

This transcript illuminates Shawn's misconceptions about the book and the way he monitors, regulates, and repairs his comprehension ideas and misconceptions. Shawn is a proficient third-grade reader, so he may have engaged in this rich thinking anyway, but it is also possible that the act of thinking aloud had an effect. Simply slowing down and publicly ruminating about the reading likely deepened his reflection.

My colleagues and I have been exploring these techniques for many years, and it is clear that think-alouds can produce insights into students' approaches to text reading, and also that they can improve students' reading comprehension when used over time. Think-alouds—especially supported think-alouds—help students comprehend better. We have had very good luck using a list of possible prompts for thinking aloud. (See Figure 3.11.) Of course, these things are much more likely to be used if we model them during our own read-alouds.

Think-Aloud Prompts

- I wonder . . .
- I was surprised by . . .
- I don't understand . . .
- This reminded me of . . .
- I didn't like it when . . .
- This part must mean . . .
- I think the author is saying . . .
- I am picturing . . .

FIGURE 3.11 Think-aloud prompts

Into the Classroom

Among the schools where my colleagues and I work (see Lipson et al., 2004), there is a marked difference when teachers take time at the beginning of the year to build community and teach students how to become participants in that community. This is done in a number of ways:

- Creating a climate in which substantial amounts of reading and writing can and do occur

- Teaching techniques and routines that will be used every day during literacy block

- Supporting students as they learn what and how to think and talk about their reading

We accomplish these goals through workshops and mini-lessons.

Getting-Started Workshops

In my estimation, nothing is more important than teaching students how to be members of a productive and literate community, yet we seldom plan carefully enough for this instruction, nor do we allow enough time. Good, explicit instruction and lots of time to practice are essential. Talented educators from primary to middle grades have been developing and advocating preparatory workshops for some time. See Taffy Raphael and her colleagues' useful ideas in the Book Club series; Irene Fountas and Gay Su Pinnell's in *Guiding Readers and Writers, Grades 3–6* (2000), and Kathy Collins's *Growing Readers* (2004).

When students do not know how to manage classroom routines and procedures, it affects their ability to read and write; their confusion gets in the way. In his study of one successful teacher, Doug Kaufman concluded that the teacher "focused on organization and procedures not at the expense of quality literacy instruction but in order to achieve it" (2001, p. 122). Generally, it's a good idea to spend the first two to four weeks of school on teaching students how to be members of a productive and literate community by showing them how to:

- Choose an appropriate book
- Sustain themselves during extended reading periods
- Write in response to their reading

- Prepare for literature discussion by selecting portions of their text and identifying questions they want to address
- Understand the activities that are available to them during the literacy block

In our schools, teachers have found it helpful to start with a series of workshops. There is no magic number, although a month of these at the beginning of the year is about right (4 days/week x 3 weeks for a total of 12 days; 4 days/week x 4 weeks for a total of 16 days, and so on). Although desirable, it is not necessary that these come at the beginning of the school year. If you are ready to start something fresh and make some changes, you can provide this instruction at any time. We have introduced the getting-started workshops in November and in January with excellent success.

The important thing is to plan carefully and allow enough time to really establish habits and routines. A list of workshop topics that will help you meet these goals is presented at right. Of course, the importance of any of these will depend on who your students are and what types of experiences they have had up to now. There will very likely be other mini-lessons you will want to teach over the course of the year; these are simply meant to get you started.

Topics for Getting-Started Workshops

Building Community

- Who are we as readers?
- Building stamina
- Sustaining writing
- Reading as thinking
- Preparing for talk: How to discuss and debrief in the whole group

Procedures for Literacy Block

- How to choose a book
- How to write a response
- Talking among ourselves: How to have a discussion
- Getting ready for literature groups
- How to have a peer conference

Making the Most of Our Reading

- Author's craft
- Characterization
- Narrative story structure

Troubleshooting

- What do I do when I'm stuck?

Mini-Lessons

Mini-lessons are an especially useful instructional technique during the getting-started workshops. Mini-lessons differ from full-blown lessons in the following ways:

- They are *brief*, focused lessons led by the teacher (5–10 minutes).
- They are designed to provide a common frame of reference for the whole class (they make thinking public).
- They are focused on collaborative problem solving.
- They immediately precede engagement—subsequent reading and writing are meant to support the lesson's focus.

Following is a mini-lesson by Megan Johnson, adapted from Kathy Collins's *Growing Readers* (2004). Megan teaches in an extremely diverse school, and it's important to her that she establish a good climate for reading, but she is also interested in having the students respect one another right from the beginning of the year.

MINI-LESSON: Building a Community of Readers

Goal: Establish the importance and value of reading
Materials: Clipboards with paper

Connection

1. "One of the neat things about being here is that you'll get time to read every day—reading is built right into your job! You can count on reading every morning." [Megan wants students to value the opportunity to read.]

2. "This is something that we will all do together. It's like being part of a sports team and we need to learn how to cooperate—sort of like learning our positions." [By making the connection to something most students know something about, she increases the focus on community.]

Teaching Points

1. "Since we will be reading every day, it is important to know what kinds of things are available to read in our classroom."

2. "There are things to read all over the room, and you're all going to be Print Detectives and find them." [The idea here is that students will see that they have access to text materials throughout the classroom, and it will encourage them to seek them out.]

3. "There are many things to read in this classroom—a good detective will find them in unexpected places." [Megan wants students to use a rich variety of textual materials, including charts, newsmagazines, poetry on the walls, science materials.]

Engagement/Practice

1. Students pair up and get a clipboard to share.

2. Pairs record all the kinds of things they can read in the classroom. Megan tells them, "You can draw and label or make a list of your discoveries. You will be helping us learn about all the different things we can read." [Megan wants students to be familiar enough with materials to help each other during the school year.]

3. Megan reminds students to notice how the materials are organized and where they are located. [She has organized some materials by levels, and others by author or genre; still others are exhibited as part of science displays.]

Assessment/Debriefing

1. Students read their lists and record their responses on a chart.

2. Megan notes how many choices they have for reading.

3. She reminds them that they can choose from many of these during reading workshop.

4. She encourages them to talk to each other about which things they like to read best.

On the next page, I provide a mini-lesson that I created as a model for one of the fourth-grade teachers in our project. I wanted to focus on sustained silent reading and building stamina. When students can read independently for a fairly long time, they get the amount of practice they need to improve comprehension; they can read authentic literature and prepare for discussion; and it creates a quiet, productive environment for small-group instruction. Since most of the students in this fourth-grade classroom had not engaged in sustained silent reading, I knew we would need to focus on it right away.

MINI-LESSON: Building Stamina for Reading

Goal: Building stamina with sustained silent reading
Materials: Several different books

Connection

1. Talk about building muscles through exercise and the fact that musicians find it easier to play an instrument after they have practiced. Note how important it is to spend time on something before you get really good at it. The ability to stick with something is called *stamina*.

2. Remind students that we are reading some longer texts during our literacy block, so we need to develop more stamina.

3. It's a lot like many things in life. Use doing push-ups as analogy—doing one or two is no problem, but 100 is hard! Reading is a lot like that—you have to practice and build up "mental muscle" to stick with the reading so that instead of just five or ten minutes, you can read for an hour. *Stamina* is another word for "endurance" or "stick-to-itiveness."

4. Point out that mature readers can stick with texts quite easily. Readers in fourth grade should have more stamina than readers in grades 1 or 2.

Teaching Points

1. Evaluate yesterday's silent reading performance: "How long did we read silently yesterday? We lasted, as a class, about nine minutes. That's not bad for a first time. But we want to do better than that."

2. On an anchor chart, generate a list of things that affect our stamina for reading. Don't be afraid to add things that students fail to mention, such as:

   - Length and difficulty of text
   - Surrounding noise or other distractions
   - Interest

3. Ask students, "If we were going to try to build up our stamina as a class, what could we do?" Possible answers include:

Help each other by . . .	Set goals for longer reading
Find a good spot so we can concentrate	Check to see how we're doing with concentration and endurance
Start small with short periods of time	

4. Remind students that you're after sustained reading practice—not just a quiet room!

Engagement/Practice

Ask students, "Today we'll see if we can add just a little bit of stamina. What's a realistic goal given that we sustained ourselves for nine minutes yesterday?"

Assessment/Debriefing

1. Ask students to consider what went well today (focusing on the group; "we're all in this together").

2. Anticipate tomorrow. "What do we need to do?"

It may seem as though your students should already have learned how to do many of these things, but many students, even sixth graders, have not. Instruction like this is an investment that pays off all year long.

Question Answer Relationships

Taffy Raphael developed a method for improving students' ability to answer comprehension questions more than twenty years ago (1982, 1986). Question Answer Relationships (QAR) has proven an effective technique since then. Recently, however, in collaboration with Kathy Au, she has placed QAR in the context of an overall school-improvement plan (2005). The teachers in our project have found that QAR provides an excellent beginning-of-the-year framework for reading instruction. Andrea Murnane had almost given up on literature discussion groups in her sixth-grade classroom. In previous years she had felt that students got stuck in "roles," and the level of their conversation and text engagement was disappointing. After reading Raphael and Au's article "QAR: Enhancing Comprehension and Test Taking Across Grades and Content Areas" (2005) however, she decided that the technique might be a way to set her students up for success.

Question Answer Relationships help students understand how to ask and answer two major types of questions:

- In the Text: The answer to the question is in the book or article.

- In My Head: The answer to the question requires information from my own prior knowledge and experience.

For students in grades 3 and above, these two types of questions are divided into two other types of questions:

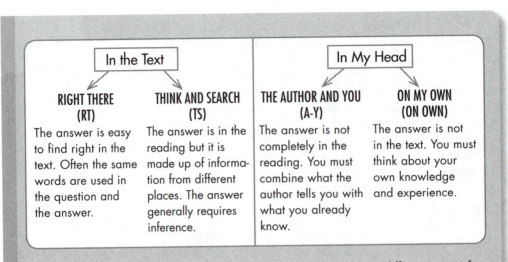

The demands of these different question types can help generate different types of thinking. For example, in the following excerpt from Ann Cameron's *Stories Julian Tells* (1981), we get a good picture of Julian's father.

> My father is a big man with wild black hair. When he laughs, you can almost see his thoughts sitting on all the tables and chairs. When he is angry, me and my little brother, Huey, shiver to the bottom of our shoes. (p. 2)

Here are four QAR questions that might be asked about this passage:

RT: What kind of a man was Julian's father?

TS: Does Julian's father have an even temperament?

A-Y: When do you think Julian likes to be around his father?

ON OWN: Why do Julian and his brother shiver when their father is angry?

Here's how Andrea Murname introduced QAR to her students.

1. **TEACHER MODELING.** Andrea provided questions, answers to the questions, QAR label (for example, TS), and an explanation for the label.

2. **SOME RELEASE.** Andrea provided questions, answers to the questions, and QAR label. The students provided the explanation for the label.

3. **MORE RELEASE.** Andrea provided questions and answers. Students provided the QAR label and the explanation for it.

4. **GUIDED PRACTICE.** Andrea provided questions. Students provided answers, the QAR label, and the explanation for it.

5. **APPLICATION.** Students developed and asked their own questions and supplied the QAR label and the explanation for it.

Andrea linked the last step—in which students develop and ask their own questions—to the students' reading of their literature circle books. Each evening, students were expected to generate one or more questions for their group. At the end of the literature discussion group, the students evaluated their questions and set goals for the next day. By the end of their literature circle rotation, students did not need to label their questions—they were on their way to thoughtful reading and authentic discussion.

Real-World Experiences

John Guthrie's research on motivation and engagement reinforces lessons we have learned since John Dewey: children are more engaged and involved in their learning when they examine real objects, participate in real discussions, do hands-on activities, conduct experiments, and create projects (Dewey, 1938). In such a context, students use their reading and writing abilities to accomplish authentic tasks.

Even very reluctant readers can become excited and work hard. For example, two years after I met Tuno, I was still teaching in Washington, D.C., working with a group of students who were in grades 5 and 6 but who were reading at the first-grade level. Luckily, the Washington Redskins were on a winning streak and my students were fascinated. So, every Monday we recapped the weekend's football game, writing our own play-by-play. The boys (the group was all boys) were deeply committed to getting their facts straight. They willingly debated the "main ideas" of the game and organized the details under each of these main ideas. On subsequent days, we reread the material we had written and did additional activities. Within weeks, the boys had a sight vocabulary that included words like *quarterback, tackle, tight end*, and *half-time*. These and many less interesting words (*first, second, next, after*) became highly familiar. They began to turn their attention to the daily newspaper accounts and found they could read some of the sports page. We began to publish a newsletter for our team and a retrospective of our "articles." Their enthusiasm for this work never waned and they began to see themselves as readers and writers.

I have been fortunate to work with many teachers who believe in active, engaged, and authentic learning. Eve Gordon, whose classroom I described in Chapter 2, is one of those teachers. Her students routinely conduct "I Searches," based on Ken Macrorie's book entitled *The I-Search Paper* (1988). Students select a personally relevant topic to investigate. Eve's students start with what they already know about it and build background knowledge for themselves. This requires that they read all sorts of material, interview people, go on field trips, decide how they will share their information, and produce a final written report. Among the I-Search papers that Eve's students produced were these three:

- "What It Means to Be a Marine" (the girl's father was a marine)
- "Poisonous Snakes" (the student thought snakes were cool)
- "Owning a Small Business" (this girl interviewed all of the small business owners in the village)

Barb Sclafani, a veteran teacher, conducted a yearlong theme study, "Realizing Your Dreams." The students in her high-poverty school identified their own "dream" and engaged in an investigation. Figure 3.12 lists the table of contents from one student's Dream Book, *I Want to Be a Teacher*.

Table of Contents

Figure 3.12 The table of contents from a student's Dream Book

Concluding Thoughts

Our own satisfaction in teaching derives in no small part from our involvement with our students. The stronger our sense of community within the classroom, the greater pleasure we take in our students and their accomplishments. Too often, however, we leave this developing sense of community to chance. Some years are better than others. There *are* things we can do, however, to strengthen students' connection to us and to each other. We shouldn't leave this to chance—we need to plan for it, teach for it, and support it.

Importantly, our efforts to create this community through discussion and "public thinking" are also the best ways to enhance students' motivation and engagement, thereby improving their performance and achievement. This double return on our investment is worth our time and effort.

Discussion and Reflection

- List all the ways you build community in your classroom. Check with colleagues to see what they do. Which practices would you like to add to your list?

- Tape a book discussion with your students. Listen to it to see how closely it meets the guidelines for discussion presented in this chapter.

- Think about the books you have been selecting for read-aloud; which meet the criteria described in this chapter?

- Collect three to five reading responses from your students. Write to each student to begin a dialogue.

- Discuss the getting-started workshops with a colleague. What would be the benefits to running these? Do you see challenges? How might they be addressed?

Digging Deeper

For more information on building community and engaging students, check out:

- *Book Club: A Literature-Based Curriculum*, 2nd ed., by Taffy Raphael, Laura Pardo, Kathy Highfield, and Susan McMahon. Lawrence, MA: Small Planet, 2002.

- *Book Club Student Reading Log* by Taffy Raphael, Laura Pardo, Kathy Highfield, and Susan McMahon. Lawrence, MA: Small Planet, 2002.

- *Building Literacy Through Classroom Discussion* by Mary Adler and Eija Rougle. New York: Scholastic, 2005.

- *Classroom Discussion* by Dixie Lee Spiegel. New York: Scholastic, 2006.

- *Guiding Readers and Writers Grades 3 to 6: Teaching Comprehension, Genre and Content Literacy* by Irene Fountas and Gay Su Pinnell, Portsmouth, NH: Heinemann, 2000.

- *Improving Comprehension with Think-Aloud Strategies* by Jeffrey Wilhelm. New York: Scholastic, 2001.

- *100 Quickwrites* by Linda Rief. New York: Scholastic, 2003.

- *102 Reading Response Lessons* by Kristin Noelle Wolfgang. Thousand Oaks, CA: Corwin Press, 2005.

- *QAR Now* by Taffy E. Raphael, Kathy Highfield, and Kathryn H. Au. New York: Scholastic, 2006.

- *Response Journals Revisited* by Les Parsons. Portland, ME: Stenhouse, 2001.

CHAPTER 4

Develop Background Knowledge, Vocabulary, and Higher-Order Thinking

When children reach grade 3, they begin to encounter new types of texts, new purposes for reading, and more complex tasks. Patrick Clinton has noted: "The fact is that reading isn't learned once and for all in grades one to four. When a child has achieved fluency, it's only a start—there's much more to learn, and most of it has to do with comprehension" (2002, p. 5).

This is a relatively new insight. Research shows that "many children who read at the third-grade level in grade 3 will not automatically become proficient comprehenders in later grades" (RAND Reading Study Group, 2002, p. xii). There are several reasons why it has taken researchers

Kara

I was sitting next to Kara, a struggling fourth-grade student, listening to her read a nonfiction selection that traced the steps in the paper-making process. Periodically, I stopped Kara to engage her in discussion of the text. Things were not going well. She simply did not understand what was going on. Although her word recognition was not terrific, this did not seem to be the main reason for her difficulty. While she seemed to understand each individual event (e.g., she understood how trees were cut down, how logs were floated downstream), none of this understanding led to an appropriate answer to the question "Where does paper come from?" As I pressed her, I gradually began to understand what the twofold problem was. First, she had serious trouble managing cause-effect inferences. The text never *stated* that trees are used to make paper, but suggested it, which would be clear to a capable reader. Second, a significant vocabulary weakness made it impossible for her to make those inferences. For example, she did not know the meaning of the word "logs." Therefore, when the author stopped talking about "trees" and referred, instead, to "logs" her comprehension broke down.

so long to arrive at this conclusion. First, the data from early interventions is quite new. As studies began to show that good word recognition was important but not enough to improve and sustain the achievement of older students, researchers began to look elsewhere. At the same time, we began to take a much closer look at the role of prior knowledge and experience. (See M. Y. Lipson, 1982, 1983.) These studies produced startling results showing that people with a lot of prior knowledge and experience consistently performed better than those without—even when they had the same "skills." Now, of course, a great deal of attention is being paid to these conclusions. Since 2000, three full issues of the *American Educator* have been devoted to the topic of language, knowledge and achievement. (See Summer 2001; Spring 2003; Spring 2006.)

Instruction designed to change this situation needs to be multifaceted and complex, partly because it depends so much on students' preexisting knowledge, experience, and vocabulary. There are at least three things that committed teachers can do to make things better for preadolescent students and to build the cognitive capacity and motivation necessary to do well in the future: (1) teach vocabulary and build background knowledge; (2) provide high-quality classroom instruction that promotes higher-order thinking with engaging texts and tasks; and (3) promote learning with challenging content and themes. So in this chapter I turn my attention to developing vocabulary, developing background knowledge, and promoting higher-order thinking. You'll find lesson frameworks, questioning strategies, and ideas for integrating content and literacy within units and themes.

Lessons From Research and Practice: What We Know About Developing Background Knowledge, Vocabulary, and Higher-Order Thinking

Developing Background Knowledge

Kara is not unusual. She is a city girl with limited experiences outside of her local neighborhood. As with all readers, her prior knowledge helps her understand some things with great sophistication and her lack of it prevents her from understanding others. Decades of research in this area have demonstrated how powerfully prior knowledge impacts comprehension (M. Y. Lipson, 1982, 1983). When students with greater prior knowledge read a familiar text, a number of positive things happen:

- They are more likely to use effective strategies (Lundberg, 1987).

- They recall it more completely later on (Addison & Hutcheson, 2001).

- They read more accurately with fewer miscues (Wixson, 1979).

- They can summarize more accurately (McConaughy, 1982).

- They answer more questions correctly (Wixson, 1983; Addison & Hutcheson, 2001).

- They are better able to make inferences (Lipson, Mosenthal, & Mekkelsen, 1999; McNamara, Kintsch, Songer, & Kintsch, 1996).

In other words, students' prior knowledge can have a critical impact on their ability to comprehend.

The cumulative effects of limited prior knowledge are only now being understood. The research has shown that students who have a storehouse of background knowledge not only read specific texts better, they accumulate knowledge in organized networks. These networks allow them to behave more like "experts" in applying and using the information in new settings. In other words, they get smarter. But students who've struggled to learn to read in the primary grades have spent so much time learning how to read that they have not acquired the vocabulary and concepts that would have been introduced during content instruction or acquired during wide reading. (See Hirsch, 2003.)

Students who enter fourth grade with weaknesses in the area of vocabulary are much more likely to experience serious reading comprehension problems than those with stronger oral language development (Biemiller, 2003). Fortunately, reading instruction that provides an in-depth, long-term focus on content knowledge improves general vocabulary (Moss, 2005). (I cover vocabulary development in greater depth later in the chapter.) This conclusion, coupled with the evidence that general background knowledge is critical for both comprehension and learning, means we need much stronger curriculum in the intermediate grades. A stronger focus on content actually increases motivation as well (Ivey & Fisher, 2006). Here are some suggestions for building a stronger curriculum:

Ensure All Students Have Access to Conceptually Challenging Texts

Students need access to conceptually challenging material so they can develop their abilities to "think with print" and expand their background knowledge. According to Andrew Biemiller (2003):

> Current school practices typically have little effect on oral language development during the primary years. Because the level of language used is often limited to what the children can read and write, there are few opportunities for language development in the primary grades. (p. 2)

Of course, students must be able to apply new or difficult skills in relatively easy material. In addition, it is clear that a great deal of reading in ability-appropriate materials is the best way to build fluency (Pikulski & Chard, 2005; Rasinski, 2003). However, students also need regular access to challenging content in age- and grade-appropriate texts.

Ensure All Students Have Access to Authentic and Diverse Texts

Because the texts used for beginning readers are designed to promote decoding skills (and not comprehension skills), they are often contrived. As they enter grade 3, most students have not had enough experience reading authentic and diverse texts. As a result, they generally have not developed very sophisticated comprehension skills. For example, students in grades 3 and 4 often do not understand the motives or goals of characters. In fact, we find that students often pay such close attention to the action in narrative stories that they may not even be able to identify the theme (M. Y. Lipson et al., 1999).

Even the narrative stories they read are beginning to change in the intermediate grades. For example, while they may understand and like simple realistic fiction, they may not have encountered historical fiction or sophisticated fantasies. These more complex narrative stories demand more from readers. In Figure 4.1, I provide an illustration of how challenging texts can be during these intermediate years. Richard Peck's terrific story, *A Long Way From Chicago* (1998), should interest many students, but the references to events and vocabulary from another era can be a barrier to comprehending historical fiction like Peck's. Without good instructional support, students may abandon these texts before they have a chance to find that they might enjoy them. Both exposure and good instruction are usually needed to help children read and understand a broad range of different genres.

To compound matters, there is some research that actually suggests that intermediate teachers avoid using substantive texts—either textbooks or challenging original documents (Clinton, 2002; Sewall, 2000). Recognizing that their students struggle with complex texts, and concerned about content, teachers may actually avoid using the very materials that students need in order to acquire information and learn to work with text. In other words, practices designed to help students in some areas may actually interfere with their development in others.

Excerpt From Historical Fiction

"You wouldn't think we'd have to leave Chicago to see a dead body. We were growing up there back in the bad old days of Al Capone and Bugs Moran. Just the winter before, they'd had the St. Valentine's Day Massacre over on North Clark Street. The city had such an evil reputation that the Thompson submachine gun was better known as a 'Chicago typewriter.'

But I'd grown to the age of nine and my sister Mary Alice was seven, and we'd yet to see a stiff. We guessed that most of them were where you couldn't see them, at the bottom of Lake Michigan wearing concrete overshoes." (p. 3)

The reference to a dead body is likely to pique interest.

These references to Al Capone and Bugs Moran are obscure for today's students.

Students may pick up on the submachine gun, but what is a "typewriter"—much less a "Chicago typewriter"? The sound of an old typewriter and its relationship to the sound of a machine gun will go unnoticed.

Students love gory detail and death, but these colorful references—to a "stiff" and to "concrete overshoes"—are likely to confuse students more than interest them without some help from the teacher.

Figure 4.1 *A Long Way From Chicago* by Richard Peck. Opening paragraphs of Chapter 1: "Shotgun Cheatham's Last Night Above Ground 1929"

Ensure All Students Have Access to Nonfiction Text

Primary students have a great deal less opportunity to hear and read nonfiction texts than intermediate students (Duke, 2000a, 2000b; Duke & Bennett-Armistead, 2003). One of the reasons that it is so important for teachers to use nonfiction texts with students is that they are so different from narrative stories. (Although some educators and researchers make distinctions between the terms "nonfiction" and "informational text," I use these terms interchangeably here. I reserve the word "exposition" for text *structure* and discuss it shortly.) We need to give special attention to nonfiction texts for several reasons:

- Students do not get enough exposure.
- Students need to read them in order to expand their background knowledge and vocabulary, and grapple with challenging ideas (Clinton, 2002).
- The breadth and depth of students' learning is enhanced by integrated study/use across domains (Guthrie, Wigfield, & Perencevich, 2004; M. Y. Lipson, Valencia, Wixson, & Peters, 1993).
- Students need them to advance their own pursuit of knowledge and fuel their curiosity (Alexander, 1996; Dreher, 2003).
- Students need experience and instruction with multiple types of texts in order to be successful throughout their school careers.

Many students who are capable and thoughtful readers of narrative stories, struggle to understand nonfiction. Shawn is a good example. You may remember Shawn's think-aloud of *Yang the Youngest and His Terrible Ear* on page 74. In that think-aloud, he revealed an excellent ability to read with meaning and make inferences that propelled him through text. More than a year later, in fourth grade, Shawn's written summary indicates that he has less ability to manage ideas from informational text related to social studies. (See Figure 4.2.) He was asked to summarize information from an informational text on Samuel de Champlain. His writing shows engaged thinking, but it also reveals weak organizational skills and some inability to focus on the big ideas.

Shawn's reading and writing are quite typical of students this age. He grabs on to various interesting tidbits (Patricia Alexander calls them "seductive details") and strings them together. This is not a summary at all; certainly not as sophisticated as his narrative summary of *Yang the Youngest*, which appeared in Chapter 3. Shawn, like many of his peers, needs support if he is going to get the most from informational texts. Explicit instruction helps but so does support.

Social Studies

2/17/

① Samuel De Champlain — name ring a bell? Lake Champlain. Did you ever think maybe it was named after him? Well guess what, it was.

Samuel De Champlain discovered Lake Champlain in the year 1609.

② Hey, did you know before Fort Ticonderoga was called Fort Ticonderoga it was called Carillon.

③ Now I thought that was pretty cool considering thats something I've never thought about. If y__ about its interesting t__ something we've called __ same thing our whol__ before people did'nt __

④ 1756 was a p__ interesting to most p__ think considering

[continued note]

was the year the French and Indian War started. Imagine being seltteled with a nice family and having to move because two different kinds of people can't sit down and talk something out peacefully. Now when that war **⑤** ended England owened most of the land. I don't see why they could'nt just share in peace. But obviously they could considering they had a 5 year war.

March 4th 1791. Big day Vermont joins the United States as the 14th State!!!

✱ French and English

---

① Shawn is attempting to create an interesting lead using information from his reading. This blending is acceptable in the first several sentences.

② Next, Shawn inserts information about Fort Ticonderoga—an interesting detail that is not coherently linked to the rest of the material. Like many students, Shawn pays more attention to "seductive detail" than important information.

③ The next paragraph reads like a journal entry—while interesting, it is definitely not appropriate for an informational summary.

④ An abrupt introduction of a fact (1756 as the start of the French and Indian War) is quickly overwhelmed by an editorial comment about getting along.

⑤ A major concept—English ownership over a vast amount of land—is not developed at all, and he ends with another unrelated fact—that Vermont joins the United States thirty years later.

Figure 4.2 Shawn's social studies paper on Samuel de Champlain

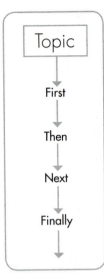

Topic

First

Then

Next

Finally

Helping Students Access Text Using Graphic Organizers

One of the best ways to support students in accessing text is to provide them with a graphic organizer. Even a simple sequence organizer like the one shown to the left would improve Shawn's summary.

Guided reading, read-alouds, discussion or question guides, and story maps or structured overviews are all good ways to help students understand—especially when the material is difficult or very important. For example, I find that students are often confused as they read about the Civil War for the first time. Who is fighting—the Confederates? the South? the Union? the North? Why are they fighting—slavery? economic purposes? states' rights? The more tailored to the specific context the support is, the better for the students. In Figure 4.3, you can see the type of graphic organizer that would be helpful for reading a social studies text on the Civil War.

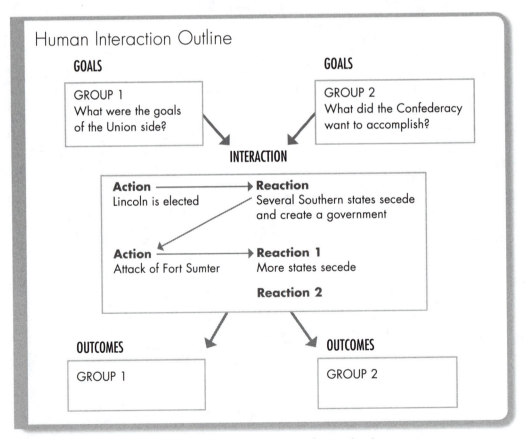

Human Interaction Outline

GOALS

GROUP 1
What were the goals
of the Union side?

GOALS

GROUP 2
What did the Confederacy
want to accomplish?

INTERACTION

Action ⟶ **Reaction**
Lincoln is elected   Several Southern states secede
and create a government

Action ⟶ **Reaction 1**
Attack of Fort Sumter   More states secede

Reaction 2

OUTCOMES

GROUP 1

OUTCOMES

GROUP 2

Figure 4.3 A graphic organizer to help students get the most out of a social studies text

An effective graphic organizer helps students assign importance as they read through the text. In effect, it shows them how to think about the relationships between the ideas.

Other Ways to Help Students Access Text

Not all students will be able to read grade-level texts by themselves. There are a number of ways that we can provide these students with access to demanding texts. Teacher read-alouds are the most obvious method. But we can also give them opportunities for partner reading, or we can have them read portions of text while a supporter (an adult or older student) reads the rest. Specific instructional supports such as preteaching and graphic organizers are still other ways to make these texts more accessible. Other ways to help students access grade-appropriate texts include these:

- **Shared reading:** An interactive technique in which both students and teacher have a copy of the same text. (Short texts can be placed on an overhead projected or copied onto a chart.) Students follow along as the teacher reads. Wherever possible, the students join in, reading in unison.

- **Paired reading:** A student listens to an adult read until he or she feels ready to join in. After a time, the adult fades her voice, and the student reads alone. If the student's reading falters, the adult joins in again.

- **Taped read-alongs:** This technique entails students' listening to and following along with a tape recording. The advantage, of course, is that the teacher doesn't have to be present for the students to read along. Also, students can listen more than once if they need to. A number of commercial programs provide taped versions of their core literature.

- **Parallel texts with mixed-ability discussion groups:** Using this method, students access the same general content but in material that is easier than what others are reading. This technique should be used cautiously. If the material is too simplified, it defeats the purpose. On the other hand, even simplified material can prepare students for whole-group discussions that may be quite challenging.

We need to provide ample opportunity to acquire grade-level cognitive competencies. Texts that are appropriate for comprehension and cognitive development are:

- Cognitively complex enough to challenge students' comprehending abilities

- Diverse enough to introduce students to a wide range of authors, genres, and text structures

- Interesting enough to intrigue and motivate students

- Well-suited to teaching specific comprehension skills and strategies. (See Chapter 5.)

Developing Vocabulary

Educators and researchers have understood for a very long time that there is a relationship between vocabulary and comprehension (see Nagy & Scott, 2000). Kara's story shows that reading is difficult without appropriate prior knowledge and that vocabulary is really a marker for prior knowledge. Words are labels for objects, concepts, ideas, and relationships. Words tend to be stored in a network of connected concepts, labels, and so on. It is not impossible to think about an idea without vocabulary, but it is much easier to manipulate ideas when we have the vocabulary associated with them. Decades of research have revealed just how important vocabulary is (see review by Nagy & Scott, 2000):

- Vocabulary knowledge is one of the single best indicators of verbal ability.

- Vocabulary difficulty strongly influences the readability of text.

- Lack of vocabulary can be a crucial factor underlying school failure.

The relationship between vocabulary and reading is reciprocal—benefits flow in both directions. Wide reading clearly promotes vocabulary development (Snow et al., 1998) and a large, well-organized vocabulary improves comprehension (Nagy, 1988). The average fifth-grade student who reads 25 minutes a day will encounter one million words of text a year, including twenty thousand unfamiliar words. She will learn about a thousand new words from text reading alone (Jitendra, Edwards, Sacks, & Jacobson, 2004). Unfortunately, many students do not read enough to broaden their vocabulary in this way.

Although this "incidental" acquisition of vocabulary is essential for reading development, students can also benefit from vocabulary instruction. Unfortunately, research suggests that most vocabulary instruction is not as helpful as it could be. It is too teacher directed and overly focused on definitions; too often the instruction relies on commercial materials that introduce words in some arbitrary order, whether students need to know the meanings or not. It is not unusual for students to look up the dictionary definitions of words that are not meaningful to them. This is unlikely to result in long-term learning. A fellow teacher, recognizing the folly, once told me it was like looking up and memorizing the phone numbers for people you didn't know and didn't want to talk to!

So what words should we teach? There is no easy answer. Word meanings are generally learned incrementally over time and with multiple exposures. Similarly, all words are not created equal. Some words are so common that virtually every native speaker knows them, such as *jump* or *yellow*. Other words are quite obscure and typically used only in connection with specific content domains, such as *exponent* or *factorization*. Recognizing these differences, Isabel Beck and her colleagues have developed a categorization scheme for helping teachers understand what words are worth spending time on (Beck, McKeown, & Kucan, 2002).

For maximum vocabulary development, teachers should spend considerable time working with Tier 2 words because they are used in general reading and speaking. Students need this wide reading of general material to improve their overall cognitive ability—to get smart. In reading science and social studies texts, for example, students encounter many words that are sophisticated, but not content specific. In the book *Graham Hawkes: Underwater Pilot* (Beatty, 2004), there are many content-specific Tier 3 words, such as *submersible, vertical, aeronautical*, and *engineer*. But there are also many Tier 2 words, such as *inaccessible, simultaneously, enveloping*, and *tinkering*. Children are

Types of Words

Tier 1 words are "basic" words, commonly found in students' everyday language and reading materials. Examples: *jump, bright, run, ball, is*

Tier 2 words are "sophisticated" words that are more precise terms for ideas students already have (for example, students know the concept of *funny* and can learn a more sophisticated word like *hilarious* without having to add a new concept). Examples: *frolic, luminous, absurd, reluctant, convince*

Tier 3 words are "low-frequency" words that are needed to understand specialized content and concepts. Examples: *quadratic, exponential, metacognitive, phonemic*

Beck, McKeown, and Kucan (2002) identify three types of words.

Wildland Fire in Ecosystems: Effects of Fire on Fauna

Fires <u>affect</u> animals mainly through <u>effects</u> on their **habitat**. Fires often cause short-term increases in wildlife foods that <u>contribute</u> to increases in populations of some animals. These increases are <u>moderated</u> by the animals' ability to <u>thrive</u> in the <u>altered</u>, often simplified, structure of the postfire environment. The extent of fire effects on animal communities generally depends on the extent of change in habitat structure and **species composition** caused by fire. **Stand-replacement fires** usually cause greater changes in the **faunal** communities of forests than in those of grasslands. Within forests, stand-replacement fires usually alter the animal community more <u>dramatically</u> than **understory fires**. Animal **species** are **adapted** to <u>survive</u> the pattern of fire frequency, season, size, <u>severity</u>, and <u>uniformity</u> that characterize their habitat in **presettlement** times. When fire frequency increases or decreases <u>substantially</u> or fire severity changes from presettlement patterns, habitat for many animal species <u>declines</u>. (Smith, 2000)

This passage shows how vocabulary can create barriers to comprehension. Tier 2 words are underlined. Tier 3 words are boldfaced.

likely to know these concepts but have vocabulary representations that are less sophisticated (*out of reach, at the same time, surrounding, fooling around*). Unless children learn these Tier 2 vocabulary words, they may have a hard time comprehending texts, even when the ideas are within their grasp.

The passage to the left shows how vocabulary can create barriers to comprehension. In this brief text on wildfires, there are certainly some Tier 3 words that contribute to its difficulty, such as *habitat, species, composition, stand-replacement, faunal,* and *adapted*.

While the Tier 3 words make the passage difficult, the many Tier 2 words pose at least as great a challenge to comprehension. Despite their difficulty, most students in grades 5 and 6 actually know concepts connected to those words. Even if students do not know a specific word—*contribute*, for example—they likely know the concept. They know about contributing to the collection plate at church, contributing to a food drive, or contributing to a group project in school.

When we teach Tier 2 words, we help students understand the specific text they are reading—but students are likely to understand *other* texts as well because these Tier 2 words have general applicability (Beck et al., 2002). With the right focus, vocabulary instruction builds background for other materials and improves students' overall comprehending ability. This is why time spent on these words is likely to be at least as useful as time spent on content-specific words, especially during grades 3 to 6.

Good vocabulary development requires an instructional program that is multifaceted and intentional. The following principles of vocabulary instruction should be kept in mind as we plan (see Beck, Perfetti, & McKeown, 1982; Blachowicz & Fisher, 2000; Nagy & Herman, 1987; NRP, 2000):

- Engage students in active learning and provide multiple exposures.

- Make connections to known concepts.

- Select words carefully and vary instruction according to purpose.

TIER 2 WORDS	KNOWN CONCEPT
affect	influence, impacts
effects	results, happenings
contribute	add to
moderated	slowed down
thrive	succeed
altered	changed
dramatically	seriously, noticeably
survive	last, live on
uniformity	evenness, regularity
characterized	common to, like
substantially	a great deal, to a large extent
declines	lowers, gets smaller

A sampling of Tier 2 words and their known concepts

Engage Students in Active Learning and Provide Multiple Exposures to Words

One of the reasons that active learning is so important is that students need multiple exposures to words before they really have a grasp of the meaning. The number of exposures needed to learn a new word ranges from 5 to 16. Word learning varies so much because it depends on such things as context, interest, knowledge of other, and related words (Meara, 1997; Nation, 1990).

Word walls and word associations are examples of active learning. Other types of active engagement include word sorts and semantic mapping of all types. (See next page.) Other ways to engage students and increase word experience include relationship charts, cloze activities, skits, and competitions.

Vocabulary Word Sort

Directions: Instruct students to use the words in the word bank to create two lists of words that go together based on their meaning. Then, have students label their two lists.

Word Bank: altered, habitat, simplified, community, adapted, environment, decreases, forests, grasslands, moderated, increases, ecosystems, declines

Words that have to do with where animals or people live	Words that have to do with change
habitat community	altered simplified
environment forests	increases decreases declines
grasslands ecosystems	adapted moderated

Semantic Map

Directions: Direct students to create a semantic map or web for words. The example here uses a technique suggested by Robert Schwartz and Taffy Raphael (Schwartz, 1988; Schwartz & Raphael, 1985). The three questions—*What is it? What is it like? What are some examples?*—help students see the relationship between new words and more familiar terms. These maps help both teachers and students organize concepts.

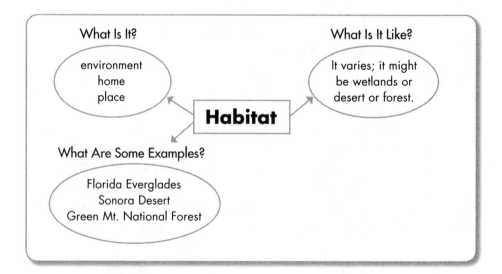

One common practice that does *not* help students very much is looking words up in the dictionary. According to Louisa Moats (2004), this activity is not effective for the following reasons:

- Reading a definition does not tell us how a word is actually used.

- We need examples in context to infer the range of meanings for a word.

- Dictionary definitions can be truncated and incomplete.

In addition, many dictionary definitions contain words that are unfamiliar to students. For example, here is the definition for the word *jib*:

> **Jib:** a triangular sail set upon a stay or halyard extending from the foremast or fore-topmast to the bowsprit or the jib boom. Large vessels often carry several jibs; as inner jib; outer jib; flying jib; etc. (*Webster's Revised Unabridged Dictionary*, 1913. Retrieved February 10, 2006 from http://dict.die.net/jib/)

Rivet

It is clear that simply looking a word up is not going to be helpful for most readers! Other techniques will be needed if the word is really critical to comprehension. One fun technique is Rivet, which can be done with very little preparation.

1. Choose 4 or 5 vocabulary words that are important to the text students are about to read.

2. Select a word and on a blank sheet of chart paper or on the board draw several blank lines, one for each letter in the word.

3. Give a clue to the word that is related to its meaning; for example, if the word is *habitat*, you might say, "This word means 'home.'"

4. Ask students to try to guess the word (they do not guess individual letters as in the game hangman). If they need more clues, you can provide more meaning-related hints, or you might write one of the letters (*h*, for example) on the corresponding line. Every time students guess an incorrect word, *you* get a point. Students get points for guessing correctly, though the number of points awarded decreases with each clue after the first. If they guess based on one clue, they get five points; after two hints, they get four points, and so on.

5. Continue playing with the remaining vocabulary words.

(Cunningham, Hall, & Cunningham, 2000)

Teachers can control the conversation and "clues" that are offered during the guessing. On a recent visit to Cathy Smith's fifth-grade class, students were preparing to read an article from *Time for Kids*, and Cathy had chosen the following words*: iPod, maximum,* and *poll.* The point of this activity is to focus on the words themselves and their relationship to the upcoming reading. Because students do not guess letters, but whole words, they are generating concept labels. In addition, the clues that teachers provide are designed to move students toward the *meaning* of the word, not the spelling. Using these words, students ended up making very good predictions about the articles they would read—and got an extra exposure to the words as well. It also offers an opportunity to notice spelling patterns, prefixes, and so on.

Make Connections to Known Concepts

Another great way to help students acquire new vocabulary is to help them see how new words are related to words that they already know. In the case of *jib*, most students do know what a sail is and, in a general way, what it does. Using this knowledge, we can build a more complete understanding by pointing out that different sails perform different functions and that a jib is one kind of sail. We may wish to limit our explanation to the key elements that may be critical to understanding the word's use in the current selection—for example, that it moves and therefore might hit someone. Of course, pictures, sketches, and objects can be very useful in introducing new concepts.

At other times, students may understand the basic concept quite clearly but may not know the new word being used. Words like this might include: *scarlet* (red), *lorry* (truck), *despondent* (very sad), and *euphoria* (very happy). Generally, students should need both fewer exposures and less explicit instruction to add such words to their vocabulary, although it might take longer for them to use them independently. When both the word and the concept are alien, much more instruction is needed. *Disdain, disillusionment,* and *veto* are examples of words where conceptual development would need to accompany vocabulary development.

One strategy that I have found very useful, since it can be easily included in guided reading is a technique called the Vocabulary-Language-Prediction (VLP) activity (Wood & Robinson, 1983), which I illustrate on the next page.

Vocabulary–Language–Prediction (VLP) Activity

VOCABULARY Step 1	Select vocabulary. Decide what skill(s) will be addressed in this lesson and how vocabulary is related to the skill(s). Write the words on individual cards with their page number from the story on them.
Step 2	The words are laid out so the students can see them. They are told these are words from the story they are about to read.
ORAL LANGUAGE Step 3	Engage students in discussion or activities related to the words. Discuss context, synonyms, or structural aspects. (See Chapter 6.)
PREDICTION Step 4	Use the words to predict what the story will be about. Write predictions on the board/chart.
Step 5	During reading, ask students to confirm, reject, or modify their predictions.

If I were to use the VLP before reading Chapter 3 of *Yang the Youngest and His Terrible Ear*, I would do the following:

1. Select words: *attention, snigger, loneliest, wistfully, audition.*
2. Place words on cards so that I can manipulate them.
3. Discuss:
   - Which words might describe how the main character is feeling in this chapter.
   - Which words might show action.
   - Which words might tell about the setting.
4. Ask students to predict: "What do you think will happen in this chapter? Use what you already know about this story and think about these new words."
5. Help students monitor their predictions during reading.

Select Words Carefully and Vary Instruction According to Purpose

Students learn new words through exposure and through explicit instruction, so our literacy programs should include both types of opportunity. Wide reading and extensive oral language experiences are the best ways to teach words indirectly. However, some words require direct, explicit instruction. It is important to decide both which specific vocabulary words we want or need to teach and what level of treatment we will give them. Not all words require, or deserve, the same intensity of focus.

The idea that vocabulary instruction does not have to mean the same thing all the time was brought home recently in a conversation I had with a fourth-grade teacher in one of our project schools. She had been teaching the westward expansion and expressed frustration about how much time it was taking to teach and test vocabulary like *Conestoga wagon, prairie schooner, sod, Oregon Trail* and *manifest destiny*. Of course, there were many names and places to be learned as well. As we talked, she suddenly realized that she had spent so much time on these Tier 3 concepts that she had neglected more universally important words such as *expansion* and *settlement, freight* and *frontier.* Of course, Tier 3 vocabulary is important, but the amount of time and attention we want to devote to those words should be balanced against their long-term power for the learner. Larger concepts such as "frontier" or "expansion" will be essential in studying other aspects of social studies or science like Hitler's expansion during World War II or the concept of a new frontier in space.

In order to decide how much time and attention to give to vocabulary, I think about the vocabulary in relation to the text the students are reading. There are several reasons to teach vocabulary, and the treatment is different for each.

- **Remove barriers to comprehension.** For this purpose, I choose words that are essential for understanding the text but may not be very important to the overall ideas I want students to know/learn. I usually spend very little time, just enough so that students' comprehension won't be disrupted.

- **Enhance comprehension of the topic or theme.** For this purpose, important and unfamiliar vocabulary are selected, and I am likely to spend time before, during, and after reading, making sure that students learn and use these words.

- **Teach interesting, useful vocabulary.** I want students to take an interest in words and generally expand their vocabulary. If the words are interesting, but not central to comprehending the specific text, I may teach them after reading the text, or I might ask students to identify several interesting words to share with others.

Removing Barriers to Comprehension

In "Wildland Fire in Ecosystems" (page 98), words like *stand-replacement* and *faunal* need to be introduced in order to remove barriers to comprehension. It is not necessary to spend much time on these words and others like them— I often just provide synonyms or quick definitions. I don't really expect children to remember these words; I just don't want them to stumble because of them. On the other hand, words like *species* and *habitats* are words that will help students comprehend the bigger ideas in the passage, and I would likely provide a more substantial treatment of them. The box below illustrates this approach.

REMOVING BARRIERS

- "Today, you are going to read about 'fauna' [write on board or have prepared word cards]. This is a technical, scientific word that means 'animal life.' Sometimes you might hear people talking about 'flora and fauna'— that means the plant life and the animal life. So, what does *fauna* mean?"

- "Another word that you are going to encounter is . . ."

SUPPORTING COMPREHENSION

- Plan to do a read-aloud using Seymour Simon's *Wildfires* (1996). This introduces the ideas and some of the key concepts that will be needed to understand the later reading.

- Highlight words such as *habitat* and *species* as the book is read and discussed.

- Create a word wall (chart) and add important vocabulary to it for reference later on.

- During and after reading, support students' understanding and use of key concepts by doing word sorts and semantic maps.

Enhancing Comprehension of the Topic or Theme

When students are reading a selection as part of a larger unit or theme, vocabulary should be introduced to advance comprehension of major concepts—some of which may appear in the passage and some of which will help them link the passage information with other concepts and ideas. For example, "Wildland Fire in Ecosystems" would probably be read within a larger unit of "bionetwork," so the word *ecosystems* would be pulled from the title and introduced as a superordinate concept. I might use a semantic map like the following to build the class's understanding of the term "ecosystems."

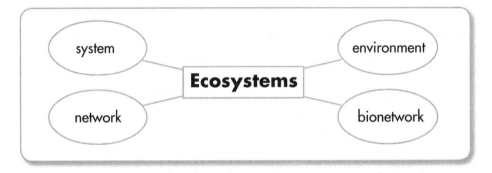

Another concept that could be mapped is "environment" and the impact of human actions on natural systems.

Teaching Interesting, Useful Vocabulary

In the passage on wildfires, there are also Tier 2 words like *moderated, contribute*, and *dramatically*, which are interesting and useful words that I would like to work with. These might become a part of an ongoing study of interesting words. With vocabulary words that are generally interesting or important and with some of the comprehension-support vocabulary, I recommend the type of "robust" vocabulary instruction described by Isabel Beck and her colleagues (Beck et al., 2002). Robust instruction provides rich information about words and their uses, as well as frequent and varied opportunities for students to think about and use them. Here's how to bring robust instruction to your vocabulary lessons:

1. Identify three to five Tier 2 words from the text.

2. Create a student-friendly definition for each word (this can be done in discussion with students).

3. Use the words in discussion, examples, and nonexamples.

4. Extend the examples to other contexts.

5. Expand students' experience with the words by using them in fun or interesting ways. Timothy Rasinski suggests ringing a bell every time a new word is used in class. Students might write word poems or play word games. The idea is to use these words frequently.

To teach vocabulary deeply, we need to explain the meanings of words directly and then provide thought-provoking, playful, and interactive follow-up. In the illustration below, I apply the steps listed above to the challenging vocabulary from the passage on wildfires.

Extending Vocabulary Instruction
(Example from "Wildland Fire in Ecosystems," page 98)

1. Identify words: *habitat, contribute, moderated, dramatically, declines*

2. Create student-friendly definitions:
   - A *habitat* is the area where someone or something lives.
   - If I *contribute* that means I give something or add more.
   - Something that is *moderated* becomes smaller or less severe.
   - When things happen *dramatically*, they grab our attention.

3. Use the words in discussion with examples and nonexamples
   - Ask students if the woods is a habitat for a squirrel. Is a birdcage a habitat for a bird?
   - Does rain contribute to the growth of flowers? Does planting a garden contribute to the wilderness?

4. Extend examples to other contexts:

   Joey's last-minute basket *contributed* to our win last night. His fine play helped us to survive the other team's excellent shooting. In the end, he *dramatically* flung the ball to his parents in the stands.

5. Expand students' experience with the words. Use the words in playful ways for multiple activities:

   HAVE YOU EVER?
   Ask students questions such as:
   - Have you ever contributed to a discussion? How?
   - Have you ever altered your parents' mind?

   WORD ASSOCIATIONS
   Play this word-association game:
   - Which word goes with diet? (declines)
   - Which word goes with speed bump? (moderated)

Promote Higher-Order Thinking

Simply exposing students to high-quality, challenging text is certainly not enough. Students need to think with print and be able to engage in vigorous reflection on unfamiliar (and familiar) information. How we ask our questions is a key to how richly students respond.

Ask Questions That Promote Deep Thinking About Text

Barbara Taylor and David Pearson, in their study of "beat the odds" schools (Taylor et al., 2003), found that teachers who had the highest levels of student achievement ("accomplished teachers") were much more likely to ask higher-level questions than less accomplished teachers. (See Figure 4.4.)

Accomplished Teachers' Approach to Comprehension Instruction

	PERCENTAGE OF TEACHERS ASKING QUESTIONS		
	Text-based questions	Higher-level questions	Writing in response to reading
Most-accomplished teachers	48%	31%	48%
Least-accomplished teachers	24%	0%	18%

Figure 4.4

We have known for quite a long time that questioning strategies are associated with greater student growth, *especially* in the poorest schools. Three decades ago, Barak Rosenshine and his colleagues found that teacher questions were related to student achievement (Rosenshine, 1971). More recently, research suggests that combining both basic skills/strategy instruction and higher-order questioning leads to better comprehension among high-poverty students (Knapp, 1995; Puma et al., 1997).

Over the years, several categorization schemes have been proposed to classify questions. Most have attempted to capture the idea that some questions are more demanding and difficult than others—that there are higher-level and lower-level questions. Lower-level questions demand little of a reader except verbatim recall of information from the text. Higher-level questions, on the other hand, require readers to manipulate information from various places in the text or to use information from prior knowledge in combination with the text.

Among the systems for classifying questions, Bloom's taxonomy is the best known (from Huitt, 2004). (See Figure 4.5.) As you generate questions about texts, don't worry too much about which category a question fits. What is important to notice is the type of *thinking* that is promoted by different levels of questions.

Types of Questions and the Thinking They Promote

QUESTION TYPE	THINKING
Knowledge	• Students recall, list, memorize, or recognize information. • Who, what, where, when?
Comprehension	• Students understand or interpret information based on text and prior knowledge. They might also organize information for retelling.
Application	• Students use information and concepts to construct understanding, solve problems, etc. • Why is ___ significant?
Analyze	• Students select and connect information—to identify concepts critical to responding to a question or understanding a system. They might also identify motive. • What evidence can you list for...?
Synthesize	• Students integrate and/or combine ideas to create something that is new to them. • What solution do you predict? If you combine two things....
Evaluate	• Students assess or critique. They must develop opinions, judgments, and decisions. • How would you decide? What would be the highest priority?

Figure 4.5 Adapted from Huitt, W. (2004).

In the box below, I provide an excerpt from the wonderful book *Passage to Freedom: The Sugihara Story* (Mochizuki, 1997), recounting the story of Hiroki Sugihara who helped hundreds of Jewish refugees escape from Poland in 1940. Multiple types of questions help students gain deeper meaning from the text. Many struggling students actually perform better when they receive

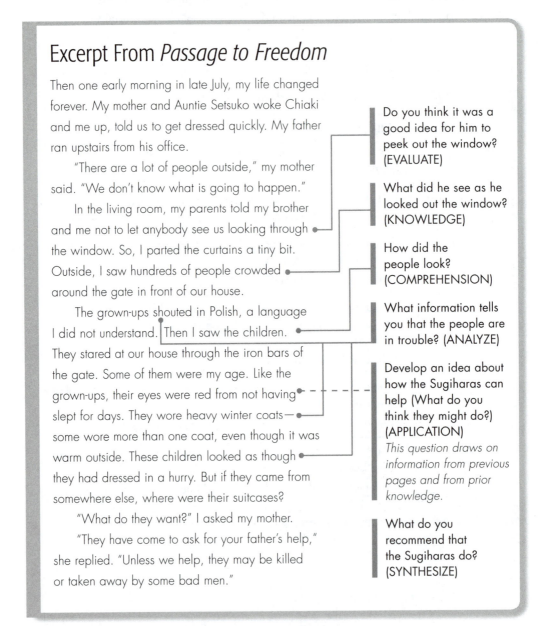

Excerpt From *Passage to Freedom*

Then one early morning in late July, my life changed forever. My mother and Auntie Setsuko woke Chiaki and me up, told us to get dressed quickly. My father ran upstairs from his office.

"There are a lot of people outside," my mother said. "We don't know what is going to happen."

In the living room, my parents told my brother and me not to let anybody see us looking through the window. So, I parted the curtains a tiny bit. Outside, I saw hundreds of people crowded around the gate in front of our house.

The grown-ups shouted in Polish, a language I did not understand. Then I saw the children. They stared at our house through the iron bars of the gate. Some of them were my age. Like the grown-ups, their eyes were red from not having slept for days. They wore heavy winter coats—some wore more than one coat, even though it was warm outside. These children looked as though they had dressed in a hurry. But if they came from somewhere else, where were their suitcases?

"What do they want?" I asked my mother.

"They have come to ask for your father's help," she replied. "Unless we help, they may be killed or taken away by some bad men."

Do you think it was a good idea for him to peek out the window? (EVALUATE)

What did he see as he looked out the window? (KNOWLEDGE)

How did the people look? (COMPREHENSION)

What information tells you that the people are in trouble? (ANALYZE)

Develop an idea about how the Sugiharas can help (What do you think they might do?) (APPLICATION)
This question draws on information from previous pages and from prior knowledge.

What do you recommend that the Sugiharas do? (SYNTHESIZE)

instruction that sends them in this direction, perhaps because higher-level questions often focus on making either personal or real-world connections (Newmann et al., 1998).

Ask Questions That Promote Thinking About the Reading Process

Most of the time, we ask questions because we want to know whether students are understanding something or to check whether they have read the material—it's assessment not instruction. However, questioning can be a potent instructional tool, and there are several excellent techniques to use in helping students think more deeply about text.

Questions can focus on a variety of different aspects of reading. We are accustomed to focusing on content, but questions can also direct students' attention to process and personal response. Here are some examples of process-focused questions:

- How does this information fit with earlier text information?
- What could you do that would help you to understand this?
- Which part is difficult for you?

Questions that are focused on response are more likely to look like this:

- Did this remind you of a time in your own life?
- Was there anything that surprised you?

These different types of questions cause students to think about the text differently and support them in entertaining new ideas.

The timing and location of questions also affects students' comprehension. For example, when students know the questions before reading, they are much more likely to be able to answer them than if they receive the questions afterward. On the other hand, prereading questions tend to narrow the focus for readers—students are more successful at answering those questions, but not others that might also be important. Questions that are asked after reading can serve an integrative function, if they are good ones. For example, asking readers to think about how two characters are alike causes them to revisit the text and think about aspects that they may not have considered before. Questions asked during reading are especially good for helping students monitor their reading and can help shape comprehension.

No one type of focus for questions is the best. These questions should be used intentionally to promote and develop varying approaches to text and different types of comprehension for different purposes.

Questioning the Author

Questioning the Author (QtA) is an instructional approach developed by Isabel Beck and her colleagues. QtA is designed to promote text comprehension, and it has a proven track record. (See Beck, McKeown, Hamilton, & Kucan, 1997.) Key features of the approach include:

- Occurs *during* text reading (not before or after)
- Involves group discussion
- Focuses on clarifying and understanding ideas in the text
- Relies on prompts (or "queries") that are designed to:
  - help students manage and understand text, or
  - advance group discussion

Some queries are designed to initiate discussion, while others extend and focus it. Based on the *Passage to Freedom* excerpt on page 110, the following questions might be used during group discussion:

- What is the author trying to tell us in this part?
- Why do you think the author includes details about the red eyes and the Polish language?
- The main character wonders about suitcases. Why is he thinking about that?
- How does the author want us to feel?

Simpler questions might include *What did he see? What language did the people speak? What were they wearing?* The problem with these questions is that students may be able to answer them and still not really understand the message the author is trying to convey. Students who read at the surface need help digging deeper. I have found the QtA questions to be an excellent way to do that.

Variations on this approach can be used to promote dialogue journals about texts. Liz Fothergill also uses dialogue journals to stretch her students' thinking. In Figure 4.6, you can see an exchange that she and 11-year-old Corey had about the book *Bigger* (Calvert, 1994). When he didn't fully respond, she modeled a bit of thinking the next day and posed the question again.

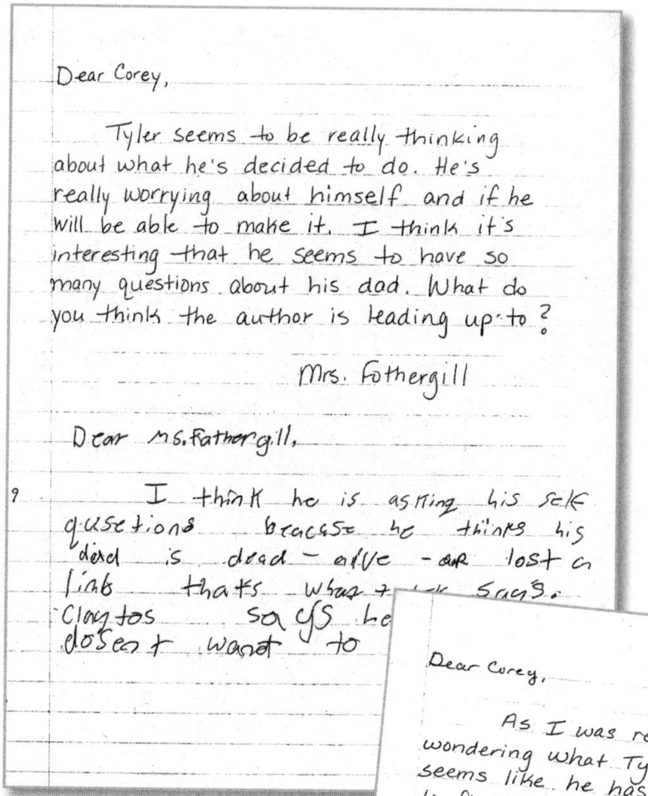

Dear Corey,

   Tyler seems to be really thinking about what he's decided to do. He's really worrying about himself and if he will be able to make it. I think it's interesting that he seems to have so many questions about his dad. What do you think the author is leading up to?

                          Mrs. Fothergill

Dear Ms. Fathergill,

9   I think he is asking his self qusetions beacese he thinks his dad is dead - alive - our lost or liak thats what tylr says. Claytos says he dosent want to

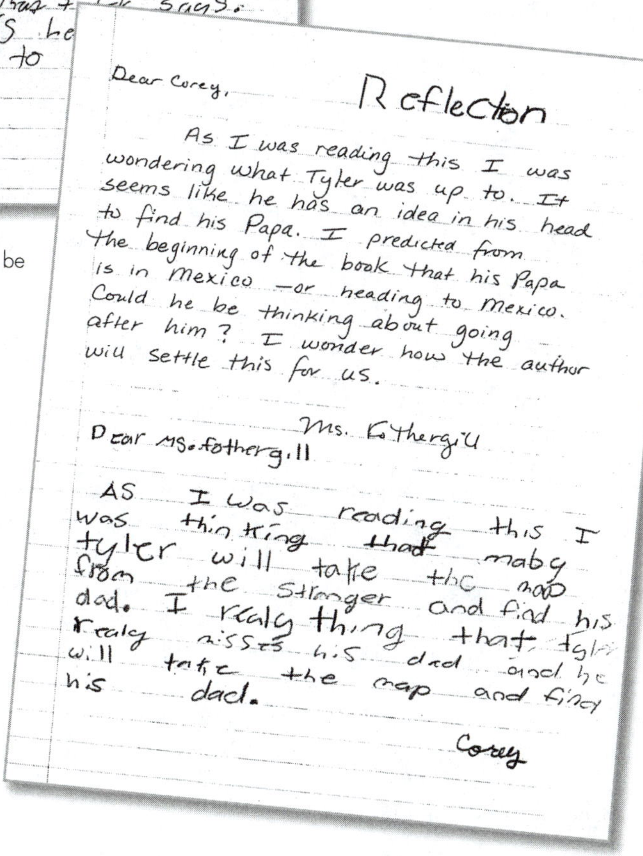

Figure 4.6 Dialogue journals can be used to stretch students' thinking.

Dear Corey,   Reflection

   As I was reading this I was wondering what Tyler was up to. It seems like he has an idea in his head to find his Papa. I predicted from the beginning of the book that his Papa is in Mexico — or heading to Mexico. Could he be thinking about going after him? I wonder how the author will settle this for us.

                          Ms. Fothergill

Dear Ms. Fothergill

   AS I was reading this I was thinking that maby tyler will take the map from the Stranger and find his dad. I realy thing that tgh realy misses his dad and he will take the map and find his dad.

                          Corey

Into the Classroom

Good teachers are always looking for the places where students may have difficulties—for example, not recognizing the setting of a story or lacking background knowledge for reading a social studies chapter—and planning instructional support. Unless they do, these difficulties become barriers to comprehension. On many occasions, students' comprehension of a particular story will be enhanced if we stop periodically to discuss how the text is similar to one they have read already. Guided reading is exceptionally useful in helping students comprehend text and acquire new ideas.

Lesson Frameworks

Effective reading instruction revolves around a three-phase framework: before, during, and after reading. The framework has proved useful over the years because it allows for such a wide variety of activity within each phase. Possible activities during each phase include:

BEFORE READING

- Activate prior knowledge and/or build background
- Set purposes and/or predictions
- Preteach vocabulary
- Preteach strategy
- Introduce graphic organizer

DURING READING

- Support comprehension with effective questioning
- Clarify and/or redirect
- Introduce additional vocabulary or demonstrate strategy

AFTER READING

- Respond
- Synthesize or summarize
- Integrate
- Apply

Teacher-guided reading should only be used when it is needed. If students do not need this high level of support, don't give it to them because they are likely to become too dependent on it. Especially in grades 3 to 6, we want students to start managing their own reading cycles. In addition, not all students need the full cycle of support. Some students may only need support before reading—to activate or acquire a bit of prior knowledge or focus their purpose for reading. After this initial instruction, they can read independently. Other students may need support both before and during, but can complete response activities on their own. Finally, some students need support at all three phases. And, of course, this will vary depending on the particular text being read. The more unfamiliar the topic or genre, the more likely students will need support. Figure 4.7 shows a sample lesson framework for guided reading for the narrative text *Yang the Youngest and His Terrible Ear*.

Guided Reading Planning Guide

Group: David, Justin, Isabel, and Haley Week: _____ Book: *Yang the Youngest and His Terrible Ear* Focus/Objectives: _____

MONDAY	TUESDAY	WEDNESDAY	THURSDAY	FRIDAY
Chapter 2 (pp. 17–26)	Chapter 2 (pp. 26–end)	Chapter 3 (up to p. 47)	Chapter 3 (finish and/or reread)	Chapter 4 (pp. 54–70)
VOCABULARY attention, snigger, loneliest, wistfully, audition	VOCABULARY approval, apologetically, sympathetic	VOCABULARY Self-selected words in vocabulary notebook (possibles: genius, admiration, convinced)	VOCABULARY N/A	VOCABULARY startled, spacious, stunned, annoyed, shocked, sympathetic
BEFORE READING 1. Review what we know about Yang and his family. 2. Preteach vocabulary using VLP.	BEFORE READING 1. Review what we know about Yang and his family. 2. Reread portions of yesterday's reading for fluency. 3. Generate predictions for today's reading.	BEFORE READING 1. Note that things change in this chapter—be looking for these changes; read to p. 47.	BEFORE READING Review vocabulary notebooks. Do word sorts.	BEFORE READING Tell students that all the vocabulary words on the board describe people's ideas, feelings, or reactions. Let's see if we can use them to get an idea about this chapter.
DURING READING 1. Read pp. 17–18 to find out what it was like for Yang in the early weeks of school. 2. Discuss how Yang feels; were we correct about how the vocabulary relates to Yang? 3. Read to p. 23 to see what happens to make Yang feel a bit better. 4. How is the next part (pp. 23–26) related to what we read earlier?	DURING READING Monitor predictions.	AFTER READING 1. Group discussion: what changes occurred in the story? How will they affect the characters and the story? 2. For tomorrow, have students finish the chapter: some things stay the same; watch for them.	DURING READING Buddy reading and think-aloud. Stop periodically and discuss any confusions, surprises, etc.	DURING READING Stop periodically to discuss how Yang and Matthew are doing; in this chapter their cultural differences definitely cause problems. Help students notice this.
AFTER READING 1. Have students summarize the story and write about it in their Reader's Notebook.	AFTER READING 1. Compare and contrast Yang and Matthew in small groups. 2. Word Work: Students choose five words from the vocabulary (Mon–Tues). Then, they find the base words and create new words by adding different endings.		AFTER READING Have students write an entry in their Reader's Notebook	AFTER READING 1. Have students summarize the story so far. 2. Word work: students use vocabulary to describe characters in the book.

Figure 4.7

Work With Challenging Content and Integrated Themes

In Chapter 2, I described some of the work by researchers such as Fred Newmann and Judith Langer that indicates how a focus on challenging and productive work can improve students' achievement—even in high-poverty schools. In the past decade, it has become very clear that improving students' comprehension is dependent on improving general knowledge and critical-thinking abilities (Hirsch, 2003; Walsh, 2003) and that content area reading can do just that. Across the country, state standards are focusing more and more on critical thinking, authentic inquiry, and the ability to use information from multiple sources to arrive at informed conclusions.

To meet these goals, the teachers I work with have been planning instruction with two ideas in mind: (1) adding more informational text to classroom libraries and displays and (2) seeking opportunities to teach literacy during content periods and vice versa.

A display of expository texts in a grade 5/6 classroom

Adding More Informational Text to Classroom Libraries and Displays

Even if the school library has an excellent collection of nonfiction materials, it is imperative that students have access to these types of texts right in the classroom. A wide array is important, too: expository texts, newspapers, biographies and autobiographies, news and information magazines, atlases, and other resource materials. Some authors write a great deal of nonfiction and they can serve as excellent author studies. (See box below.)

Some Authors of Nonfiction for Grades 3 to 6

AUTHORS	SAMPLE TEXTS
Michael L. Cooper	*Remembering Manzanar: Life in a Japanese American Relocation Camp* • *Bound for the Promised Land: The Great Black Migration* • *Dust to Eat: Drought and Depression in the 1930s* (and many more)
Peter Golenbock	*Teammates* • *Hank Aaron: Brave in Every Way*
James Haskins	*African Beginnings* • *The Story of Stevie Wonder* (and many more)
Stephen Kramer	*Eye of the Storm* • *Tornado* • *The Dark Zone: Exploring the Secret World of Caves* (and many more)
Patricia Lauber	*The News About Dinosaurs* • *Volcano: Eruption and Healing of Mount St. Helens* • *Who Came First? New Clues to Prehistoric Americans* (and many more)
David Macaulay	*Castles* • *The New Way Things Work* (and many more)
Ken Mochizuki	*Baseball Saved Us* • *Passage to Freedom: The Sugihara Story*
Walter Dean Myers	*At Her Majesty's Request* • *Malcolm X: A Fire Burning Brightly* • *Antarctica: Journeys to the South Pole* • *Now Is Your Time*
Andrea Davis Pinkney	*Duke Ellington* • *Ella Fitzgerald* • *Let It Shine: Stories of Black Women Freedom Fighters*
Seymour Simon	*Destination Jupiter* • *Wolves* • *Wildfires* (and many more)
Diane Stanley	*Good Queen Bess* • *Michelangelo* • *Bard of Avon: The Story of William Shakespeare* • *Shaka: King of the Zulus* (and many more)

The National Council of Teachers of English presents the Orbis Pictus Award every year for the best nonfiction title. These books are selected because they are useful in classroom teaching, serve as models of exemplary expository writing, and encourage critical thinking. In addition to the winning title, there are as many as five Honor Books, and other titles are also recommended. The following criteria are used in the selection process—criteria that are generally helpful for selecting informational texts to be used in instruction:

- **Accuracy**: facts are current and complete; contains a balance of fact and theory; point of view varies; stereotypes are avoided; author's qualifications are adequate; scope is appropriate; details are authentic

- **Organization**: development is logical; sequence is clear; interrelationships are indicated; patterns are provided (general-to-specific, simple-to-complex, etc.)

- **Design**: attractive, readable, illustrations complement text; placement of illustrative material is appropriate and complementary; media format and type are appropriate

- **Style**: writing is interesting, stimulating and reveals author's enthusiasm for subject; encourages curiosity and wonder; uses appropriate terminology and rich language

These books are excellent examples of high-quality nonfiction, and the full listing is available online at http://www.ncte.org/elem/awards/orbispictus.

Seeking Opportunities to Teach Literacy During Content Periods and Vice Versa

One of the best ways to get the most out of both literacy and content programs is to work with integrated units and themes. Traditionally, instructional units have been organized around a specific topic such as "oceans" or "the westward movement." In such content-driven units, literacy usually takes a backseat—we ask the students to use reading and writing, but we are not expressly teaching them literacy-related skills or strategies. For example, we might use historical fiction as part of a unit on the westward movement. While this is very good practice, we can't limit our literary reading in the intermediate grades to historical fiction! When literacy is taught only through topic units, there is a risk that students do not get a broad enough range of text types.

More than a decade ago my colleagues Sheila Valencia, Karen Wixson, Charlie Peters, and I studied and taught with themes. (See M. Y. Lipson et al., 1993.) Theme units are different from topic units in several ways:

- They are organized around one or more of the following:
  - **A universal literary concept** (such as "change" or "freedom") that is a central idea, message, concern, or purpose of a literary work
  - **A big idea** (such as "Change can be difficult but rewarding"), rather than a content topic
  - **An essential question** that prompts higher-order thinking and interdisciplinary connections (such as "How does pollution affect our state?")
- The theme is represented in more than one way across content domains—for example, the idea of change might be examined within realistic fiction or within a social studies topic.
- The theme organizes the multiple genres that are used.
- The theme is used to frame student inquiry and promote critical thinking; it is not linked only to factual content.
- Provocative, real-world subject matter is chosen.

Themes are generally universal concepts such as "freedom," "belonging," "responsibility," and big ideas or essential questions are related to these concepts. In one upstate New York school district, for example, teachers organize their studies around yearlong themes; for sixth graders one year, the theme was "Culture: Values, Beliefs, and Rituals." Essential questions related to that theme included *What factors shape our values and beliefs?* and *What happens when belief systems of societies and individuals come into conflict?* (See Greece Central School District's "Themes and Essential Concepts" Web page at http://www.greece.k12.ny.us/instruction/ela/6-12/Essential%20Questions/Index.htm.)

Not only can thematic units be much more motivating for students, they can deepen and broaden students' knowledge. States all across the country are realizing how important it is to study and comprehend ideas across content boundaries, and standards often reflect this. Here, for example, are two of the fourth-grade standards for the state of Kentucky:

- Students will identify the interrelationships (themes, ideas, concepts) that are developed in more than one literary work
- Students will analyze the ways in which similar themes or ideas are developed in more than one text.

Similarly, in Vermont students in grade 4 are expected to:

- Analyze and interpret informational text, citing evidence as appropriate by connecting and synthesizing information within or across text(s)

And, finally, the San Francisco Unified School District cites these expectations for fourth-grade students:

- Compare and contrast the treatment of a common theme or recurrent idea by different authors reflecting diverse culture (i.e., family relationships, friendship, loss)
- Identify universal themes prevalent in the literature of different countries

Cross-disciplinary units of substantial depth and breadth are needed to prepare students for such demanding work. Although thematic units have great potential, if we are not careful when planning integrated themes, the result is that these are not "meaty" enough to help students understand important underlying ideas—the sorts of ideas that will build genuine background knowledge and cultivate the ability to think deeply.

With a bit of thoughtful and creative reflection, however, some really spectacular things can be done. The teachers I work with have taught hundreds of thematic units with great success in the past 15 years. (See Valencia & Lipson, 1998.) They find that orienting toward themes opens the door to using mixed-genre texts. Coupled with a framework for thinking about universal themes and big ideas, this approach offers a way to break away from trivial topics that too often provide a cute, but not deep or broad, focus to learning. Figure 4.8 shows how we organize our thinking in planning for thematic teaching.

1. **Think big.** Identify a theme that is relevant for the content/grade you are teaching. Sometimes we start with a topic and think about the essential questions related to that topic. Other times we start with a book or books that we are about to teach and consider its theme. In either case, we are trying to think about big ideas instead of the "smaller" objectives that will be developed along the way.

2. **Make a connection.** We look for opportunities to link this theme, big idea, or essential question to another content area. If we have started with a reading/language arts narrative, we think about science or social studies. If we have started with content, we think about reading/language arts.

3. **Create a plan.** Locate materials and begin to create a unit plan that involves more than one way to look at the theme.

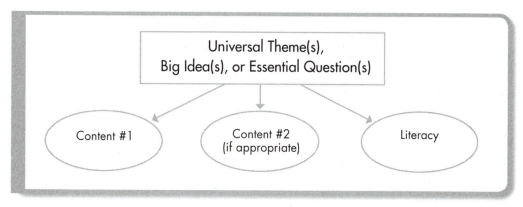

Figure 4.8 How to organize our thinking in planning for thematic teaching

Using this framework, one of my undergraduate students did a delightful integrated theme some years ago. Charged with teaching the American Revolution in a fifth-grade class, she was tempted to add historical fiction to integrate literacy with social studies. However, she took a different tack—one that increased the power of the theme immensely. She decided to work from the conceptual theme "Perspective." (See Figure 4.9.) Her big ideas included:

- "There is always more than one way to look at things."
- "Conflict is often the result of different perspectives."

Her students studied the American Revolution using these ideas. In this way, she was able to dig deeply into major points of conflict in the Revolutionary period and help students see what challenging decisions people had to make. Her students really understood this period well after this theme study—and were in a better position to bring the idea of perspective and point of view to their other social studies units. Importantly, her students deepened their understanding of perspective by examining it in varying contexts. During literacy periods, for example, they considered the perspective and points of view of various characters as they read realistic fiction (*The View From Saturday*, *Because of Winn-Dixie*, and

The Jacket). They considered questions such as *Whose perspective, or point of view, is represented?* and *How does that affect how we think about the events?* They also wrote persuasive essays during writing time and, in addition, they studied the notion of perspective in art.

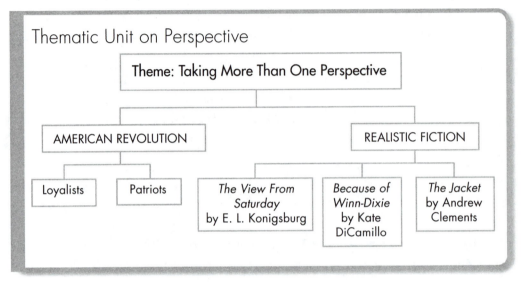

Figure 4.9

Among the many universal themes, the following are ones that we have found useful in grades 3 to 6:

Change	Power
Taking Responsibility	Cooperation
Exploration and Discovery	Relationships
Interdependence	Freedom

Big ideas and essential questions provide a more refined focus for our instructional planning. Figure 4.10 displays a chart of possible themes, big ideas and texts appropriate in these grades. As John Guthrie and his colleagues have noted: "The practice of using content goals for reading instruction is motivating because such goals provide fascinating topics for reading (e.g., animal competition and survival in harsh environments) . . . Simultaneously, such content goals in a conceptual theme provide a rich substantive domain in which to learn strategies" (2004, p. 426). In addition, taking two or more approaches to big ideas deepens and extends students understanding of important themes—in other words, they get smarter.

Universal Themes and Big Idea Statements

UNIVERSAL THEME	BIG IDEA STATEMENTS	CURRICULAR AREA	POSSIBLE TEXTS
Change	• Change is a part of life. • People change over a lifetime. • Change in one area leads to change in other areas (e.g., seasonal change impacts the plants and animals in the environment). • Change often causes growth.	Science Mathematics Social Studies Language Arts	*Chemistry for Every Kid* by Janice VanCleave *Mosaic and Tessellated Patterns* by John Wilson *Sarah Plain and Tall* by Patricia MacLachlan *Lily's Crossing* by Patricia Reilly Giff *Unfinished Dreams* by Jane Breskin Zalben
Taking Responsibility	• People have personal, community, and global responsibilities. • People who take responsibility can make a difference. • There are consequences when people do not take responsibility. • Responsibilities change over a lifetime.	Social Studies Science—the Environment Language Arts	*Kids Explore Kids Who Make a Difference* by Westridge Young Writers Workshop *The Lorax* by Dr. Seuss *Keeping Barney* by Jessie Haas *The Composition* by Antonio Skarmeta *Red Scarf Girl* by Ji-li Jiang
Exploration and Discovery	• Exploration leads to new ideas and ways of life. • Exploration often leads to discovery. • Exploration involves risk. • Explorers must be able to overcome obstacles. • Exploration may lead to unexpected consequences.	Science Social Studies Literary Works—Self-Discovery	*Miracle's Boys* by Jacqueline Woodson *The Usborne Book of Explorers* by Felicity Everett *Bridge to Terabithia* by Katherine Paterson *Shanghai Messenger* by Andrea Cheng *Half and Half* by Lensey Namioka *Spotlight on Cody* by Betsy Duffey

Figure 4.10

Concluding Thoughts

As teachers we need to help our students "get smart," by building background; using thoughtful, high-level questions; and teaching with excellent texts. The careful selection of content and the integration of literacy with other content areas can go a long way toward improving students' reading/writing abilities *and* content knowledge. Some changes, though small, can make a big difference in students' performance and achievement. Increasing the proportion of high-level questions that we ask, for example, can have big payoffs in their ability to comprehend. Similarly, selecting both content texts and narrative stories for our instructional program can expose them to big ideas and important themes.

There is very little we could do that would be more helpful for students than to build their conceptual vocabulary and improve their ability to think with print. In the next chapter, I discuss how we can help students to gain control over this knowledge and skill in order to build independence.

Discussion and Reflection

- Before your next discussion, list the questions you want to ask. Do they represent a range of questions, including higher-level ones?

- Describe some ways you support students as you teach with text.

- Are there other ways you could do more?

- Analyze one or more of the selections you teach for vocabulary opportunities.

- List the Tier 2 and Tier 3 words in a nonfiction selection. Which words will pose the greatest challenge for your students?

- How do you currently integrate content and literacy? What topics and themes lend themselves to doing more?

Digging Deeper

To find out more about building background and developing vocabulary, check out these resources:

- *Bringing Words to Life* by Isabel Beck, Margaret McKeown, and Linda Kucan. New York: Guilford Press, 2002.

- *Building Background Knowledge for Academic Achievement: Research on What Works in Schools* by Robert Marzano. Alexandria, VA: Association for Supervision and Curriculum Development, 2004.

- *Guided Reading in Grades 3–6* by Mary Browning Shulman. New York: Scholastic, 2006.

- *Reading for Information in Elementary School: Content Literacy Strategies to Build Comprehension* by Nancy Frey and Douglas Fisher. Upper Saddle River, NJ: Pearson, 2006.

- *Teaching Reading in Social Studies, Science, and Math* by Laura Robb. New York: Scholastic, 2003.

- *Teaching Vocabulary in All Classrooms*, 3rd ed., by Camille Blachowicz and Peter Fisher. Columbus, OH: Allyn & Bacon/Merrill.

- *The Vocabulary-Enriched Classroom* by Cathy Collins Block and John Mangieri. New York: Scholastic, 2006.

- *Vocabulary Handbook* by Linda Diamond and Linda Gutlohn. Berkely, CA: CORE, 2006.

- *Word Savvy* by Max Brand. Portland, ME: Stenhouse, 2004.

CHAPTER 5

Teach Comprehension and Build Independence

"We read novels to immerse ourselves in the stories and to gain meaning that is personally significant—not to memorize the names of the characters or the sequence of the events. We read informational text to satisfy and stimulate our own curiosities as we discover and learn more about our world—not to regurgitate information. . . . In short, we choose to read actively and strategically because to do otherwise means that we must relinquish our rights as readers and submit to the meanings, beliefs, and purposes advocated by others."

(Villaume & Brabham, 2002, p. 673)

I have high expectations for students in grades 3 to 6. I want them to do more than remember the information and skills they learned in the primary grades. I want them to have so much control over that information and those skills that they can use them for a variety of purposes:

- To comprehend a wide range of genres, such as science fiction, newspapers, biography, original documents, and poetry

- To derive personal pleasure, gain information, participate in civic life, and fulfill curriculum demands

- To accomplish a variety of tasks, such as exploring their own thoughts and feelings, supporting an opinion with evidence from texts, writing research reports, and evaluating information to arrive at a reasonable solution or conclusion to a problem

This may sound like a tall order, but in my experience, it is not impossible— even for struggling readers and writers. In fact, recent summaries of brain research suggest that students actually need the challenge (Solomon & Hendren, 2003).

In their groundbreaking book *How People Learn: Brain, Mind, Experience, and School*, John Bransford and his colleagues summarize a wealth of knowledge about brain development and learning (Bransford, Brown, & Cocking, 2000). They conclude that different areas of the brain develop at different times—creating sensitive or prime times for certain types of learning. During these "windows of opportunity," experience is extremely important because people may find it easier to learn key information and acquire critical abilities. The areas of the brain that govern higher functioning develop over a long time, all the way through intermediate grades and into middle and high school. Starting at around age 10, development is focused on integrating the various systems and in gaining control over physical and cognitive functions.

We expect our students in grades 3 to 6 to become increasingly self-reliant and planful, but neither the curriculum nor our teaching tactics generally provide instruction in these areas. As we have seen, there is no guarantee that students, even those that have been successful in school previously, will develop into powerful and self-directed learners beyond the intermediate grades. Most experts had previously believed that students who were capable readers in the third grade had "learned to read" and could then move on to "reading to learn" (RAND Reading Study Group, 2002). Clearly the matter is more complicated than that.

Teaching comprehension is among the most rewarding aspects of teaching students in the intermediate grades. They are capable of wonderful insights, terrific humor, and deep grief. These students are also hungry for interesting information. We can help them get the most out of their reading with powerful instruction in *how* to comprehend and how to manage different texts and tasks. This chapter is designed to show you how to do that. There is quite a lot of agreement about what good comprehension instruction looks like—and I start by describing it. I begin with a close look at how good readers comprehend. From there, I examine the kind of instruction necessary to move students toward independence in reading. Since students need explicit instruction in comprehension strategies, opportunities to use those strategies, and opportunities for self-regulated learning, these topics will be discussed in turn. I also present ideas for selecting texts as well as examples of instructional plans to help you get started right away.

Lessons From Research and Practice: What We Know About Teaching Comprehension and Building Independence

Although educators often disagree about many other aspects of literacy, there appears to be universal agreement that the primary goal and purpose of reading is to comprehend text—to understand what we read. Comprehension is not just the by-product of accurate word recognition; instead it is a complex process that requires active and intentional cognitive effort on the part of the reader.

As a result, comprehension instruction is inherently complicated and requires a flexible and adaptive approach. The National Reading Panel noted that teaching comprehension is more difficult than teaching other aspects of reading. Teaching and practicing skills apart from real reading simply do not work in the complex arena of text understanding. In fact, the knowledge and skill needed to comprehend doesn't even tend to "look" the same on a workbook page as it does during actual use.

Comprehending single sentences or even short paragraphs is a completely different matter than comprehending longer, more complex texts. It relies quite a lot on "opportunistic teaching"—finding and capitalizing on "teachable moments." This, in turn, places significant demands on us. The more we understand comprehension, the more likely we will be able to recognize "teachable moments" when they arise or prod them into being when they don't occur naturally.

How Good Readers Comprehend

This section is designed to provide specific information about comprehension. Reading comprehension has been a focus of research for the past 25 years, and we know a great deal more about how it works than we did in the past. Comprehension instruction needs to capitalize on this new information. So, how do good readers comprehend?

- By recognizing words and their meanings
- By connecting known and new information
- By engaging actively and intentionally with text
- By using strategies flexibly

Recognizing Words and Their Meanings

All readers comprehend text by recognizing words and thinking about the words and ideas as they read. Paying attention to meaning is a great deal easier when you know all, or most, of the words. The reader must be fluent as well as accurate; word recognition must occur quickly and rapidly with enough automaticity that it allows the reader to attend to meaning. (See Chapter 6, where I discuss these issues in greater detail.) However, accurate, and even fluent, decoding does not ensure that we know word meanings. Many young readers, for example, would be able to read the following sentence accurately but would not be able to comprehend it or use the information in any meaningful way since, most likely, they would not know the meaning of some words:

> Around the cell body are nerve fibers called axons
> and dendrites.

Even when readers know the meaning for each word, it may not be enough to ensure comprehension. Comprehending is more than recognizing individual words and their meanings. The excerpt below appears in a law textbook cowritten by my husband, Michael Lipson (M. H. Lipson & Katz, 1988). It is from a Supreme Court decison written by Potter Steward (Fuentes v. Shevin, 407 U.S. 67 (1972). Even if I had definitions for several words (*replevy, replevin, chattels*), I have little confidence that I would understand this passage.

> The right to a prior hearing, of course, attaches only to the
> deprivation of an interest encompassed with the Fourteenth
> Amendment's protection. In the present cases, the Florida
> and Pennsylvania statues were applied to replevy chattels in
> the appellant's possession. The replevin was not cast as a final
> judgment; most, if not all, of the appellants lacked full title to

the chattels; and their claim even to continued possession was a matter in dispute. Moreover, the chattels at stake were nothing more than an assortment of household goods. Nonetheless, it is clear that the appellants were deprived of possessory interests in those chattels that were within the protection of the Fourteenth Amendment. (p. 89)

Connecting Known and New Information

Readers comprehend by connecting known and new information. It would be difficult to overestimate the influence of children's prior knowledge and experience on their comprehension of text. In their review of children's learning from text, Patricia Alexander and Tamara Jetton (2000) concluded that of all the factors involved in learning from text, "none exerts more influence on what students understand and remember than the knowledge they possess" (p. 291). The text above brings home this point clearly. For example, I certainly understand both the words *prior* and *hearing*, but this passage seems to suggest a specific meaning for "prior hearing" that I don't possess. Similarly, I know the words *deprivation* and *interest*, but I have never thought of an interest being deprived. I bring a layperson's knowledge to this reading that is simply not up to the task. While I have a general understanding of what the Fourteenth Amendment says (it actually has several provisions, although I think about it as being the one having to do with "equal protection under the law"), I clearly do not understand what it has come to mean in a *legal sense*. The problems go on and on as I try to read this paragraph. My comprehension is minimal, my memory for the text nonexistent. Unless I had some personal self-interest in reading this case law, I would give it up quickly without trying very hard.

Students in grades 3 to 6 are more interested (really, everyone is) when they can connect their reading with our own lives or interests. For example, they often enjoy realistic fiction because they like to connect the events or actions of the characters in books with their own problems. When new text information is challenging, it is even more important that these connections can be made. Analogies are often helpful. For example, science teachers often use a machine analogy to explain the function of cells. By comparing information about the cell with another idea that is well-understood, it is easier to understand how a cell functions and why it is important.

Engaging Actively and Intentionally With Text

It is clear that comprehending is not passive. Rather, it requires an active construction of meaning. Good readers *intend* to understand, and they flexibly recruit a variety of strategies as they interact with text (Anderson, Hiebert, Scott, & Wilkinson, 1985; NRP, 2000). One of the major reasons why some students struggle with reading is because they have adopted a compliant but disengaged approach to reading (Dweck, 1975). Some years ago, I was talking to Michael, a sixth grader, as his tutor was preparing for a session with him. His mother was very worried about his plummeting grades. The conversation I had with Michael went like this:

> **MARJORIE:** Why do you think you're here at the clinic?
>
> **MICHAEL:** Because of a reading problem.
>
> **MARJORIE:** So, you have trouble with reading?
>
> **MICHAEL:** I must—my mother's making me come here.
>
> **MARJORIE:** What's the hardest part about reading for you?
>
> **MICHAEL:** The long words
>
> **MARJORIE:** The long words . . . Do you mean *saying* the long words or knowing what they *mean*?
>
> **MICHAEL:** Saying them.
>
> **MARJORIE:** Okay, so if you can say or read the words, you usually know what they mean?
>
> **MICHAEL:** No.
>
> **MARJORIE:** Is that a problem?
>
> **MICHAEL:** No.

Michael lacks engagement, certainly, but also is clearly focused on word recognition. It is easy for young students to get the wrong idea about the purpose of reading. We pay so much attention to decoding and fluency in the early years (understandably so) that children sometimes come to believe that flawless and rapid word recognition *is* the point. As texts get more demanding and/or unfamiliar, some of the "good readers" in our classes begin to struggle because they are not sufficiently engaged in constructing meaning. They may not even know that they should be! The combination is a deadly one—lack of engagement and intentional effort make it impossible for students like Michael to be independent during reading.

A student engaged in reading

Using Strategies Flexibly

More than a decade ago Gerry Duffy concluded, "the best way to pursue meaning is through conscious, controlled use of strategies" (1993, p. 223). In the years since, this conclusion has been reaffirmed many times. A relatively short list of strategies has repeatedly been shown to be essential to effective comprehension (Dole et al., 1991; Fielding & Pearson, 1994). The very same strategies are used by very young and much older readers. (See Figure 5.1.) Ideally, as students mature, they refine these strategies to understand increasingly difficult, complex, and/or unfamiliar texts. Certainly students' success in using strategies varies developmentally—younger children are less skilled at selecting and recruiting appropriate strategies than older and more mature readers. But it is important to know that "the data suggest that students at *all* skill levels would benefit from being taught these strategies" (Rosenshine, Meister, & Chapman, 1996, p. 201).

Seven Strategies Capable Readers Use

MAKE CONNECTIONS: Bridge from new to known, connecting text to self, world, and other texts

QUESTION: Ask questions to enhance understanding, find answers, solve problems, find specific information, etc.

MAKE INFERENCES: Connect ideas and/or fill-in information to make sense of unstated ideas

VISUALIZE: Generate mental images to stimulate thinking and heighten engagement

SUMMARIZE: Synthesize and organize key information to identify main points and major themes, distinguish important from unimportant information, enhance meaning

MONITOR/REGULATE: Pay attention to meaning, clarify or correct comprehension difficulties, and/or promote a problem-solving stance during reading

EVALUATE: Make judgments about the text to form new ideas and opinions and/or determine author's purpose

Figure 5.1 Comprehension strategies and their functions

Helping students in grades 3 to 6 to become more strategic is absolutely essential. Compared with the content of earlier grades, the texts and tasks that they now regularly encounter are more conceptually demanding and more complex in both form and function, and they often address topics or domain knowledge that is unfamiliar. Exposure and experience alone do not appear to ensure controlled knowledge and use of strategies (M. Y. Lipson & Cooper, 2002; Paris et al., 1983). Happily, there is absolutely no question that "text comprehension can be improved by instruction that helps readers use specific comprehension strategies" (Armbruster, Lehr, & Osborn, 2001, p. 55), and methods for teaching these strategies are relatively well-developed.

Providing Explicit Instruction in Comprehension Strategies

The individual strategies listed in Figure 5.1 are not as important as taking a "strategic approach" that allows readers to respond differently to different topics, texts, genres, and tasks. Highly skilled, mature readers use a repertoire of skills and strategies to enhance comprehension. A strategic approach, which involves teaching children to use strategies flexibly and in a coordinated, problem-solving fashion (Duffy et al., 1986, 1987), has a greater impact on students' comprehending abilities. In grades 3 to 6, it is not generally a good idea to try to focus for too

Explicit instruction in action

long on an individual strategy. I prefer to introduce all of the strategies and discuss the fact that "these are the things good readers do." Below I list some general guidelines for effective strategy instruction.

Guidelines for Effective Strategy Instruction Across the Year

- Introduce core strategies early in the year to provide a basis for conversation and encourage a *strategic approach* to reading.

- Display a poster showing the strategies that good readers use. Use Figure 5.1 as a starting point.

- Provide clear descriptions of the steps in a strategy and keep them readily available.

- Although you may focus on teaching one strategy, encourage students to use a repertoire of strategies.

- Connect skills to strategies. For example, summarizing (a strategy) often requires locating important details. These can and should be taught together.

- Model strategy use during read-aloud.

You can make the most of explicit instruction in comprehension strategies by keeping the following two goals in mind:

- Identify opportunities for strategy instruction
- Help students acquire and use strategies

Identify Opportunities for Strategy Instruction

Different texts demand different strategies, and individual students will need to use different strategies depending on their background knowledge and familiarity with the genre, text structure, and so on. That said, it is sometimes important to examine individual strategies closely through explanation, modeling, and guided practice. This exploration needs to be done in the context of authentic texts.

With practice, it becomes easier to identify texts that provide good opportunities for strategy instruction. I recommend taking a reflective stance on your own reading—What do you think is the most important thing about this book/section? What does the author provide and what have you brought to this reading? What strategies did you need in order to comprehend the text? What strategies might a less-knowledgeable reader need? I also recommend talking about books or articles with your colleagues. Ask them to read a book with you. Talk about what you *did* as well as what you *thought*.

Picture books are especially useful for introducing strategies because they can be read in one or two sittings and everyone can participate in the discussions. Later, students can be asked to apply (or do guided practice) with longer or more-challenging texts. The box below offers several examples of books to use with your students. For each strategy I recommend a picture book and one or more longer books. For more ideas, I highly recommend the book *Strategies That Work* by Stephanie Harvey and Anne Goudvis for its extensive listing of books linked to strategies.

Sample Books for Teaching Strategies

STRATEGY	BOOKS THAT INVITE USE
Make Connections	Text-to-Self: *The Two of Them* by Aliki Text-to-World: *Immigrant Kids* by Russell Freedman Text-to-Text: *Quake* by Joe Cottonwood (narrative fiction) and *Earthquakes* by Seymour Simon (nonfiction)
Question	*Passage to Freedom* by Ken Mochizuki *The Story of Ruby Bridges* by Robert Coles *The Giver* by Lois Lowry *The City of Ember* by Jeanne DuPrau
Make Inferences	*Arnie the Doughnut* by Laurie Keller *Chato's Kitchen* by Gary Soto *Holes* by Louis Sachar
Visualize	*Chato's Kitchen* by Gary Soto *Autumn Street* by Lois Lowry *Al Capone Does My Shirts* by Gennifer Choldenko
Summarize	*Raising Dragons* by Jerdine Nolen *Sweet Clara and the Freedom Quilt* by Deborah Hopkinson
Monitor/Regulate	*Jumanji* by Chris Van Allsburg *Van Gogh Café* by Cynthia Rylant *The Egypt Game* by Zilpha Snyder
Evaluate	*Teammates* by Peter Golenbock *Pink and Say* by Patricia Polacco *Stone in My Hand* by Cathryn Clinton

Help Students Acquire and Use Strategies

Strategy instruction requires both explicit discussion (see later in the chapter for more about this) and interactive discussion during reading. The sample lesson in Figure 5.2 shows how I introduce a strategy and also how I link strategies with more-specific skills, in this case, sequencing. We often use strategy journals as a way to focus students on a particular strategy that is being addressed instructionally. Unlike response journals, these journals give students a chance to focus on applying and refining their use of comprehension strategies. Typically, we create a series of journal pages and put them together with plastic spiral binding. (See the reproducible on page 138.) Alternatively, some teachers like to have three-ring binders that students use for many purposes.

A literacy coach in one of our schools recently described what she observed in a fifth-grade classroom:

> Mindy, the teacher, had just completed a lesson on comprehension monitoring. Her students were in the middle of a partner-read where they were documenting in their reading journals the problems they encountered while reading and the solutions they used to solve them. The students were using a reference sheet that the teacher had made for them. After about 25 to 30 minutes of reading time the students came together and each shared the problems that arose and how they solved them. Examples included: "I was reading too fast, so I stopped and started reading aloud to slow myself down" or "I didn't know what a word meant so I made a guess based on the words around it and then reread the sentence to check if my meaning made sense."

MINI-LESSON: Summarizing

Book: *Raising Dragons* by Jerdine Nolen (1998)

Synopsis

A young girl discovers a huge egg and falls in love with the dragon that is hatched from it. She takes Hank home, where neither of her parents wants anything to do with him. He makes many marvelous contributions to their farm life, however—fanning the tomato plants so they don't die of the heat and making popcorn with his fiery breath. Eventually Hank draws so much attention that he has to leave, but the little girl knows that raising dragons is in her blood.

Explain

Good readers summarize stories and articles so that they can remember the information. That way they can use it in their own reading and writing and they can tell others about it. Summarizing can be especially helpful when an article is complicated. Using the text organization of the piece you are reading can really help you summarize. For example, many stories are organized by the sequence of events.

You already probably know that this means the author relates the events in time order, describing what happened first, then the next thing, and so on. The types of stories you read now that you are older are more complicated than those simple stories. For example:

- Sometimes the author provides background information before the sequence begins. Your job as a reader is to find where the sequence, or story, really begins.

- Sometimes the events are spread out over a long period of time. You must really follow the time order carefully to understand what is happening.

- Remember, when you summarize you tell only the most important information.

Model

In *Raising Dragons*, the author started by telling us about her father and her mother and how they didn't know anything about raising dragons. It takes more than a page before the main story begins and the author uses the following words:

"I remember the day my life with dragons began. I was out for my Sunday . . ."

Provide Guided Practice

Then, the author uses other sequence cues to carry on with the story. Let's find these:

Day after day . . .

One night . . .

At the first hint of dawn . . .

Whenever . . .

It did take a little time, but . . .

Up until then . . .

Encourage Application

Using your strategy journal, complete the story and create a summary.

Figure 5.2

Strategy Journal

Strategy _____ Date _____

Book Title _____

While you are reading, look for cues that tell the sequence of events.
Use this journal page to help you.

EVENT	SEQUENCE WORDS:
Event 1 _____	_____
_____	_____
Event 2 _____	_____
_____	_____
Event 3 _____	_____
_____	_____
Event 4 _____	_____
_____	_____
The Final Event _____	_____
_____	_____

Look at your events and circle the ones that are very important to telling
the story. Use those to write your summary:

_____

_____

_____

_____

_____

_____

_____

_____

_____

_____

It is important to keep in mind that strategies need to be adapted to the particular text. The mini-lesson on page 137, for example, is designed to be used with narrative text. Summarizing nonfiction requires a somewhat different approach. I have found that the magnet summary technique, developed by Doug Buehl (2001) works very well. It is designed to help students focus on important concepts and supporting details. The key concepts are called "magnet words" because, as I explain to students, they attract the important information to them; all the main concepts are gathered around. A guide to help you introduce this technique is provided in the box below.

Magnet Summary

What is a magnet summary?

A magnet summary is a way for you to identify key concepts—magnet words—from your reading and use them to organize important information into a summary.

Steps to creating a magnet summary

1. Look for a "magnet word" in your reading. These are key terms or concepts that attract information to them, information that is important to the topic and connected to the main idea.

2. Write the magnet word down on a piece of paper or index card.

3. Write related terms, related ideas, and supporting details around the magnet word:

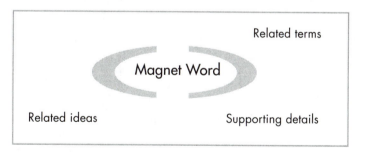

4. Use the information around your magnet word to summarize orally the information from your reading. Be sure to leave out any unimportant details.

5. Write a single sentence that summarizes all of that information. The magnet word should be a main part of the sentence.

Adapted from *Classroom Strategies for Interactive Learning* (2nd ed.) by Doug Buehl, 2001

It's often a good idea to use short pieces of text from newspapers or magazines to introduce difficult skills and strategies; they're excellent for teacher modeling. In Amber Profitt's classroom, she and students had been using that type of material for some time when she decided her students were ready to attempt something more challenging. Because she teaches many struggling readers, she decided to use a leveled reader entitled *Severe Weather,* which she downloaded from the online reading program Reading A–Z (http://www.readinga-z.com). She knew her students would need support, so she created a graphic organizer (Figure 5.3) and modeled how to use it, and then they completed the first one together. Then, Amber showed students how to use the information they compiled in their organizers to write summaries. These reflected their ability to summarize important information about tornadoes, including how they form and how they affect people and buildings.

Although short and/or contrived texts can be helpful in introducing a skill or strategy to students, most children are not able to use comprehension strategies like monitoring, summarizing, and self-questioning unless they practice using longer and more complex material. We need to introduce and model the use of multiple strategies within the context of actual text reading for students to reach independence (Brown, Collins, & Deguid, 1989; Duffy, 1993; Resnick, 1987).

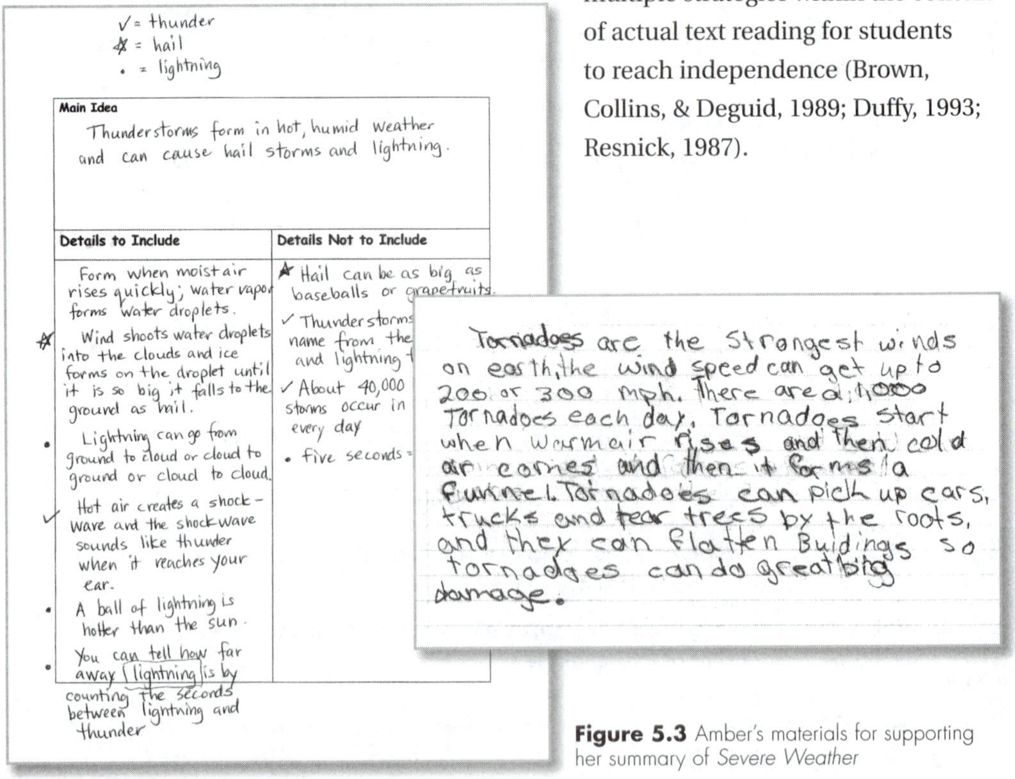
✓ = thunder
★ = hail
• = lightning

Main Idea	
Thunderstorms form in hot, humid weather and can cause hail storms and lightning.	
Details to Include	**Details Not to Include**
Form when moist air rises quickly; water vapor forms water droplets.	★ Hail can be as big as baseballs or grapefruits.
★ Wind shoots water droplets into the clouds and ice forms on the droplet until it is so big it falls to the ground as hail.	✓ Thunderstorms name from the and lightning
• Lightning can go from ground to cloud or cloud to ground or cloud to cloud.	✓ About 40,000 storms occur in every day
✓ Hot air creates a shock-wave and the shockwave sounds like thunder when it reaches your ear.	• five seconds =
• A ball of lightning is hotter than the sun.	
• You can tell how far away lightning is by counting the seconds between lightning and thunder	

Tornadoes are the Strongest winds on earth, the wind speed can get up to 200 or 300 mph. There are a 1,000 Tornadoes each day. Tornadoes start when warm air rises and then cold air comes and then it forms a funnel. Tornadoes can pick up cars, trucks and tear trees by the roots, and they can flatten Buidings so tornadoes can do great big damage.

Figure 5.3 Amber's materials for supporting her summary of *Severe Weather*

Providing Opportunities to Use Comprehension Strategies

Before anyone realized the importance of strategies, reading instruction focused almost exclusively on the content. Students read the words, and teachers checked to make sure that they understood by asking questions that almost always focused on the information in the text. The idea seemed to be that students would figure out how to comprehend by being questioned in this way. And, in fact, some students do become excellent readers under these conditions. Many, however, do not.

Children can be taught to be better "comprehenders." But effective comprehension instruction is as complex as comprehension itself. Explicit instruction is one effective method of teaching students various strategies (NRP, 2000; Paris et al.,1983). However, research also suggests that instruction in specific strategies may not be enough. Students also need to use those strategies *during cooperative activities embedded in content learning* (Moore, 1996). In other words, students need teachers to help them learn the strategies in service of other purposes— to learn why the Civil War was fought; to understand why Charlotte wove words into her web; or to figure out why marbles roll off the table the way they do.

To teach this way—in service of purposes—we need to focus on two areas that are central to comprehension: author's craft and text structures and genres.

Teach Author's Craft

Powerful comprehension and profound enjoyment of texts comes only when readers appreciate and use an array of devices employed by authors to build meaning. The techniques and devices listed below are used by authors to add interest, but they are also critical for comprehension. Readers who do not, or cannot, perceive author's craft effectively are likely to struggle with both comprehension and motivation.

Many of us have not been well prepared to recognize and use the elements of author's craft to teach and/or support comprehension. We simply have not been encouraged to identify how authors use language and literary devices to increase interest, tension, or enjoyment. Nor have we been trained to identify aspects of author's craft such as metaphor, irony, and flashback, or to think

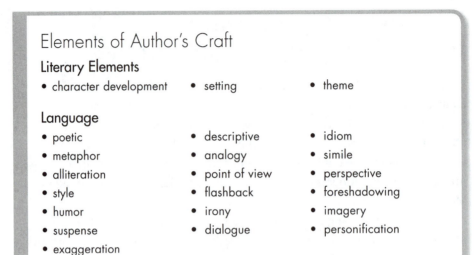

Elements of Author's Craft

Literary Elements
- character development
- setting
- theme

Language
- poetic
- metaphor
- alliteration
- style
- humor
- suspense
- exaggeration
- descriptive
- analogy
- point of view
- flashback
- irony
- dialogue
- idiom
- simile
- perspective
- foreshadowing
- imagery
- personification

about how these may make reading more challenging. Yet young and less-skilled readers often fail to understand a selection because they do not notice or understand features intentionally used by the author to enhance meaning or make the text more interesting.

In Chapter 4, we examined an excerpt from Richard Peck's novel *A Long Way From Chicago* (page 91). In Figure 5.4, we examine this excerpt again, looking at the ways in which he makes use of various elements of author's craft.

Because we are experienced and capable readers, we are often unaware of these features of text at the conscious level, but we enjoy the books precisely because we understand how they work—we're "in the know." If we want our students to read deeply and passionately, we need to link the specific considerations of author's craft to particular stories or pieces of informational text—removing barriers by helping children understand the use of various devices, or deepening enjoyment by pointing them out. We want to put students in the driver's seat, but it will take time.

Identify Elements of Author's Craft in Texts

The texts we use in grades 3 to 6 are often complicated enough that we have choices about where to focus our attention—depending on our students and the particular textual demands. For example, the outrageous book *Dogzilla* by Dav Pilkey (1993) demands quite a lot of readers. This story is an exaggerated spoof of horror movies of the 1950s and 1960s, featuring a community of mice and a

Excerpt From Historical Fiction

"You wouldn't think **we'd have to leave** Chicago **to see a dead body**. We were growing up there back in the bad old days of Al Capone and Bugs Moran. **Just the winter before, they'd had the St. Valentine's Day Massacre over on North Clark Street.** The city had such an evil reputation that the **Thompson submachine gun was better known as a 'Chicago typewriter.'**

But I'd grown to the age of nine and my sister Mary Alice was seven, and we'd yet to see a stiff. We guessed that most of them were where you couldn't see them, at the bottom of Lake Michigan **wearing concrete overshoes.**" (p. 3)

This reference to a dead body foreshadows the events of the rest of the chapter.

The author is establishing the setting here—time and place are very important in this novel.

The metaphor is used to bring home the point that at the time of this story, Chicago was a dangerous city.

This idiom—a signature reference to "concrete overshoes" as an indicator of mobster activity—will be unfamiliar to most students.

Figure 5.4 *A Long Way From Chicago* by Richard Peck. Opening paragraphs of Chapter 1: "Shotgun Cheatham's Last Night Above Ground 1929"

menacing creature in the form of an oversized dog with bad breath. Authentic comprehension of this story requires that students make inferences about the events in the story, use their knowledge of realism and fantasy to draw conclusions, and evaluate the events by drawing on past experience and the author's use of language. The author has used exaggeration to entertain and amuse; words and phrases like *depths of the earth, terrifying, dreadful, heroic,* and *monstrous* all contribute to our appreciation of the humor and drama of the story. (See Figure 5.5.) Any one of these aspects could be the focus on instruction. This type of text analysis is a critical first step to teaching author's craft and is not as difficult as it might first appear. A good first question is, "What is my reaction to this text and how did the author make that happen?"

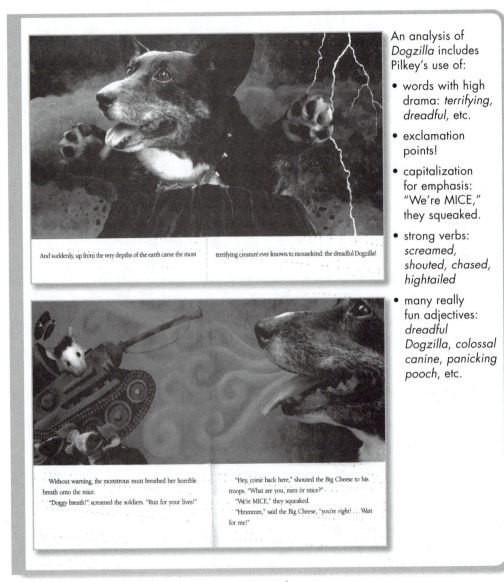

An analysis of *Dogzilla* includes Pilkey's use of:

- words with high drama: *terrifying, dreadful,* etc.

- exclamation points!

- capitalization for emphasis: "We're MICE," they squeaked.

- strong verbs: *screamed, shouted, chased, hightailed*

- many really fun adjectives: *dreadful Dogzilla, colossal canine, panicking pooch,* etc.

And suddenly, up from the very depths of the earth came the most terrifying creature ever known to mousekind: the dreadful Dogzilla!

Without warning, the monstrous mutt breathed her horrible breath onto the mice.
"Doggy breath!", screamed the soldiers. "Run for your lives!"

"Hey, come back here," shouted the Big Cheese to his troops. "What are you, men or mice?"
"We're MICE," they squeaked.
"Hmmmm," said the Big Cheese, "you're *right!* . . . Wait for me!"

Figure 5.5 Text analysis helps focus instruction in author's craft.

Help Students Identify and Use Author's Craft

Because author's craft must be taught in the context of authentic text, it is often a good idea to teach it after a first reading. Instruction in author's craft gives us an excellent reason to *revisit* text—to reread all or portions of a story to enjoy an author's style, to understand more deeply what he or she intended, or to clarify meaning. During an initial reading of *Dogzilla*, readers are likely to focus on the *action*—and there's a lot of it. We always want to focus on the story line first. During a second or third read, however, readers can see how it is that Dav Pilkey used language to increase our enjoyment of the characters and our feelings about the events. Discussion might look something like this:

> **First, I focus the topic.** "Many of us were laughing as we read this story. What does this author do that makes it funny?" Students often talk about the mice having a barbeque, they love the references to "doggy breath," "fleabag," and so on.
>
> **I look for instructional opportunities.** During the discussion, I watch for students to make some reference to language. Then, I might say, "Let's look at that page again. Dav Pilkey uses really interesting words here. For example, 'And, suddenly up from the very depths of the earth came the most terrifying creature ever known to mousekind: the dreadful Dogzilla!' He uses words that are really meant to get us excited and funny-scared. What are some of those words? Where else do we see him using words that are funny and dramatic?"
>
> **Then I wrap up and extend.** Depending on the students, we might explore one or more of the other craft elements noted above. Once students have noted these elements in a piece of text, we might post examples on an anchor chart or begin to use them in the students' own writing. Students can really see the impact of author's craft when they start using it to improve their own writing.

Teach Text Structures and Genres

None of us is always a "good reader." We are always reading *something*, and our success in comprehending it depends on what that is. (Remember the law book material earlier?) The topic of the material certainly has an impact on our comprehension, but so does the *type* of text. Generally speaking, educators and researchers organize texts in two large categories: narratives (stories) and exposition (explanations of facts and concepts). These two types of text are different in both purpose and organization. Understanding these differences is important because it helps readers to:

- Select ideas and events—to know what's important
- Organize ideas and events—to see how things are related

- Integrate ideas and events with prior knowledge and texts they've already read—to make sense of the world around them

Narratives

Narratives typically share a common set of features and structures called a "story grammar" (Stein & Glenn, 1979). Readers who understand how stories are organized can use this information to help them understand better. Narrative texts have the following five elements:

- A setting, either physical or psychological (time/place/ mental state)
- Characters, the major players in the story
- A problem or initiating event, something that gets the story started
- Important events related to the problem
- An outcome or resolution

In addition, most narratives have a theme, a major idea or important concept that the author is trying to convey. There may be more than one theme in a complex narrative, and these ideas are generally more universal than concrete (for example, "friends stand by each other and help out when needed"). Generally speaking, we read stories for pleasure, to gain insight into ourselves and others, and/or to learn about the actions and events of life around the world.

Exposition

Expository texts are typically read and written for various purposes—to inform, describe, or explain. So our purposes usually run parallel, we read to acquire information, confirm or disconfirm ideas, answer questions, or understand our world. Nonfiction texts can be structured in any number of ways. Common text structures are cause-effect, compare-contrast, chronological order, and description. When children do not understand the organizational structure, they generally struggle to understand and remember the information.

There is good evidence that teaching students explicitly about text structure and helping them see how ideas are organized in expository text improves their comprehension (Armbruster, Anderson, & Ostertag, 1989; RAND Reading Study Group, 2002). Within expository texts, certain organizational patterns are easier to grasp than others (Armbruster, 1984). For example, cause-effect is more challenging for children than chronological order. The following passage from Charlotte Wilcox's *Mummies and Their Mysteries* demonstrates how challenging

Excerpt From Expository Text

"A **mummy** is the body of a human or animal in which some of the soft tissues (skin, muscles, or organs) did not decay after death. This makes a mummy different from a skeleton or a fossil. A skeleton is only bones, with no soft tissues at all. A fossil keeps the shape of the human, animal, or plant, but the body itself has hardened into rock. Mummies are made naturally or by **embalming**, which is any process used to preserve a dead body.

While we are alive, our bodies fight off bacteria and fungi, but after death these germs and molds eat the body's tissues, causing decay. **Mummification** happens when bacteria and fungi cannot grow in the dead body. Most mummies, whether natural or embalmed, result when the body quickly dries out after death, because bacteria and fungi need water to live. Mummies can be dried in the sun, with chemicals or with fire and smoke."

Drying isn't the only way to turn a body into a mummy. Taking away all air from around the body will stop decay, since bacteria and fungi need air as well as water to live." (pp. 1–2)

The boldfaced words signal key concepts.

References such as "this" are ambiguous for many students. What makes a mummy different?

The connector "because" in this sentence doesn't really help most young readers understand how drying relates to bacteria and mummification. Students must be able to connect information across paragraphs to infer the relationship between bacteria, soft tissues, and mummification.

Readers must infer how an airless environment would cause mummification.

Mummies and Their Mysteries by Charlotte Wilcox. From Chapter 1, "What Is a Mummy?"

understanding cause and effect can be, since the causal connections must be inferred and connected across many paragraphs. Within the first several pages of this text, the author also employs description and chronological order as well as cause-effect structures.

Other features set expository texts apart from narrative stories. Features such as headings, subheadings, graphs and tables, diagrams, bulleted information, sidebars, word glosses, labels, and captions can be very helpful to readers. However, intermediate-grade students often do not know how to make good use of them (Goldman & Rakestraw, 2000). These features are meant to support readers' comprehension. If students do not use them, however, their comprehension may actually suffer, especially if, for example, the author is relying on the tables and figures to convey key information.

Children have a great deal less opportunity to internalize expository text structures because they hear and read so little of it during the primary years (Duke, 2000a, 2000b; Duke & Bennett-Armistead, 2003). An effective reader needs to be looking for the ways in which ideas are connected in text—and inexperience with these text structures can hamper these efforts.

Identify Elements of Structures in Texts

Previewing texts can help identify which structures or genres will be challenging and/or interesting to teach. Think about which aspects of genre could be helpful in promoting comprehension or important for promoting wider reading. The International Reading Association and the National Council of Teachers of English have a wonderful Web site that offers lesson plans on a wide variety of topics—many of them featuring different genre types. As well, one section of their site studies genre directly. I have found it very useful: http://readwritethink. org/lessons/lesson_view.asp?id=270.

Common narrative genres for grades 3 to 6 include historical and realistic fiction, mystery, fantasy, and tall tales. It is important to identify the text structure or genre because the type of text is very likely to influence which strategies students use. For example, reading Zilpha Snyder's terrific mystery *The Egypt Game* (1997) requires a different approach and strategy than reading John Christopher's science-fiction/fantasy *The White Mountains* (1967). In *The Egypt Game*, students need to engage in close reading with attention to details to keep track of several different characters, and they need to look for gaps in the narrative that provide clues. Readers should attend to the suspense and also author's craft such as foreshadowing. On the other hand, *The White Mountains*, like most fantasies, requires creating and maintaining an alternate world. Visualization is helpful, as is making connections. Inferring the theme is critical as well.

Help Students Identify and Use Structures

Mature readers have a number of "mental maps" stored in memory that are useful in reading new texts (Dickson, Simmons, & Kameenui, 1995a, 1995b; Goldman & Rakestraw, 2000). Mental maps are internalized frameworks that parallel various text structures and/or genres. These mental maps, or organizational frameworks, act as a support or scaffold for new information and ideas, giving readers a place to put the information as they are reading. As I have noted elsewhere:

> When students become highly familiar with particular text structures or genres, reading is easier because those frameworks help them to anticipate text and make rapid, accurate inferences, which frees them to attend to other, more novel aspects of the text. This is, of course, one of the reasons children love series books so much: They become familiar enough with the structures that they can enjoy (comprehend) the text more easily. (Lipson & Wixson, 2003, p. 582)

Of course, when children are *unfamiliar* with a genre or text structure, reading is more difficult. Teaching children explicitly about genre attributes provides needed support and hastens their acquisition of appropriate mental maps.

A good map will help children see the relationships between the events in a story or informational piece. Students are guided to understand the selection because the map directs their attention. Creating text-specific maps is a great deal of work. Gerald Fowler (1982) and Bonnie Armbruster et al. (1989) both suggest a different tactic—using more-generic "story frames" to focus students on different elements. I have adapted these for use with both narrative and expository texts.

Narrative Example

Our story starts when _____. The most important characters(s) think/feel that _____. They decide_____ _____. The problem is _____. The problem is solved when _____.

Expository Example, Cause-Effect

In this chapter/article, the author is talking mostly about the causes of _____

_____. S/he lists _____ causes and their effects. Some of the

effects are _____ and _____

and_____. The causes are_____,

_____, and _____. The

author thinks_____. I think _____.

Expository Example, Compare-Contrast

1. _____ and _____ are

similar in several ways. They both _____, and they also

both _____. Finally, both _____

and _____.

2. _____ and _____ are

different in some ways. _____, but _____.

In addition, while _____, _____.

Of course, these relatively simple frames can be expanded as students become more capable.

Into the Classroom

The implications are clear: We need to provide a wide variety of text types for students in our reading instruction and classroom libraries. And then we need to teach students how to read strategically, how to recognize and understand different types of text, and how to use various aspects of author's craft to comprehend them.

Teach Comprehension Explicitly

We need to teach students what is involved in understanding texts, how good comprehenders understand text, and how students can do it for themselves. Although explicit instruction is common when teaching phonics (for example), it is less often used when teaching comprehension, in part because we haven't really had good information about comprehension processes until quite recently.

Good, explicit instruction can be very useful in introducing students to critical elements of any new skill or strategy and in helping them identify important attributes of a task. No matter what is being taught, effective explicit instruction involves the following:

- **Explaining:** Provide information about how and why to use skills, strategies, or tasks.

  How: Clearly describe the tasks and skills you want students to do or use.

  Why: State the purpose and its meaning for you as a reader.

- **Modeling:** Show students what this looks like in action via think-alouds or demonstrations.

- **Providing guided practice:** Support students as they attempt the new strategy or use the new information.

- **Encouraging application:** Provide students with appropriate opportunities to practice in new settings (Baker, Gersten, & Scanlon, 2002; Paris, Cross, & Lipson, 1984).

Students are much more likely to remember and use the information you present if you help them understand how to use it *and* why it is important. This "conditional knowledge" appears to make a major difference in students' sense of the utility of skills and strategies they are taught (Paris et al., 1983). This does not need to be a time-consuming matter. Simply saying something like "Good readers pay attention as they read to see if things make sense" significantly improves students' comprehension and use of (in this case) the monitoring strategy.

As an example of explicit instruction, we might:

- **Explain** that good readers have to "pay attention" (or monitor) as they read. In order to do this, good readers usually stop periodically and check to see whether the ideas are fitting together or whether they make sense with what they already know. Readers keep checking to see whether the text is making sense so that they can fix things right away if they need to and don't run into bigger problems later on.

- **Model** monitoring for the students as we read aloud. I might say things like "I'm not sure what this means right now; I thought _____, but now I'm thinking that maybe _____. In general, this makes sense to me, but there is this one thing I'm not sure about. I may need to go back, but I'm going to keep reading and see if I can figure this out."

- **Provide guided practice** by having a reading guide that asks students to stop periodically and reflect on their reading. Initially this might be done as a class or in small groups as I guide their thinking.

- **Offer feedback** as students begin to try monitoring themselves. This is easier to do in small groups. Group think-alouds provide one of the few reasons to do oral reading with intermediate-grade students. As they read aloud, they can stop periodically to think aloud—in this case, to monitor. I provide feedback on the quality of their monitoring and challenge their choice of "stopping points."

- **Encourage application.** During their reading workshop, I remind students to use their monitoring skills and note (e.g., put a sticky note) places where they are unclear.

These explicit episodes of instruction happen recurrently. As students get good at doing some things, we move to the next challenge. Once students are comfortable with particular skills or strategies, we introduce new ones.

Using authentic materials and tasks (as opposed to contrived or controlled ones) can be a messy business, and we should *expect* that sometimes students' comprehension will not be what we would wish. And this is fine. To teach students how to comprehend, we need to be quite knowledgeable about and expert at using texts to teach. There are certainly many techniques that can help teachers prepare themselves. However, there is no recipe for understanding all texts, no tricks that always help. Sometimes, we just need to leave a story or a piece of text without arriving at "complete comprehension." Of course, our role is to observe and assess very carefully so that new, explicit instruction and/or additional supportive opportunities can be planned.

Providing Opportunities for Self-Regulated Learning

The research on comprehension highlights the active and intentional nature of good reading. We all know, though, that not all students are active or intentional. Left to their own devices, many intermediate-grade students cannot read with understanding, synthesize information across texts, or extend their thinking. Instead, without strong teacher support, they focus on literal and/or lower-level meaning.

Unfortunately, teacher support can actually be detrimental. Monique Boekaerts (1999) notes that too much external regulation (in the form of teacher support and direction, for example) can be dangerous. Students who are not good at planning, monitoring, or evaluating their own performance rely on the teacher to do this for them.

> Clearly, many students consider external regulation as bliss, viewing it as essential to extend their knowledge and skills. They expect the teacher to tell them what to do, how and when to do it, and when to stop doing it. . . .The point is that dependence on teachers works only as long as a teacher is available to take over, or to activate the students' poor self-regulatory skills. However, a decrease in achievement will be noticed as soon as these students have to study in an environment where they have to steer and direct their own learning process (Kurtz & Weinert, 1989). (Boekaerts, 1999, p. 447)

Motivation and engagement are intimately linked to self-regulation and independence. Remember in Chapter 3 how Andrew's compliant attitude led him to wait for the teacher to direct him.

For some students, ongoing and continuous teacher support actually leads to a phenomenon known as *learned-helplessness* (Dweck, 1975; Peterson, Maier, & Seligman, 1993) in which students feel so incompetent that they do not try—even when the tasks are doable for them. Recent research suggests, however, that these types of self-defeating feelings can be turned around by teachers and parents when they convince students that they are capable and teach them the knowledge and skills they need to be successful.

It has become very clear over the past 25 years that really good learners know more than skills or even strategies. They know how to recruit and apply strategies when they need them, they know how to change their approach depending on the task at hand, and they know how to manage their own responses. Metacognition is a critical part of these abilities. (See research summaries by Israel et al., 2005; Paris, Wasik, & Turner, 1991.) Metacognition is thinking about one's own thinking or controlling one's own learning, and it includes elements of both knowledge and self-regulation. It includes knowledge about:

- Ourselves as learners

- Task demands

- How text, prior knowledge, and reading strategies affect comprehension

In addition, metacognition involves self-regulating abilities such as:

- Coordinating various types of knowledge

- Intentional planning

- Monitoring understanding

- Identifying comprehension failures and using "repair" strategies

Too much guidance can cause students to become dependent on us. For students in these critical intermediate grades, we need instruction that will help them become more independent and self-directed in their reading. Instructional events need to be planned that help students acquire the knowledge and skills they need for the *next* time they read.

Instructional Techniques to Build Independence

In this section, I discuss three techniques that I and the teachers I work with have found particularly effective for moving students toward independence in reading:

- Helping students manage their own learning

- Reciprocal teaching

- Selecting books with an eye toward instructional opportunities

Helping Students Manage Their Own Learning

Increasing students' control over their reading and achievement is a long-term proposition. Students need to learn how to manage their own learning. To help that process along, we can teach students to do the following:

Plan: Help students choose strategies for particular texts or tasks.

Monitor: Teach students how to "pay attention" as they read— how to check their comprehension against the demands of the text and the task.

Identify comprehension failures: Encourage students to recognize when they have not understood, but also to figure out the source of the problem. (Is it unfamiliar vocabulary? Poor word reading? Incomplete information?)

Recruit repair strategies to remediate those failures: Provide students with tactics for addressing these comprehension difficulties. "Fix-up" strategies include rereading, summarizing, discussion. For more information on repair strategies, read Linda Baker's excellent chapter on metacognition in *Comprehension Instruction* edited by Block and Pressley (2001). For specific teaching ideas, I recommend Ellin Keene and Susan Zimmerman's *Mosaic of Thought* (1997), or check out the collection of ideas in *50 Strategies for Improving Vocabulary, Comprehension and Fluency* by Adrienne Herrell and Michael Jordan (2006).

Reciprocal Teaching

One of the most widely used approaches to building independence in comprehension is reciprocal teaching. Originally conceived by Annemarie Palincsar and Ann Brown (1994), "reciprocal teaching is a scaffolded discussion strategy that is built on four strategies that good readers use to comprehend text: predicting, questioning, clarifying, and summarizing" (Oczkus, 2003, p. 1). While reciprocal teaching has elements in common with explicit instruction, teachers demonstrate the strategy with modeling and students get guided practice in a small group. What distinguishes this approach is that it allows students in small groups to gradually assume the role of the teacher.

As students read a selection—usually proceeding a paragraph at a time—the teacher demonstrates how to, for example, summarize or clarify during reading. Then, students take turns being "the teacher," while the teacher provides feedback about the strategy use. Over time, the teacher gradually phases out the support.

During student-teacher dialogue the teacher initially demonstrates by thinking aloud. After students have seen the teacher demonstrate a strategy (usually over several days), the teacher asks one student to take over the role of teacher. During this time, it is essential to support students with useful prompts and feedback. Remarks like the following are used to guide students as they become more expert and independent:

> **Prompting:** "What question do you think a teacher might ask?"
>
> **Instructing:** "Remember, a summary is a shortened version, it doesn't include a lot of detail."
>
> **Modifying** the activity: "If you're having a hard time thinking of a question, why don't you summarize first?"
>
> **Requesting** the help of other students: "Who can help us out with this one?"
>
> **Modeling:** "A question I might have asked is. . ."

Research shows that the most important part of the reciprocal teaching technique is this gradual release of control (Pearson & Gallagher, 1983). Little by little, the process is turned over to the students (Englert & Mariage, 1991).

This type of learning takes time. We need to be sure to shift the responsibility gradually and also to monitor text difficulty to make sure that students can actually apply their strategic approach to material. Finally, of course, we need to be constantly assessing students' progress to see whether we need to reteach. For more information on reciprocal teaching, see *Reciprocal Teaching at Work* by Lori Oczkus (2003).

Selecting Books With an Eye Toward Instructional Opportunities

We choose books for many instructional purposes, including to help students find pleasure in reading, to help them develop their understandings of concepts, and to expose them to new authors. So they need to be selected with care. We need to read with an eye to the *instructional opportunity* offered by the text. Comprehension of a particular story may be enhanced if students are encouraged to make connections to a previously read text. Alternatively, a news article may be just the right vehicle for introducing summarization. Because we want to use instructional texts to "make reading public," we should examine and select texts for their power in helping us teach strategies, text structure, and author's craft. (See the section on author's craft, pages 141–145, for some suggestions).

Not all texts are good for all purposes. In the past, commercial programs were quite notorious for teaching skills or strategies that were not required for in the assigned text! If students cannot see the need for a particular skill, strategy, or new piece of information, they will obviously not develop greater expertise, nor will they use it in the future. On the other hand, most books that are appropriate for grades 3 to 6 have the potential to be used for multiple purposes. I keep running documentation of books as I read them and/or hear about them from my colleagues. Below are a few of the novels from my list. Because students may be reading these novels over several weeks, it is possible to have more than one objective in mind.

Teachers can expand their own repertoire of book opportunities by partnering with colleagues. Share what you know with others—particularly other teachers at your grade level. Read books together. Talk about them. Identify their potential.

Identifying Instructional Opportunities in Books

BOOK	OPPORTUNITY
Lily's Crossing by Patricia Reilly Giff	**Genre:** historical fiction **Author's Craft:** characterization **Skill:** cause–effect **Strategy:** evaluating and/or making connection **Possible Theme:** change, growing up
Out of the Dust by Karen Hesse	**Text Structure/Author's Craft:** free verse **Author's Craft:** role of setting in establishing plot **Strategy:** making inferences, monitoring **Possible Theme:** relationships
Yang the Third and Her Impossible Family by L. Namioka	**Genre:** realistic fiction **Strategy:** visualizing, text–self connections **Possible Theme:** similarities/differences, changes
The White Mountains (part of the Tripod Trilogy) by John Christopher	**Genre:** fantasy **Author's Craft:** setting **Strategy:** visualizing, making inferences, evaluating **Possible Theme:** journeys, wilderness

Putting It All Together in the Classroom

Good teachers do not use only one instructional technique. As Pat Cunningham and Dick Allington note in their book, *Classrooms that Work:*

> The most effective teachers provide all the important ingredients that go into creating thoughtful, avid readers and writers. Exceptional teachers teach skills and strategies and also provide lots of time each day for children to read and write. (2007, p. 7)

Explicit instruction, readers' workshop, and guided reading are not incompatible approaches to instruction. The sample literacy-block planning framework shown in Figure 5.6 demonstrates how the "clear and direct explanations of skills, strategies or tasks" can take place during a mini-lesson prior to readers' workshop. Similarly, modeling (of that same skill, strategy, or task) can occur during read-alouds or guided reading, while guided practice may occur during individual conferences or small groups—either guided reading or flexible groups. Of course, the application in new settings may occur as teachers remind students to use a recently learned skill or strategy during silent reading or as they engage in reading during another time of the day.

Although readers' workshop is associated with a much more student-centered, less teacher-directed type of teaching, many students would benefit from some more explicit instruction. This can be done in a way that is consistent with the overall climate of the classroom. The key is to make some instruction more intentional, focused, and recursive—students need information, support, and feedback as they acquire new, complicated reading abilities (Baker et al., 2002).

Another possibility is to provide explicit instruction to all students who are reading a particular text (whether it's the whole class or small reading groups). I have provided a comprehensive lesson plan to demonstrate what explicit strategy instruction looks like in this context, especially when using complex text that offers rich opportunities for discussion.

Sample Literacy Block

		DAY 1	DAY 2	DAY 3
WHOLE GROUP 15–20 minutes		**Mini-Lesson:** Direct explanation of a skill, strategy, aspect of craft or text structure **Read-Aloud:** Model skill, strategy, etc.	**Guided Practice:** Revisit skill, strategy, etc. with group text or with new example. Shared reading and/or discussion.	
SMALL GROUP 30–60 minutes		Application of Knowledge and Skill: Independent Reading and/or Small Groups and/or Writing	Independent Reading Instructional Groups • Guided reading • Flexible groups (as needed) • Review and reteaching • Extra support Conferences • Teacher • Peer	Independent Reading Instructional Groups • Guided reading • Flexible groups (as needed) • Review and reteaching • Extra support Conferences • Teacher • Peer	Independent Reading Instructional Groups • Guided reading • Flexible groups (as needed) • Review and reteaching • Extra support Conferences • Teacher • Peer
		⬅ **Whole-Class Debriefing** ("community share") ➡		
		Share examples of skill, strategy, etc.	Discuss (theme, insights, etc.)	Discuss (theme, insights, etc.)
		Writing 20–40 minutes (can overlap with reading)		

Figure 5.6

MINI-LESSON: Making Inferences

Goals: Students will understand that inference requires "filling in the gaps"; identifying cause–effect events in a text; using cause–effect to infer the relationship between events and characters' actions.

Book: *Chato's Kitchen* by Gary Soto (1995)

Synopsis

Chato is a sneaky, low-riding cat who is delighted when a large family of "fat, juicy mice" move next door. He decides to invite them over for dinner, apparently intending to eat them. He begins to prepare a tasty feast, and Chato's friend, Novio Boy, comes over to help him cook. The mice ask whether it would be okay if they brought a friend, and Chato is even more delighted, thinking that it will be another mouse. When the friend, Chorizo, arrives, we see that he is a dog, and they all make their way to Chato's home. We see another side of Chato and Novio, who are terrified of Chorizo and run to hide. After Chorizo reassures them, they all settle down unhappily to eat the original feast the cats have prepared.

Explain

I tell students that authors usually don't tell us everything we need to know in order to understand their stories. Good readers fill in the gaps and make connections across the text. This is called "making inferences." We make inferences by reading what the author says, thinking about what we know already and putting those things together to make a conclusion or arrive at an insight. To help students visualize this, I show them the graphic in Figure 5.7.

Model

I demonstrate how this works using a brief excerpt from a familiar text. I read aloud an excerpt from *Yang the Youngest*:

> "Before I got used to the American school, the other kids laughed at some of the things I did. Each morning, as soon as the teacher came into the room. I jumped to my feet and stood stiffly at attention. That was how we showed our respect to the teacher in China. The first time I did it here, the teacher asked me whether I needed something. I looked around and saw that nobody else was standing up."

Then, using the format in Figure 5.7, I demonstrate how I made inferences about the text.

STORY CLUES: "The author tells me that no one else jumped up."

WHAT I KNOW: "I know from my own experience that being the only one to do something, especially if it's not right, makes me feel really embarrassed."

MY CONCLUSIONS: "I think that Yang feels embarrassed, but he also feels like he's an outsider; he doesn't know how to fit in with the other kids. He must feel bad going to school each day. The author doesn't tell me that he feels this way, but I can make an inference about it."

Provide Guided Practice

Now I want students to get a feel for making inferences themselves. I say, "Today we are going to read a wonderful book and we will have to make inferences if we are going to really enjoy it." I start reading *Chato's Kitchen* aloud, stopping at appropriate points to model the inferring process. After two or three pages (I stop after page 6) I provide guided journal pages and have students work together to complete one sequence as I read the next portion. Guided practice can be provided with graphics like the one shown in figure 5.7 or through discussion, open-ended prompts, charts, and so on.

Offer Feedback

Discuss students' work, individually and/or in small groups. Be sure to provide specific feedback that will help students clarify any misunderstandings. For example, if students did not understand why Chato wanted the mice to come to dinner, help them find the clues in the text (and in their own background) to make an informed guess.

Encourage Application

Ask students to use the journal page to clarify as they finish the book for themselves.

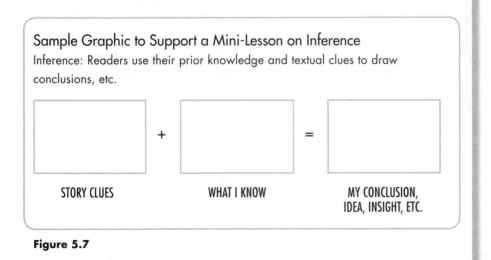

Sample Graphic to Support a Mini-Lesson on Inference
Inference: Readers use their prior knowledge and textual clues to draw conclusions, etc.

STORY CLUES	WHAT I KNOW	MY CONCLUSION, IDEA, INSIGHT, ETC.

Figure 5.7

Mini-Lesson continued

On subsequent days, we continue using this strategy with other texts. A strong emphasis on *when* and *why* helps students internalize and use these techniques. Questions like the following support the ongoing shift to student independence:

> Did anyone make an inference about this part?
>
> What information from the text did you use to help you?
>
> What did you know already?
>
> How did that help you understand the story?
>
> Why was that a good thing to do with this material?

I might want to revisit *Chato's Kitchen* to accomplish other objectives. For example, I would likely revisit this text for a lesson on how the author helps us understand characters and their motivations. This lesson would be supported by a character map like the one on page 163. We would reflect, for example, on how the author has described Chato (he's "a cool, low-riding cat") and how he talks (he says things like "no problema, home boy") to get the idea that Chato is the coolest cat in East L.A. But the fun really begins as we examine Chato's thoughts. His plans to eat the new neighbors, a family of mice, is revealed in his thoughts about the "tasty family." Finally, of course, we learn about characters by their actions and Chato's are hilarious—he dances and sings "La Bamba" while cooking up chorizo and beans. I use stories like *Chato's Kitchen* because the rich characterizations can help students see how important character development is to a story and also how paying attention to characters can help us understand and enjoy stories more fully. This new awareness of character development can then be applied to more-challenging texts.

Character Map

What the Character Is Thinking
Examples from text:

How the Character Talks and What He or She Says
Examples from text:

What the Character Looks Like
Examples from text:

What Other Characters Say About Him or Her
Examples from text:

How the Character Acts
Examples from text:

Concluding Thoughts

Teaching reading in grades 3 to 6 requires quite a lot of knowledge and expertise on our part. And while there is always more to learn, the good news is that this is rich and rewarding work. It's fascinating to understand the process of comprehension and to begin using text to explicitly teach strategies or author's craft; what's more, the texts themselves are inherently engaging. Finally, there is nothing more important than helping students in these grades begin to learn how to govern their own learning.

I highly recommend starting with texts that you already know well. Reexamining them with the idea of teaching more intentionally and explicitly will reveal new opportunities. Then, we must remember that these abilities grow in our students over a very long time. If you are teaching in grade 3, your students are just beginning the journey. If you are teaching in grade 6, there is still a worrying amount to learn. New texts and new tasks await in middle and high school. However, building independence for the abilities students have *now* will help them learn how to learn more.

Discussion and Reflection

- How aware of your own comprehension are you?

- Which strategies do you use? When do you use them?

- Are there some aspects of comprehension that you already teach explicitly? Share those with others.

- Identify two to five books that you use regularly that are good candidates for explicit teaching. Complete a chart like the one on page 157.

- Consider what step(s) you might take to increase your students' independence and self-control.

Digging Deeper

If you are looking for more information on comprehension instruction, check out these resources:

- *Craft Lessons* by Ralph Fletcher and JoAnn Portalupi, Portland, ME: Stenhouse, 1998.

- *Guided Comprehension: A Teaching Model for Grades 3–8* by Maureen McLaughlin and Mary Beth Allen. Newark, DE: International Reading Association, 2001.

- *Nonfiction Craft Lessons* by JoAnn Portalupi and Ralph Fletcher. Portland, ME: Stenhouse, 2001.

- *Nonfiction in Focus* by Janice Kristo and Rosemary Bamford. NY: Scholastic, 2004.

- *Reading and Writing Literary Genres* by Kathleen Buss and Lee Karnowski. Newark, DE: International Reading Association, 2000.

- *Reading and Writing Nonfiction Genres* by Kathleen Buss and Lee Karnowski. Newark, DE: International Reading Association, 2002.

- *Reciprocal Teaching at Work: Strategies for Improving Comprehension* by Lori D. Oczkus. Newark, DE: International Reading Association, 2003.

- *Self-Regulated Learning.* Dale Schunk and Barry Zimmerman. New York: Guilford Press, 1998.

- *Strategies That Work* by Stephanie Harvey and Anne Goudvis. Portland, ME: Stenhouse, 2000.

CHAPTER 6

Extend Word Identification, Fluency, and Spelling Skills

Word study is an important component of reading instruction for all students in the intermediate and middle grades. Approximately 3 to 5 percent of students are genuinely disabled readers and need further, intensive help in phonics and fluency. (See M. Y. Lipson & Wixson, 2003.) Many more students than that struggle with reading at the word level. Some need work in word recognition accuracy, others need to focus on meaning vocabulary. In addition, a great many need continued work on automaticity and fluency. Students

Kaylie and Jordana

Kaylie and Jordana were both enrolled in our summer clinic. They were both scheduled to enter sixth grade in the fall, and they had remarkably similar abilities and difficulties. Both could read sixth-grade text with accuracy. However, they were very slow and, not surprisingly, assessments of developmental spelling revealed weak knowledge of spelling patterns. Both girls spelled *fortunate* as "forchenit," for example. Their reading rates were slow and their comprehension was much weaker than their word accuracy scores, despite average and low-average verbal abilities. In short, they were hanging on by their fingernails! They *could*, with a great deal of effort, read grade-level materials. But it took a lot of time, and their motivation sometimes wavered in the face of the difficulty. We knew that when they got to middle school and the demands of the sixth-grade curriculum, they would quickly start to flounder.

like Kaylie and Jordana, profiled in the box above, are quite common in grades 3 to 6, but virtually all students in these grades, even those who are not struggling overall, will benefit from intentional and sensible word work in their literacy programs.

In this chapter we explore word-level concerns and also provide ideas for adding word work to the instructional program. I give a review of phonics elements, as these form the basis for reading multisyllabic words, and introduce additional information students need in order to become adept at using base words, prefixes, and suffixes to read challenging new words. Then I describe the strategic approach I teach to move students toward independence in word-level reading. Since word identification and spelling can inform each other at these ages, I also demonstrate how the analysis of students' spelling can enhance word reading. Finally, I present ideas for teaching and monitoring fluency. These elements can and should work together to constitute the word-study component of an intermediate classroom.

Lessons From Research and Practice: What We Know About Extending Skills in Word Identification, Fluency, and Spelling

Research and practice tell us that students are still developing both word identification and fluency abilities during grades 3 to 6. Certainly, most students will have "mastered" most of the basic phonological aspects of reading by this point—they have grasped the basics of phonemic awareness and phonics decoding. However, most students will still be acquiring control over these abilities beyond grade 2, working on automaticity in word recognition and fluency during text reading. Spelling development, which was completely aligned with phonics in the primary grades, becomes an ally to word identification in different ways during this later period, providing as it does the basis for identifying and using written spelling patterns.

According to Joseph Torgesen, the challenge of continuing growth in word identification becomes even greater after third grade:

> [Fourth], 5th, and 6th graders encounter about 10,000 words they have never seen before in print during a year's worth of reading. Furthermore, each of these "new" words occurs only about 10 times in a year's worth of reading. Unfortunately, it's very difficult to correctly guess the identity of these "new words" just from the context of the passage. Thus, it is important to have reliable decoding strategies to improve the accuracy with which "new" words are identified when they are first encountered. (2004)

Traditionally, teaching practices for grades 3 to 6 have not attended to these word-level matters, however. There has been an absence of materials and strategies appropriate for use with older, still-developing readers. Even teachers who see the need may not know quite what to do. Many teachers in grades 3 to 6 do not know enough about the structure of the language—I certainly didn't when I began teaching.

Developing Skills in Word Identification

Some people think word identification is the same as phonics, but phonics is only one part of what it takes to identify words, especially in grades 3 and beyond. Most students have all the phonics they need by the time they reach third grade. What they are missing is a repertoire of word-identification strategies that includes phonics but also structural analysis (the ability to see the syllable structure of words) and morphemic analysis (the ability to use roots, suffixes, and prefixes to decode and analyze words).

Phonics

There are two ways in which the word *phonics* is used. First, phonics is the *understanding* that there is a predictable relationship between the sounds of spoken language (phonemes) and the letters and spellings that represent those sounds. Second, phonics is used to describe a system for *teaching* reading and spelling that emphasizes the relationship between sounds and symbols. Phonics is important, but it's just not enough. Phonics analysis instruction is necessary as an aid to rapid and effortless decoding and merits a prominent place in early reading instruction.

Phonics knowledge and skill are essential building blocks for a more sophisticated repertoire of word-identification strategies, so it is important to understand basic phonics, even if you don't teach it.

All spoken languages are composed of sounds. The sounds, or phonemes, of English are summarized in Figure 6.1.

In writing, English is an alphabetic language, which means that symbols (letters) are used to represent phonemes, or sounds. For example, *y* is used to represent the initial sound in the word *yard*. Not all written languages work this way. In some languages, the symbols represent meanings and there is little or no relationship to the sounds of the language (e.g., Chinese logographs). In some other languages symbols are assigned to whole syllables (e.g., Cherokee). Several aspects of English make it challenging:

- There are between 40 and 44 phonemes (sounds) in the language but only 26 letters to represent them. This means, of course, that some symbols, or combinations, have to be used to represent more than one sound.

Phonics Content

CONSONANTS are sounds that are produced when you stop or slow the breath coming through your mouth. There are roughly 25 consonant sounds (phonemes) in English

SOUND	EXAMPLES
/b/	ball, scab
/d/	dog, bad
/f/	fog, graph, rough
/g/	game, ghoul, fig
/h/	hat, who
/hw/	white
/j/	jam, gem, wage, wedge
/k/	car, kitten, take, black, antique
/l/	lake, wall
/m/	monkey, slim, came, limb
/n/	name, pneumonia, gnat, fin
/p/	pail, sap
/r/	rain
/s/	sun, cereal, us, bass, mice
/t/	tap, cat, clapped
/v/	vote, live
/w/	wink
/y/	yoke, bastion
/z/	zoo, was, whiz, fizz, maze,
/ch/	chain, much, hutch, lecture, question
/sh/	sheet, sugar, chaise, mash, fiction
/th/	thimble, myth
/th/	them, lathe
/zh/	measure
/ng/	ring

VOWELS are sounds that are produced when air flows in an unrestricted way through your throat and opened mouth. There are approximately 16 vowel phonemes in English

SOUND		EXAMPLES
Long	/a /	make, bait, fray, table
	/e/	beet, seam, me, pony, key, receive
	/i /	bike, fight, tiny, lie
	/o /	dome, soap, no, mow, sold, total fuse, puny
	/u/	cat
Short	/a /	bed, meadow
	/e/	fit
	/i /	top
	/o /	cup, come
	/u/	
r-controlled		car
	/ar /	fir, her, fur
	/ir/	for, more, pour, door
	/or /	hair, bare
	/air/	fear, leer
	/eer/	
Other vowels		button, about, model
Schwa (ə)		foil, boy
	/oi/	owl, mouth
	/ow /	awful, taught, fall, air, bare, balk, scoff
	/aw/	food, suit, flew, sue
	/oo/	book, should
	/oo/	

CONSONANT DIGRAPHS and **CONSONANT BLENDS** require attention because they need to be visually identified by readers during words analysis; especially in more advanced decoding.

DIGRAPHS are two consonants that work together to represent one sound (phoneme): e.g., *sh, ch, gh*

BLENDS are two consonants that work together, but each continues to represent its original sound: e.g., *br, fl, scr, st, sp, ld*

Figure 6.1 From Lipson, M.Y. & Wixson, K. K. (2003)

- Some sounds are represented in more than one way. For example, the long-*a* sound is represented in several ways, including *ay*, *ai*, *a*-consonant-silent *e*, and *eigh*.

- More than one letter is used to represent some sounds— /ch/ is usually represented by the two letters *c+h* but also in the following ways: *butch, lecture, question.*

- We have many "loan" words from other countries— for example, *pecan, karate,* and *safari.*

English is more predictable than many people seem to think. In fact, at the syllable level, English is quite consistent, and decoding can be eased considerably once students are able to analyze words at that level. Very, very few students in grades 3 to 6 are at the single sound-symbol level. All but the most challenged students can read regularly-spelled, single-syllable words such as *cat, but,* and *jump.* In addition, they should be able to locate the "rime" in these words. Simple English words are comprised of an onset and a rime. Rimes are spelling patterns that include the vowel and what follows it in a one-syllable word. An onset is the consonant or consonant string that precedes the rime.

Word	Onset	Rime
rat	r-	-at
smile	sm-	-ile

Other examples of spelling patterns include:

-ake	-oat	-ile	-uke	-eam	-oat
-oil	-ork	-ail	-erm	-and	-oot

These recurrent spelling patterns make up the *orthography* of our written language—that is, the sequence of letters in conventionally spelled words.

As students move up through the grades it becomes increasingly important that they can identify these recurrent patterns in English words. Recognizing these spelling patterns allows them to read familiar words rapidly—thereby circumventing the need to sound it out. In addition, the orthographic patterns form the basis for identifying longer, multisyllabic words.

Syllabication

Using the letter-sound information from phonics to read longer words is a bit more complicated. Readers often need to engage in structural analysis *before* they can apply their phonics knowledge. In structural analysis, readers must recognize and segment by syllable boundaries, either through "rules' or by using recurrent spelling patterns (or rimes). After these patterns, or chunks, are located it is possible to use the letter-sound information. Let's consider an example:

Imagine that *constandark* is an English word. We have not seen it before. Before we can use our letter-sound information, we need to divide this word into syllables. Our experience with other English words tells us that it is probably divided this way:

con-stan-dark

Now, it's pretty easy to decode this word. Try it with these "words": *spectition, moutate, volancholy.*

When you first looked at the word *constandark*, you may have had just a second of uncertainty. While your word-recognition ability normally functions on automatic pilot, here you had to shift from automatic, take the controls, and look more closely. Now, imagine what happens when students in grades 3, 4, or even 5 encounter long words if they do not know *how* to approach reading them. Students who attempt such a word typically try the initial consonant or syllable and guess at the rest. Most others do one of three things: (1) mumble something and keep reading; (2) skip it and read on; or (3) ask.

This pattern of response is one of the reasons that so many people think that students in these grades have phonics problems. They look like they can't decode, but the problem is really that they can't *find* the phonics pattern. Until they can locate the pattern, it is simply not possible to apply decoding skills. Although humans are naturally inclined to notice patterns, "readers acquire the ability to recognize likely spelling patterns gradually. . . . [I]t is during the fourth grade that the adult ability to perceive syllables as units emerges, at this point normal readers begin to perceive syllables more quickly and accurately than single letters" (Adams, 1990, p. 125).

Teaching students some basic syllabication patterns is helpful because it may help them perceive recurrent spelling patterns. Later in the chapter, I describe a couple of different tactics for teaching students to acquire and use this information.

Syllable Types and Patterns

SIX MOST COMMON TYPES OF SYLLABLES

Type	Example
open	An open syllable ends with a single vowel; the vowel is long. Example: *to*–tem
closed	A closed syllable has a single vowel and ends with a consonant; the vowel is short. Example: *but*–ter
r-controlled	In this type of syllable, the vowel is followed by the consonant *r*; the vowel is "controlled," or changed, by the *r*. Example: *par*–take or *mor*–tal
vowel_silent *e*	The pattern in these syllables is vowel-consonant-silent *e*; the first vowel is generally long. Example: par–*take*
vowel combination	Vowel combinations make one sound in these syllables and may appear in various vowel sound forms. Examples: *fea*–ture or *found*-ling
consonant-*le*	When syllables end in -*le*, these letters attach to the preceding consonant; the vowel sound is the schwa (unaccented vowel). Example: rat–*tle* or a–*ble*

COMMON SYLLABLE PATTERNS

(Always start marking a word at the first vowel to discover its pattern)

VC/CV	Words that have a vowel-consonant-consonant-vowel pattern. Example: *flat/ter* or *cat/nip*
V/CV or VC/V	Most words that have the vowel-consonant-vowel pattern divide after the first vowel and the vowel is long (e.g., *tu/tor*); sometimes, though, the break is after the vowel and the syllable is closed (e.g., *mim/ic*).
VC/CCV or VCC/CV	Words with this pattern generally have consonant blends or digraphs that must be treated together. If it's a blend, it is usually divided before the blend (e.g., *pin/prick*); if it's a digraph, it is usually divided after the consonant combination (e.g., *graph/ic*).
V/V	If there are two vowels in a word, but there are not vowel "teams" (digraphs or diphthongs), the word is divided between them. Example: *li/on*

Figure 6.2

Morphemic Analysis

Another aspect of more sophisticated word identification strategies is morphemic analysis, in which the reader breaks down a word into smaller meaning-bearing units as an aid to identifying and understanding it. This type of analysis is absolutely essential for students in the intermediate grades as they encounter not only longer words, but words whose meanings they may not know.

Morpheme is a linguistic term for the smallest unit of meaning in our language. English morphology includes root words, prefixes, suffixes, and inflectional endings. Students in grades 3 and beyond are usually quite adept at reading or locating root words and inflectional endings, especially those in compound words such as *firefight* and *breadstick*, which each have two morphemes. Each root word carries meaning and contributes to the overall meaning of the word. Other words are more complicated and include prefixes and/or suffixes that make decoding difficult but which may also change meaning. (See Figure 6.3.) For example, the word *unmentionables* can be divided into four meaning parts: *un-, mention, -able*, and *-s*. Each part carries meaning, and the whole word is influenced by the parts.

Identifying these parts is important for word decoding. Of course, paying attention to morphemes also helps readers figure out the meaning of the words.

Common Prefixes and Suffixes

PREFIXES

a, an	Greek; without
anti	Greek; opposite
pre	Latin; before
in	Latin; in, on, into
re	Latin; again, back
pro	Latin; for, with
poly	Greek; many
trans	Latin; across
neo	Greek; new
mis	Latin; less or wrong

SUFFIXES

less	Latin; changes to opposite of base
ish	Latin; having character of
able	Latin; capable of, can do
ize	Greek; changes to noun
ary	Latin; a person, place or thing which, connected with
ance	Latin; quality or state of being, condition
tion	Latin; changes to noun
ment	Latin; changes to noun; result of, means of
or	Latin; person or thing that
y	Greek; state of, quality of

Figure 6.3

Jack Pikulski and Shane Templeton recommend systematically teaching the meaning of prefixes, suffixes and root words. "In the intermediate grades and beyond, most new words that students encounter in their reading are morphological derivatives of familiar words" (2004, p. 6). These authors note that simple prefixes like *un-* or *re-* are taught in the primary grades, but as students move into grades 3 to 6, affixes often signal changes in both meaning and word function: *govern* (a verb) becomes *government* (a noun), for example. Similarly, in these grades some morphemes form the "base" but cannot stand alone. Roots such as *spect* form the basis for many words, including *inspection, spectacles,* and *spectator.*

A simple approach to decoding can be helpful in the early stages of learning to read. Recognizing which letter(s) stand for which sounds is a critical first step. As students become more mature, however, they need a repertoire of skills and strategies that can be applied flexibly, depending on the context.

John Shefelbine has been studying word identification among fourth-, fifth-, and sixth-grade students for many years. His research (1990) suggests that direct instruction and practice with word parts help these students pronounce multi-syllabic words. "Directly teaching students how to pronounce and identify syllable units and then showing them how such units work in polysyllabic words appears to be a worthwhile component of syllabication instruction and should help reduce or remediate this source of reading difficulty among intermediate students" (p. 228).

It is important to know that good readers tend to use an "analogy approach" to decoding, in which they compare and contrast new, unknown words and word parts to words and patterns they already know (Cunningham, 1975–76, 1979). That's probably how you figured out how to pronounce *constandark* earlier. You may have done something like this:

con-	-stan-	-dark
I know the word part *con* ("convict").	I know *stand,* so this is *stan.*	I know the word *dark.*

Younger readers might make a comparison to *on, an*, and *bark.* Then, they would add initial consonants or combinations to arrive at the word.

In its comprehensive review of phonics and decoding, the NRP concluded that a program of explicit instruction in a compare-contrast approach was among the few approaches that worked for older struggling readers (Lovett & Steinbach, 1997). To use an analogy strategy successfully, readers need to be able to identify syllables and morphemes. In addition, they need to be able to use context to refine both pronunciation and meaning. I provide examples of this type of instruction later in the chapter.

Word Work for Everyone: Classroom Instruction

As we have noted, all students in grades 3 to 6 should have an opportunity to increase their word power. Most educators use the term "word work" to refer to the interrelated knowledge and skills that help students with decoding, vocabulary, and spelling. Word study is designed to teach students to examine, discover, and make use of the patterns and regularities of the English language. It requires explicit instruction, communal discussion and discovery, and independent practice. In his terrific book *Word Savvy*, Max Brand notes: "Even though intermediate-grade students come to us with a breadth and depth of word knowledge, they still need supportive instruction. It's tempting to push these students toward independence prior to readiness" (2004, p. 16).

Students engaged in word study

Good reading instruction in grades 3 to 6 should include a comprehensive plan for engaging students in word study. To maximize effectiveness in this area, the reading program should do several things:

- Interest students in words
- Teach strategies for identifying multisyllabic words
- Promote sensitivity to spelling patterns and/or syllable types
- Teach prefixes and suffixes

Interest Students in Words

No matter what their stage of development, students can benefit from an increased attention to and interest in words. The more students explore words as they talk, read, write, or play, the more likely it is they will develop the understanding and flexibility necessary to decode words while reading and encode words while writing.

If possible, the tools and techniques we use to do this should allow *all* students to participate. That is one of the reasons I like word-study notebooks so much. (See Bear, Invernizzi, Templeton, & Johnston, 2003.) Teachers can introduce a word pattern and ask students to keep an eye out for words that share this pattern, or students can discover their own. Students should be encouraged to enter words by patterns—for example, creating a page for all *-tion* words. As they enter words in their notebook, they can write the sentence that it appeared in, make notations about how it was used, and think of other words that are spelled—or pronounced—the same way. The teacher's role is important in directing students' attention to the patterns and also helping them understand how patterns operate. In addition, we can differentiate the task for different students. Some students may be asked to look for words with certain rime patterns, while others may be alerted to find words that have specific root derivatives.

Teach Strategies for Identifying Multisyllabic Words

As we noted earlier, reading and recognizing longer words can be unnerving for our students. We can help by teaching them how to approach multisyllabic words when they encounter them in print. We can teach them to break words into manageable, decodable chunks:

1. Carefully look at the word; decide how to pronounce it.
2. Remove any prefixes.
3. Identify any suffixes.
4. Look for syllable patterns.
5. Find familiar spelling patterns (or chunks).
6. Think about words you know that have these spelling patterns and decode by analogy.
7. Say the word and ask yourself whether you know the meaning or whether it makes sense in the context.

Of course, this only helps readers with pronouncing the word. Sometimes the word will be in our oral vocabulary and we can move along. Other times, more is needed. Pikulski and Templeton offer a useful additional strategy (2004). They suggest that readers try one of two tactics: (1) Look *around* the word for context clues; or (2) look *within* the word.

Look around the word for context clues:	Look within the word:
within the sentence	for prefixes and suffixes
within previous sentences	for base words
within sentences to come	for root words

These types of strategies have been shown to be very helpful to intermediate-grade students—even struggling ones (Cunningham, 2000; Gaskins, Gaskins, & Gaskins, 1992; Shefelbine & Newman, 2000).

Struggling readers often do need explicit instruction to encourage them to look through the whole word before they attempt to decode and also in applying the analogy technique. Gaskins and her colleagues teach a patterned approach that involves saying the word pattern, looking for a familiar analogue, and then saying, "If I know _____, then I know _____," as they work through the decoding process. Thus, if students came to the word *arcane* and did not recognize it, they would do something like this:

I see two spelling patterns in this word: *ar* and *-ane*

I know *car*, so I know *ar*, and I know *Jane*, so I know *cane*.

The word must be *arcane*.

Younger and struggling students need to be taught how to substitute onsets and also how to blend the parts together, but the vast majority of intermediate students catch on quickly.

Promote Sensitivity to Spelling Patterns and/or Syllable Types

Of course, this general decoding strategy requires that students can recognize spelling patterns. It is clear that in grades 3 and 4, this ability is just emerging. Therefore, teachers can aid students' recognition by pointing out the ways that words are similar and asking students to pay attention to these aspects of words. An excellent way to do this is with a word sort, a powerful tool for helping students investigate almost all aspects of words. This technique is not new. In 1979 Jean Gillet and M. J. Kita described how students could benefit from grouping and categorizing words by using their prior knowledge and experience. They described two types of word sorts: open and closed. In an open sort, no criteria for sorting are provided. Because students must impose their own organization on the words, it is possible to observe the types of relationships students recognize and use. In a closed sort, the teacher establishes the criteria for sorting. Using word cards prepared in advance (or selected by students from their own word bank), the teacher may ask students to do any of the following:

- Put the words that go together in the same pile (open sort). Name the sort.

- Put all the words together that have the same (for example) prefix. Then name the group (closed sort).

- Put all the words together that have *something* the same and label the characteristic.

- Put all the words together that have the same *feature* (for example, rhyme or spelling pattern).

According to Fountas and Pinnell (2001), word sorting helps students compare and contrast words to discover their key features. We can use word sorts to focus students' attention on sound, spelling, or meaning. In Glenn Willette's third-grade and Drew Blanchard's fourth-grade classes, students have been engaged in hands-on, discovery word study all year. It shows in the types of sorts these students do and also in the kinds of thinking evident in their summary notes.

The example in Figure 6.4 shows how students begin to notice regular sound-symbol patterns—and also the "oddballs," those words that don't follow the pattern. As students sort the words, they begin to draw conclusions. In Figure 6.5 we can see this student has begun to form an important generalization about plural endings. He hasn't got the whole story yet, but in future sorts he can begin to revise his hypothesis (when his teacher adds words like *car, heart,* and *claw*).

For teachers who need help thinking about words and their patterns, there are now a number of commercial sources for word sorts, including the *Words Their Way Word Sorts* books, for each of the developmental stages described by Donald Bear and his colleagues. Other resources are available online. For examples, check out the word sorts section on Houghton Mifflin's Kids' Place Web site (http://www.eduplace.com/kids/sv/books/content/wordsort/) for interactive word sorts at every grade level. Students can time themselves and select a level that is appropriate for them.

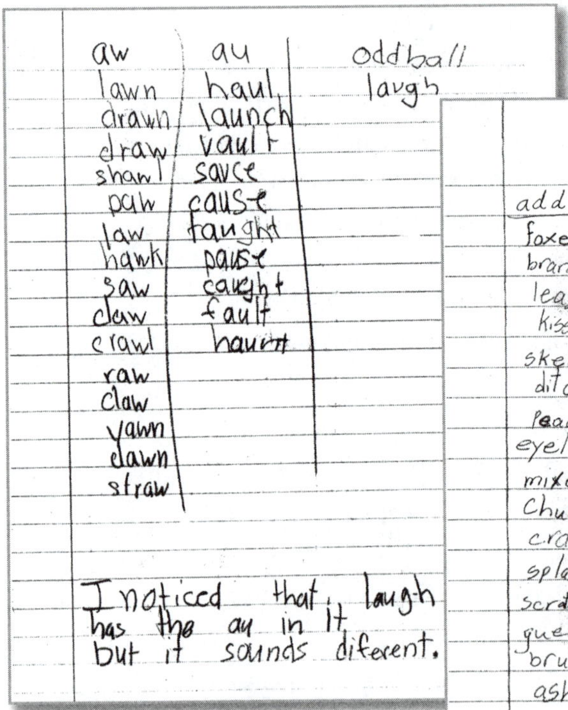

aw	au	oddball
lawn	haul	laugh
drawn	launch	
draw	vault	
shawl	sauce	
paw	cause	
law	taught	
hawk	pause	
saw	caught	
claw	fault	
crawl	haunt	
raw		
claw		
yawn		
dawn		
straw		

I noticed that, laugh has the au in it but it sounds diferent.

Figure 6.4 Word sort for -aw and -au

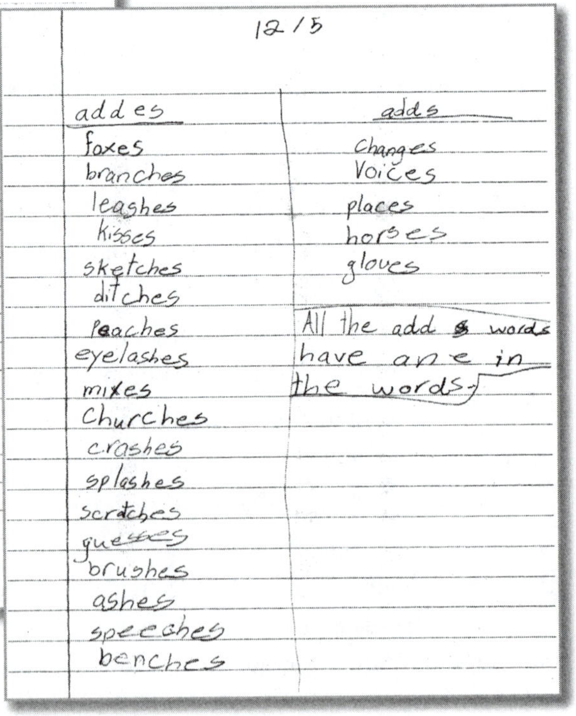

12/5

add es	adds
foxes	changes
branches	voices
leashes	places
kisses	horses
sketches	gloves
ditches	
peaches	All the add s words
eyelashes	have an e in
mixes	the words.
churches	
crashes	
splashes	
scratches	
guesses	
brushes	
ashes	
speeches	
benches	

Figure 6.5 Word sort for -es and -s endings

Teach Students to Recognize Meaning-Based Word Elements

Mature reading and writing require deep knowledge of prefixes, suffixes, and word roots. Explicit instruction is certainly required for many students as they move toward the more sophisticated derivational analysis of mature readers and spellers. Explanation, modeling, and application will all be needed. Matching definitions for common prefixes and suffixes can really help students, for example. Although many teachers are not confident themselves about Latin and Greek roots and bases, some easily accessible resources can help a great deal. I have found *Instant Vocabulary* by Ida Erlich (2005) helpful, for example, and both *Words Their Way* (Bear et al., 2003) and *Word Journeys* (Ganske, 2000) provide extensive resources for teachers who want to know more. Lisa Goetz's fifth-grade students have been doing word study that includes manipulating morphemes. Two sorts from her classroom are shown in Figure 6.6.

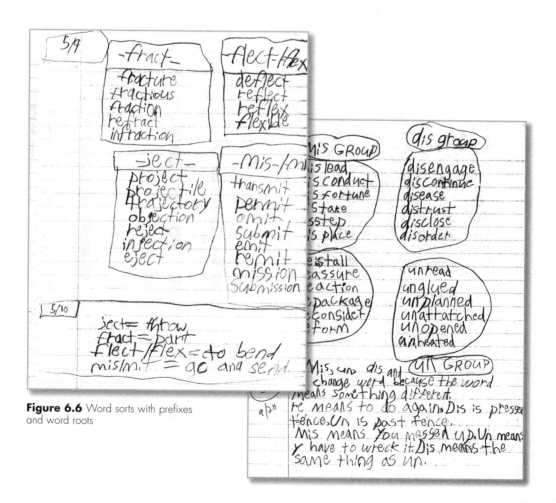

Figure 6.6 Word sorts with prefixes and word roots

Developing Skills in Fluency

Although it is important for students to be able to decode unknown words, it is not enough to ensure good reading performance. According to the NRP:

> Teachers need to know that word recognition accuracy is not the end point of reading instruction. Fluency represents a level of expertise beyond word recognition accuracy, and reading comprehension may be aided by fluency. (2000, p. 3)

It is likely, in fact, that fluency is a key ingredient of comprehension. There is increasing evidence that among older students (grade 3 and above) fluency may be a better predictor of comprehension than accuracy, although of course both are important (Kershaw, 2005; RAND Reading Study Group, 2002).

Reading fluency is often called a "bridge" between decoding and comprehension because it involves elements of both. (See Pikulski & Chard, 2005.) Fluency is the ability to read words accurately with appropriate rate in such a way as to maintain and construct meaning.

To be fluent, readers must do the following:

- Read words accurately

- Instantly recognize a large number of words without undue analysis

- Automatically read words during actual reading in continuous text

- Read words in such a way as to maintain the meaning of the text—for example, in phrases and with expression

- Maintain a good pace and speed over time

Reading fluency shows gradual improvement over time and in response to practice (NRP, 2000). As a result, in most intermediate-grade classrooms students' knowledge and skill in fluency can vary enormously. In addition, fluency probably continues to develop through adolescence, as students' knowledge about words grows. While we do not have good research evidence from grades 5 to 8 about who benefits from what types of instruction, it is certainly clear that struggling readers' fluency can be improved and also that improvements in fluency improve comprehension (NRP, 2000). In fact, Marilyn Adams (1990) argues that automaticity is the "key to the whole system. . . . The readers' attention can be focused on the meaning and message of a text only to the extent that it is free from fussing with the words and letters" (p. 207).

Fluency Instruction for Everyone: Classroom Instruction

Many intermediate-grade students are not fluent. Some are not fluent because well into grade 3 they are still developing basic decoding abilities. In later grades, though, there are many more students who are not fluent because they simply have not had enough exposure to print. Fluency relies very heavily on students' rapid recognition of common spelling patterns. Unlike many other aspects of reading, it cannot be taught explicitly. Instead, it develops through practice and repeated exposure to printed words; in other words, through reading (Barker, Torgesen, & Wagner, 1992).

Students' independent practice must be in appropriately difficult texts. If the material is too difficult or requires too much decoding, students will not attain the fluency they are trying to practice. If it is too easy, they won't benefit from improving their performance.

For instructional activities related to fluency, the text should be difficult enough to pose some challenge. Two very effective instructional approaches to developing fluency are repeated reading and Readers Theater.

Repeated Reading

There is an extensive research base supporting almost any form of repeated reading. Repeated reading benefits both good and poor readers, and students tend to maintain their gains even after the repeated-reading training ends. The most benefit, however, comes from repeated reading that involves some degree of feedback or guidance (NRP, 2000). What is especially interesting is that repeated reading practice seems to improve word identification and comprehension as well as fluency (Dowhower, 1987).

Karen Wixson and I have worked with repeated readings for many years, and we have described how to implement this approach (2003):

Select materials. Choose material that lends itself to fluent oral reading. Text that is too choppy or artificial does not result in increased fluency. Do not hesitate to select material that is somewhat challenging since it will be read several times.

Identify purpose. Help students understand why they are rereading. As with an athlete or musician, practice is a major part of improving overall performance. Emphasize that this increased fluency will help them comprehend better.

Record results. Keep track of results on individual graphs or charts. As students' fluency improves, move to more challenging material.

Once students are comfortable with repeated readings, they can practice in pairs. Partner reading has proven successful as a whole-class strategy in regular classrooms (Rasinski, 1990). Although repeated readings may seem to you like a tedious task, students are surprisingly enthusiastic about it—especially if the additional motivation of record keeping is added as a personal incentive.

Readers Theater

One way to increase students' motivation for repeated-reading practice is to use a technique called Readers Theater. Although the research base for Readers Theater isn't quite as strong as for other forms of repeated readings, it is fun to do and easy to implement. It is also a wonderful way to make stories come alive and to get students actively involved.

Choose a text. Select a narrative story with dialogue that can be divided into parts or roles.

Do an initial read-through. This may be done as a "shared reading" activity, as individual silent reading, or in pairs.

Assign and practice parts. Determine the number of parts, and then divide the class into as many groups. Be sure to help students identify the narrator ("said the snake") and assign one group to that role as well. Ask groups to chorally practice their character's dialogue. Have participants (in their small groups) discuss:

- What parts could be improved upon in terms of fluency and interpretation?
- What should be kept the same?

Have students perform. Bring everyone back together and have them perform, with each group taking its turn.

This type of activity can be done with any story that the students are reading. In addition, there are now available many sources of scripts for Readers Theater. For example, Aaron Shepard has free scripts and other resources on his Web site at http://www.aaronshep.com/rt/RTE00.html.

Developing Skills in Spelling

Many of us have vivid memories of studying spelling lists and taking Friday spelling tests. Some of us already knew the words on Monday and didn't have to study them. Others of us had to study hard to pass. As teachers, we also know that many students who pass spelling tests misspell the very same words in their own writing.

Excellent research over the past 25 years has helped us get a better grasp on spelling. Investigators like Edmund Henderson, Shane Templeton, Donald Bear, and Marcia Invernizzi have made significant contributions to our understanding.

One extremely important insight is the realization that spelling is developmental—that students progress along a fairly predictable path toward conventional spelling. The developmental stages shown in Figure 6.7 demonstrate that the spelling abilities in any given intermediate-grade classroom are likely to be highly variable.

I discuss spelling development in this chapter because it is so intertwined with students' evolving word identification abilities. Because English is an alphabetic language, students use orthographic knowledge for both decoding and spelling. Information about one area can provide insights into other areas. Of course, this is not a perfect correlation; there are some students who are good readers but not good spellers, and there are some good spellers who are not good readers (usually as a result of fluency difficulties).

Stages of Spelling Development

LETTER NAME (kindergarten to mid–grade 2)
Students have a concept of word and represent beginning and ending sounds. Example: bed – *bd*

WITHIN-WORD PATTERN (grade 1 to mid–grade 4)
Students spell most single-syllable, short-vowel words correctly; errors may appear in consonant and vowel combinations. Examples: float – *flote*; spoil – *spole*

SYLLABLE JUNCTURE (grade 3 to grade 8)
Students spell most single-syllable words correctly; errors appear at the juncture of syllables. Examples: cattle – *cattel*; cellar – *celar*

DERIVATIONAL PATTERNS (grade 5 to grade 12)
Students have mastered most frequent and common words; errors appear when combining roots and affixes and where vowels change in combinations (extreme – extremity). Examples: carries – *carrys*; opposition – *opisition*

Figure 6.7 Drawn from Templeton (1991); Bear et al. (2003)

For teachers in grades 3 to 6, progress in spelling is often related to students' growing word identification insights as well as their emerging vocabulary development.

> Among intermediate students, examination of how spelling patterns reflect meaning leads to vocabulary growth. To get a sense of how the connection works between spelling and meaning, examine the following words: bomb/bombard; muscle/muscular; compete/competition. Because the words in each pair are related in meaning, the spelling of the underlined sounds remains constant; although the sound that letters represent may change in related words, the spelling usually remains the same because it preserves the meaning relationship that these words share. (Pilulski & Templeton, 2004, p. 7)

Students may struggle with conventional spellings in their own writing, but be completely capable of reading these same words in print. In the primary grades, student writing samples can tell a great deal about students' phonics knowledge and skill. As they get older, however, this is a less-reliable method. Some students, in fact, remain weak spellers long after they have become capable and fluent readers. In their book, *Words Their Way* (2003), Bear, Invernizzi, Templeton, and Johnston have provided exceptionally good resources for students who are struggling in spelling. This important resource is especially useful for teachers who may not have acquired a deep understanding of how English words work. It offers both assessment and instructional support.

Spelling Work for Everyone: Classroom Instruction

It is beyond the scope of this book to describe a full-fledged spelling program. However, the most effective instruction would link spelling instruction to reading and vocabulary. It is clear that the traditional approach of studying lists of words is not an effective one because it promotes a random view of spelling and also one that focuses too much attention on "sounding out" words instead of using a combination of approaches, including close attention to visual patterns and meaning (Templeton & Bear, 1992). Instead, our approach needs to help students make connections and notice patterns.

As Pikulski and Templeton note: "Once students understand the spelling-meaning relationships among words, they can learn how the spelling or structure of familiar words can be clues to the spelling and meaning of unknown words, and vice-versa" (2004, p. 7).

For students in grades 3 to 6, the following guidelines are helpful for organizing a spelling program. (See Bear et al., 2003; Templeton & Morris, 2000.)

Choose words wisely. Spelling words should be selected based on the students' developmental stages and level of confusion when using them in their writing. In other words, you should include words that students "use but confuse." For example, students who are in the syllable juncture stage will be using but confusing double consonants or *-cle* endings. These patterns should be selected for instruction. (See Chapter 7 for spelling assessment tools.)

Encourage word exploration. Students should be actively involved in the exploration of words. Word sorts, puzzles, and word notebooks are all ways for them to do that.

Ensure multiple exposures. Students should have many exposures to words in meaningful contexts, both in and out of connected text. Ideally, some of the words selected for spelling instruction would be words that have been (or will be) encountered during reading. Then, students should be encouraged to locate these words (and their derivatives) in additional reading and use them in writing.

Remain sensitive to developmental stages. Teach by following a sequence of structural elements that reflects the developmental stages of spelling listed in Figure 6.7 (page 185), in relation to the specific needs of each student.

Into the Classroom

Over the past 15 years, we have gained a much better understanding of how word recognition ability matures over time. There is no question we need to bring word work and fluency into the intermediate classroom. You don't want to leave all of this to chance; opportunistic teaching is not likely to prompt you to teach the syllable patterns, for example. The question is how and when. I advocate planning a yearlong focus on word identification and fluency that is appropriate for the age and grade. Third-grade students are going to require something different from sixth graders. Although the specific content may vary, there are some practices that can provide an anchor for this activity within the literacy block.

Word Work and Fluency Within the Literacy Block

Although a systematic approach to word study would be ideal, Janet Bloodgood and Linda Pacifici (2004) found that teachers in the intermediate grades often do not have either the time or the materials to implement a full-blown program. They suggest that students can benefit from activities that fit into brief periods in the school day. Here are three places where we can embed word work right into our ongoing instruction: (1) word-study stations, (2) paired reading, and (3) guided reading.

Word-Study Stations

Depending on the particular classroom organization that is being used, the teachers I work with have either a word-study block during their literacy time (common among teachers who use a three- or four-block arrangement) or they assign independent work to be done during the literacy block. I prefer to introduce specific decoding skills and strategies to the whole group in a mini-lesson and then provide practice in various stations as part of a literacy block rotation. (For more on literacy blocks, see Chapter 2.) Among the ideas that Bloodgood and Pacifici recommend, for example, is "Root of the Day." A morphological root (*spect*, *dict*, etc.) is posted in the station, and students contribute to a list that is posted there. Students who visit the station later in the period can be charged with checking meanings in the dictionary to arrive at a conclusion about the derivation.

Whether the word study is done at stations or during a separate word-work block, the procedures need to be very clear. It is helpful to introduce a series of procedural frames that will be used all year long:

- Set rules regarding the number of students who can be at a station at one time.

- Use simple sign-in and sign-out formats.

- Establish procedures for managing materials and work. (These should remain the same all year.)
- Stock the station(s) with appropriate resources: dictionaries, books of lists, and so on.

WORD SORTS

Word sorts are easy to put in a station—simply vary the words every couple of days, depending on the focus for instruction. Once students have sorted their words, they should read them to another student or to the teacher to make sure that they are able to decode them. There are many other possible materials to use in a station.

MAKING WORDS

Word-making activities are also excellent for literacy stations. You will need to prepare cards that contain rimes and onsets, syllable patterns, or base/root words and prefixes/ suffixes. Students create and write as many words as possible using these materials. These can be recorded on sheets that are kept in the station or in the students' word notebooks or vocabulary journals.

WORD CHAINS

Word Chains is a simple word-study game that can be played in many ways. It can be played alone or in a small group. I suggest starting by asking students to list as many words as they can that have the same rime pattern:

1. Write the word *sit*.
2. Now write other words that have this same spelling pattern.
3. When you cannot make any more words using that spelling pattern, you can continue by adding, removing, or replacing *one* letter.
4. Example: sit, pit, bit, fit, hit, lit, nit, wit, spit, spat, rat, drat, drag, rag, rage . . .
5. If playing in a group, the person with the most words wins.

The game can be also be played by changing one syllable in each word: pattern, lantern, lanyard, barnyard, yardstick, lipstick, lipid, rapid.

WORD-STUDY NOTEBOOKS

Provide each student with a notebook. (Inexpensive spiral ones are good.) Divide the notebook into sections according to your purposes. Possibilities include a section for word lists, a section for content vocabulary, a section for root words, and a section for spelling words or words with certain phonic elements.

POETRY

Finally, poetry is fun and can provide good practice for students in identifying and using spelling patterns and other phonic elements. In stations, students can read poems and underline rhyming words. They can also rewrite poems with new rhyming words and/or find new patterns.

A Fly and a Flea in a Flue

A fly and a flea in a flue
Were imprisoned, so what could they do?
Said the fly, "Let us flee!"
"Let us fly!" said the flea,
And they flew through a flaw in the flue.

Some students might like to think of other words they can substitute without changing the rest of the poem—for example, where else the fly and the flea might be stuck (*stew, brew, loo*). For students who may not be able to substitute words or make new poems, you can provide word starters. For example, what might happen if the fly and flea were in a crate? A stream?

Students can collect their own versions of the poems and put them together for other students to read. Of course, reading and rereading poetry is also an excellent way to improve students' fluency.

There are some caveats, however. Word work is not very effective, for example, when it involves too much paper-and-pencil activity. The point is to improve students' word recognition and/or fluency. Keep these guidelines in mind when having students engage in word work at stations:

- Provide hands-on activities that require students to actually *read* the words (not just substitute letters or identify spelling patterns visually).

- Encourage students to practice elements that have already been taught.

- Choose activities that involve multilevel responses, so students of differing abilities can benefit.

- Select activities that allow students to have more than one response so they can return to the activity another time.

Paired Reading

Students need to practice in order to become fluent readers. One of the best ways to help them do that is to provide time for them to reread material. This can be text that was read aloud by the teacher, stories introduced during guided reading, or text that students self-selected. Koskinen and Blum designed a peer-assisted strategy for building fluency that works quite well (1986). Students read together in pairs; one student reads the text three times, and on the third reading, the other student rates the reading using a simple format (1= okay; 2 = good; 3 = great). Next, the students switch roles and continue the practice. The idea is to practice over several days until fluent.

Guided Reading

Because students are likely to be reading ability-appropriate texts during guided reading, this is an excellent time to address word-level concerns. Ideally, guided reading provides time to reinforce the skill or strategy that was introduced to the whole group, but sometimes small groups need specialized instruction. This might be explicit instruction in a specific phonics element, or it could involve supportive feedback as students read a portion of the text aloud, or it might include rereading for fluency.

Word Work and Fluency Within the Content Areas

Literacy block is not the only time to improve students' word recognition and fluency. In fact, some of the best opportunities for modeling and/or reinforcing students' knowledge and skill come during content area reading and discussion. Most fifth-grade curricula include specific vocabulary for science and social studies—words such as these:

Social Studies	Science
explorers	molecules
exploration	organism
expeditions	respiration
colonize	digestion
resistance	digestive
declaration	circulate
independence	cellular
revolution	multicellular
continental	evaporate/evaporation
ratification	condensation
empowering	vapor
government	recycling/recycle
unified	

Notice how many of the words in social studies involve base words or roots and prefixes and suffixes. This provides a perfect opportunity for us to point out recurrent endings and prefixes and show how these morphemes change meanings. Many of the science words are multisyllabic words—not all of which have a free-standing root word. Note, for example, that the base for the word *respiration* is the Latin *respirare*—"to breathe." As a result, students may have trouble both decoding this word and knowing what it means. Helping students recognize how to decode the words, however, does improve the chance that they will have the words in their vocabulary—words like *digestion* and *exploration* are likely to be understood once they are decoded.

Working With Struggling Readers

Of course, some students need more word and fluency work than can be embedded in ongoing instruction. Research by Joseph Torgesen suggests that for many struggling readers in the intermediate grades, a relatively brief dose of appropriate small-group instruction can bring their skills into the average range (2004). His research suggests that as little as 60 hours—about one and a half hours a week during the school year—is enough to accomplish this for students around the thirtieth percentile. Students with more substantial difficulties require both more time and considerably more work on fluency.

Since word-identification problems are such a common source of reading difficulty, I discuss ways to address them below.

Determine What Each Student Can Do

Because of the enormous variation among the students in any given classroom in grades 3 to 6, the first thing we need to do is make sure that we understand what they *can* do as well as what they cannot. Because most students in grades 4 to 6 actually can decode words at the syllable level, it is important to assess this ability by using the following series of prompts when a student misreads a word:

1. "Look at that word again . . ."
2. "Let's look at that word by itself—try it."
3. "Let's take off the ending (or beginning). Now try it."
4. "Let's look at the syllables in that word . . ."

If students are successful at prompts 1 or 2, they obviously possess the necessary skill to read the word but may not have done so for other reasons—poor fluency, inability to manage lots of print, weak comprehension, or nervousness. Students who require prompts 3 or 4, need instruction. They need to acquire some new strategies—how to take off the morphemes before panicking and/or how to divide words into syllables. This requires modeling, but students can learn to recognize recurrent patterns.

Provide Explicit Instruction

Of course, a very few students won't succeed even when they receive additional explicit instruction in identifying spellings and in using the compare-contrast strategy. These students likely need further help from specialized teachers. However, there are a few things that classroom teachers can do. First, a review of common onsets and rimes is in order. Second, students should be reminded of the technique of deleting and substituting different onsets. Here are the steps a student might go through when encountering an unfamiliar word:

1. I don't know the word *trump*.

2. I do know that this word is made up of *tr-* and *-ump*.

3. I know that *-ump* with a *j* in front is *jump*.

4. I also know the word *tree*, and that starts with *tr-*.

5. So, if I take off the *j* and put on the *tr*, the word must be *trump*.

Some students may not be able to think of words for comparison, so initially we have to provide them. Specialized programs like *Benchmark's Word Detectives Intermediate Program* (Gaskins, 2000, 2002) and SIPPS: Systematic Instruction in Phoneme Awareness, Phonics, and Sight Words (Shefelbine & Newman, 2000) provide this information for students as part of a coherent and systematic program. Although these programs can be helpful, they must be conducted within a more comprehensive instructional framework that incorporates many of the elements touched on in this book.

Concluding Thoughts

A comprehensive and balanced reading program for students in grades 3 to 6 must provide for word identification, fluency, and spelling. Educators have only recently paid much attention to these areas in the intermediate grades. Relatively simple yet focused instruction can make a big difference for students in the intermediate grades. Since most students have so much more experience with words than they did in the primary grades, we can use this knowledge and experience to build insights, promote an orderly approach to word identification and spelling, and help students gain control over their reading and writing.

Intermediate teachers used to be told that students should be done learning how to read when they came into these grades. We now know that is not the case. There is much to be done. At the same time, we also know that we should not be *repeating* the types of activities and content provided in grades K–2. Instead, we should be building on that earlier instruction and using it to create more-powerful insights and more-comprehensive understanding of how the English language works. This can be interesting, engaging, and even fun work. Promoting reflective thinking and an interest in words is much more exciting than the mechanical and narrow memorization that passed for spelling, phonics, and vocabulary instruction in the past. It is a happy marriage of emerging developmental abilities and task demands. At exactly the time that students are becoming more aware of patterns and more able to think metacognitively, we can gear our instruction to capitalize on these new capacities.

Discussion and Reflection

- How can you use the information about sounds and syllables from this chapter in your teaching?

- What new insights did you gain from this chapter?

- Collect reading and writing samples from three students—one who is performing above grade level, one who is performing right at grade level, and one who is below grade level. See if you can identify ways in which their knowledge and skills are similar and ways in which they are different.

- Select one aspect of word study (sound, meaning, spelling) and create a word sort for your students.

Digging Deeper

To find out more about word identification and fluency for intermediate-grade students, check out these resources:

- "Bringing Word Study to Intermediate Classrooms" by Janet Bloodgood and Linda Pacifici. *The Reading Teacher*, Vol. 58, pp. 250–263.

- *The Fluent Reader* by Timothy Rasinski. New York: Scholastic, 2004.

- *Phonics Poetry: Teaching Word Families* by Timothy Rasinski and Belinda Zimmerman. Boston: Allyn & Bacon, 2001.

- *Teaching Phonics & Word Study in the Intermediate Grades* by Wiley Blevins. New York: Scholastic, 2001.

- *Word Journeys: Assessment-Guided Phonics, Spelling, and Vocabulary Instruction* by Kathy Ganske. New York: Guilford Press, 2000.

CHAPTER 7

Make Effective Use of Assessment

Good teaching requires assessment. Without it, we are teaching curriculum, not kids. All of the studies of successful schools and effective teachers have concluded that systematic teacher and/or classroom-based assessment of student progress is a key element for success in literacy (Mosenthal et al., 2004; Taylor et al., 2000). Teachers in successful schools use assessment data to inform their teaching and to help them answer questions they have about their teaching and students' learning.

Many years ago, I got a phone call from the principal of a small rural school. The state's department of education was insisting that she and her staff do something about their students' reading performance. The reason? More than a third of their students were identified as eligible for special education! That alarming rate seemed inexplicable.

When I got to the school and began to ask questions, I found there were other red flags. For example, students were doing *very* poorly on the norm-referenced tests that were given annually starting in grade 2. Although the teachers discounted these tests as meaningless, it was hard to ignore the fact that students were *averaging* below the 15th percentile!

It was puzzling to me that the school had no other data to show me. The only assessment information it/administrators/teachers had was those norm-referenced test scores and, in general, they supported what everyone already knew—the students and the school were in trouble. The teachers weren't sure what materials to use with their students, and they weren't always sure whether their students were making good progress. Most significantly, they didn't know where to start because the only assessment information they had wasn't helping them make good instructional decisions. They were discouraged and inclined to blame their students and/or the parents, who were predominantly poor and poorly educated.

In the intermediate grades, I often hear questions like these:

- How will I know if my students are making progress in reading?
- How can I evaluate students' comprehension?
- What level of text can this student read?
- What can/should I say when parents ask about their child's reading ability/level?
- If students are really struggling, what should I do to assess them?

In this chapter, I describe the role of assessment in the intermediate classroom, examine the different purposes, content, and tools of assessment, and suggest a tiered approach with specific recommendations for classroom teachers. I will also introduce you to Tyler, a beginning fourth grader whose parents were worried that he was slipping behind and wondered if I could "take a look" and make some recommendations to the school. Throughout the chapter, I describe the assessments I used and the data that resulted from my work with him.

Lessons From Research and Practice: What We Know About Effective Use of Assessment

Teachers are often frustrated by the amount and kinds of assessment that are available to them. Sometimes that frustration is the result of simply "too much" assessment. This frustration is compounded, however, when teachers perceive that the assessment does not provide useful information for shaping their instruction.

The Purposes of Assessment

The federal government has recently identified several specific purposes for instructional assessments. (See Figure 7.1) As teachers, we are most concerned about assessments that help us teach better. Several types of tests can be used for this purpose although classroom-based and progress-monitoring assessments are probably the most useful on a continual basis.

We cannot expect any one assessment tool to meet all possible purposes. This means that we should guard against the misuse of test results. Measures designed to compare one program with another (usually large-scale tests) to determine whether large groups of children are meeting standards are generally not good at helping us to understand what, exactly, the particular children in our classroom need for instruction. On the other hand, because these assessments often have very important consequences—for teachers, children, and schools—they cannot be ignored. They should not be allowed to overwhelm your program of instruction, however. One way to guard against that result is to collect additional types of assessment information. In this chapter, I focus on the types of assessment that inform our instruction or help us monitor students' progress, because they can have the biggest impact in classrooms.

Deciding what and how to assess can be a challenge. Good assessment often starts with good questions, which may involve *description*:

- What skills and strategies does Leon use when decoding connected text?
- What is Yolanda's rate of reading?
- What books can Derrick read?

Different Types of Assessments and Their Purposes

Type of Assessment	Purpose
SCREENING READING ASSESSMENT Quick assessment procedure(s) used with all students as a first step to get an estimate of overall achievement.	Used to identify students who may be at high risk for academic failure and need further diagnosis in order to plan instruction and/or determine eligibility for special services.
DIAGNOSTIC READING ASSESSMENT Assessments that examine individual students' skills and instructional needs more closely in order to create specific instructional plans for them.	Used to (a) inform instruction (identify a student's specific areas of strengths/weakness and determine any difficulties s/he may have in learning to read and the potential cause of such difficulties) or (b) help determine possible placement decisions (instructional interventions and related special needs). Often administered by special educators or reading specialists.
CLASSROOM-BASED INSTRUCTIONAL READING ASSESSMENT Systematic observations of students' reading achievement on classroom tasks. Used to improve instruction and performance.	Used to (a) inform instruction (identify specific areas of strength and determine whether students need more support to achieve grade-level reading outcomes); (b) determine whether students are making adequate progress; and/or (c) require further assessment. These assessments may include work samples, unit tests, and/or checklists.
PROGRESS-MONITORING MEASURE Assessment conducted a minimum of three times a year using comparable and multiple test forms.	May be used to (a) estimate rates of reading improvement, (b) identify children who are not demonstrating adequate progress and require additional or different forms of instruction, and/or (c) compare the efficacy of different forms of instruction for struggling readers in order to create more-effective, individualized instructional programs.
OUTCOME MEASURE Assessments (both standardized and classroom based) that focus on grade-level performances or standards.	Used to (a) evaluate whether or not students have achieved grade-level performance or improved their achievement, (b) hold schools and teachers accountable, and/or (c) evaluate program effectiveness.

Based on Section 1208, Public Law 107–111, the No Child Left Behind Act of 2001.

Figure 7.1 Different types of assessment serve varied purposes.

To make good instructional decisions, though, we need to add an *evaluative* component to these questions:

- Is Yolanda reading as fluently as she should be for her age/grade?
- Should Leon be using a wider array of decoding strategies? How well does he use the ones he has?

These questions can and should be answered using systematic, informal assessments based in the classroom.

The Content of Assessment

Gay Su Pinnell has argued that teachers do not need more tests, rather, they "need assessment tools that help them become 'noticing teachers'" (1991, p. 81). The challenge, of course, is knowing what to notice and then being able to interpret what we are seeing in order to plan instruction based on those observations and interpretations.

The students in any grade 3 to 6 classroom often span several reading levels and an assessment plan for these years needs to take this variation into account. Despite this variation, we need to evaluate students' overall reading ability to be sure that they are achieving or are at least near grade-level expectations and also to make sure that they are making progress throughout the year. To do that, reading components like those in Figure 7.2 should be assessed. Students' abilities in any of these elements may vary depending on the level of text difficulty, so it will be important to carefully consider what level of text is being used. For example, students may demonstrate very weak fluency—but only on some levels of text. When they are moved to easier material, their so-called fluency problems may disappear. In other words, we need to specify *both* the reading component and the text level when discussing students' assessment results.

The Content of Assessment for Grades 3 to 6

1. Word recognition:
   - Accuracy
   - Knowledge of and skill in:
     - Phonics
     - Structural analysis (syllabication)
     - Morphemic analysis (prefixes, suffixes, etc.)
2. Fluency in reading age/grade-appropriate text
3. Spelling
4. Comprehension
5. Vocabulary
6. Motivation and interest

Figure 7.2

Assessment in Action: Gathering Baseline Information on Tyler

As I said at the start of the chapter, I am going to use an individual student, Tyler, to show both what and how to assess. Tyler's parents asked me to assess his reading because they felt he was not keeping up with his peers. Here are notes on my first meeting with him.

June 15

- Interview
- Word recognition check using his own book
- QRI word list and grade 3 passage for accuracy check
- Comprehension check using questions from QRI, grade 3 passage

Notes from the Session: Tyler will be in fourth grade in the fall. He likes school "okay" but much prefers athletic activity. He is the youngest of three brothers. It's an active family—both parents were competitive athletes through college—and the two older boys play baseball, soccer, and basketball. Tyler plays all three, but his real love is basketball. Despite the focus on athletics, education is highly valued in their home, and Tyler's mom (an ex-teacher) reports that she has worked with him on reading since he was in first grade. She shared his test results from the standardized test given at the end of grade 3, which revealed reading scores in the low-average range for his age and grade.

After his mom left, Tyler said that he has problems concentrating and that he reads too slowly. A quick check of both oral and silent reading comprehension, revealed weak ability to understand grade-3 texts. Although his accuracy seems fine, Tyler loses his place often and frequently reads past phrase and sentence markers (periods, quotation marks, etc.). This is frustrating him because he does notice the problems that result. Tyler's slow rate will be a problem as he enters the more-demanding fourth grade. He has a prescription for glasses but was not wearing them on this day.

Next Session: Look more closely at both word recognition and comprehension for levels 3 and 4; evaluate rate and fluency. Assess his oral language abilities as an indicator of potential. Check his comprehension under different conditions and with different texts.

As you can see, I thought Tyler's difficulties were significant enough to take a closer look. Often, I decide to examine some aspects of reading more closely—for example, I may want to find out more about fluency or comprehension. However, it may also be necessary to pay attention to some additional components. In Tyler's case, this meant that I wanted to assess his vocabulary knowledge to make sure that his oral language development was age appropriate. In addition, I needed more information about fluency and comprehension.

Although many students deserve closer attention, we need to remember that students in grades 3 to 6 often "look" different than younger readers. For example, even though many intermediate students do struggle with word-level aspects of reading, they do not generally have the same *types* of problems experienced in the primary grades. Unlike their younger peers, many students in grades 3 to 6 have adequate phonics knowledge and skill, and often they can read simple, one-syllable words quite accurately. As I noted in Chapter 6, their difficulty lies, instead, in applying this phonics knowledge to multisyllabic words (Memory, 1992; Ryder & Graves, 1980; Snow & Biancarosa, 2004).

The developmental differences between younger and older students can make assessment challenging. There are not as many tools available and those that do exist often assess students' reading too simplistically. The tools that I use to explore distinct aspects of reading for intermediate students are described in the next section.

The Tools of Assessment

Teachers can generally notice how students are doing in reading during the course of their normal instruction. I examine work samples, listen to students read, observe their responses to my questions, and examine their abilities to discuss. On the other hand, good commercial tools can be enormously helpful in clarifying matters when students are struggling. They provide us with easy access to leveled texts and they provide standardized procedures that can be invaluable in school settings.

I regularly use the Qualitative Reading Inventory (QRI) in my classroom and clinical work and have found it to be especially helpful in conducting a close examination of students' prior knowledge, comprehension, and word-level abilities. In the latest version, QRI-4 (2005), Lauren Leslie and Joanne Caldwell have added many nonfiction passages appropriate for students in grades 4 and up. Another recent assessment tool for diagnosing students is the Developmental Reading Assessment, Grades 4–8 (with a "DRA-Bridging Pack" for struggling readers) by Joetta Beaver and Mark Carter (2004). This assessment is a modification of more traditional informal reading inventories (IRIs). It, too, often allows for a comprehensive picture of students' reading abilities. One of the major advantages of the DRA is that students read much longer texts than is typical in most assessments. It also assesses students' ability to write in response to reading and provides diagnostic tools for examining strategy use.

Assessing Word Recognition

There are two aspects of word recognition to consider: accuracy and phonics/decoding knowledge and skill. When students' accuracy is adequate, we generally do not go further. However, if accuracy is a problem, a closer examination of the nature of the difficulty is in order.

Oral Reading Accuracy

Many students who struggle in grades 3 to 6 (especially in grade 3) have not developed appropriate word-recognition ability, so it is always a good idea to examine accuracy as a part of the profile for students who are struggling. Accuracy is determined by collecting a record of students' oral reading. This can be tricky because older students read more quickly than younger ones. As a result, certain tools (running records, for example) are not very practical for these students. Instead, I use a **record of oral reading**.

1. Photocopy a page or two from a grade-level book or article, or choose a reliable informal reading inventory.

2. Ask the student to read out loud from the text. Make a record of all errors or miscues on your copy. Try to capture what the student did and how she read—recording any deviations from the text and noting such things as repetitions and long pauses.

3. Count the oral reading errors, or miscues. Even though we record other things, only the following are counted as errors in this part of the process:

   - Substitutions of one word for another (e.g., reading "hamper" for "humpback")

   - Omissions (count as an error any word that is skipped)

   - Partial substitutions or omissions (e.g., reading "led" for "bled" or deleting prefixes or suffixes)

- Insertions (adding a word or part of a word that is not in the text)

4. Then, determine word-recognition accuracy using the following procedure:

  - Compute the total number of words read correctly by subtracting the number of errors from the total number of words in the passage (or total number of words read).
  - Divide the total number of correct words by the total number of words in the passage.
  - Multiply the result by 100 to convert to a percentage.

For example, here's how to compute the word-recognition accuracy for a student who made 10 errors while reading a 150-word passage:

1. 150-10 = 140
2. 140/150 = .93
3. .93 x 100 = 93 percent accuracy

Once these percentages are determined, then we are left asking how to make sense of the results. In the example above, the student's accuracy is not perfect, but is it adequate? Fortunately, we have very good guidelines for interpreting accuracy scores. In our research and practice, Karen Wixson and I have found consensus on the range that is displayed in Figure 7.3 (2003).

Reading-Level Determination	Word-Recognition Accuracy
Independent (Can be read without assistance)	97–100 percent
Instructional (Can be read with instructional support)	92–96 percent
Frustration (Can not be read or understood, even with support)	92 percent or less

Figure 7.3

Of course, students' accuracy is likely to be different if they read an easier or more difficult text, so it is important to examine accuracy across levels of text difficulty. All commercial informal reading inventories and the DRA 4–8 include clearly labeled texts of increasing difficulty.

Assessment in Action: Tyler's Word-Recognition Accuracy

In Figure 7.4, you can see a summary of oral reading for Tyler, who is just beginning fourth grade. These results show that word-recognition accuracy is *not* an area of special concern for him. Like many students his age, Tyler had mastered phonics (sound-symbol correspondence) by the time he finished third grade. His overall accuracy is very good, but Tyler does get flustered when he encounters longer words. Although he is usually successful in eventually decoding the words, this lack of confidence diverts his attention and he frequently loses his train of thought during these episodes.

Summary of Tyler's Word-Recognition Accuracy

Oral Reading	Independent Level	Instructional Level	Frustration Level
Accuracy Qualitative Reading Inventory – III (QRI-III)	Third Grade: 97 percent accuracy on narrative ("Trip to the Zoo") and 98 percent accuracy for exposition ("Wool").	Fourth Grade: 95 percent accuracy for narrative-informational text ("Johnny Appleseed")	
Accuracy DRA – Level 40 (Fourth Grade)	97 percent accuracy on Level 40 narrative ("A New School Experience"). Read orally about 300 words.		

Figure 7.4

Since Tyler's accuracy revealed that he does *not* have problems in decoding, I did not do additional assessments in this area. If Tyler had demonstrated difficulties in the area of word-recognition accuracy, I would have taken a closer look at the details of decoding knowledge and skill.

Decoding Knowledge and Skill

When students do poorly on initial tests of accuracy, we need to try to find out more about why. Students' difficulty in decoding words is usually caused by limited knowledge and skill in some aspect of phonics, structural analysis, or morphemic analysis. (See Chapter 6 for more about these topics.) Although there are many tests of isolated word-level skills, I generally find it possible to diagnose these components by looking at the record of oral reading. The record of oral reading for Kaylie, whom I introduced in Chapter 6, demonstrates how much information can be gleaned.

Figure 7.5 shows an excerpt from Kaylie's DRA. Kaylie is in sixth grade, and this passage's difficulty is rated at Level 50 (fifth-grade expectation). As you can see, her overall word recognition is not awful (her miscues on this passage place her in the instructional range on this passage for accuracy). However, the *pattern* of Kaylie's errors is what is important, and a closer analysis is revealing. (See Figure 7.6.) She

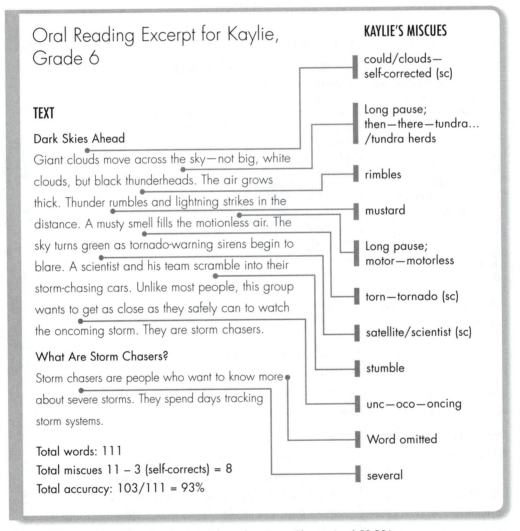

Figure 7.5 Record of oral reading for a student reading *Storm Chasers*, Level 50 DRA

TEACHING READING BEYOND THE PRIMARY GRADES

Analysis of Kaylie's Miscues

MISCUE	TEXT	ANALYSIS
could/cloud	clouds	Self-corrected, probably using meaning and syntax
then/there/tundra/ tundraherds	thunderheads	Compound, multisyllabic word; tries using grapho-phonic cues
rimbles	rumbles	Multisyllabic word, misses vowel in first syllable
mustard	musty	Suffix ending
motorless	motionless	Multisyllabic word with suffix; finally gets suffix but misses base word
torn/tornado	tornado	Self-corrected, probably using meaning
stumble	scramble	Multisyllabic word; misses vowel in first syllable (see *rumbles* above); not much meaning change
satellite/scientist	scientist	Self-corrected
unc/oco/oncing	oncoming	Multisyllabic word—prefix
(omission)	more	Deleted—no meaning change
several	severe	Multisyllabic word; mistakes base; moderate meaning change

Figure 7.6

struggles on longer and/or multisyllabic words. For Kaylie, even basic words pose problems when an ending is added and the meaning changed (e.g., *musty).*

The analysis in Figure 7.6 shows how it is possible to get a good picture of a student's abilities, even using a small sample. Kaylie tries to maintain meaning while she reads (she generally self-corrects words that would change the meaning dramatically). While multisyllabic words slow Tyler down, they completely stymie Kaylie. She seems to have a limited grasp of syllable patterns and prefixes and suffixes. As a result of her limited skills, she often abandons her search for meaning (as in "tundraherds" and "oncing." Needless to say, this painstaking decoding is also influencing her fluency and comprehension.

Many students in grades 3 to 6 have difficulties reading multisyllabic words. Because the problem is so pervasive, it is helpful to have tools for examining this more closely. John Shefelbine and Katherine Newman (2001) have created a very useful multilevel phonics program and assessment tools that demonstrate how phonics works within longer words. (See extension and challenge levels of *SIPPS: Systematic Instruction in Phoneme Awareness, Phonics, and Sight Words.*) For students who have not yet mastered basic skills of sight-word recognition or basic phonics, additional testing will be needed. This is where a special educator or reading coach can be especially helpful. Thoughtful spelling assessment can provide additional insights, because it can reveal how well students have internalized the spelling patterns (orthography) of the language. These spelling patterns are necessary in writing, but they also provide useful information for decoding unfamiliar words.

Assessing Spelling

There are several good developmental spelling assessments available today. I especially recommend that teachers explore Kathy Ganske's *Word Journeys* (2001) and/or Donald Bear et al.'s book *Words Their Way* (2003). The Developmental Spelling Assessment (DSA) in Kathy Ganske's book is excellent, as is the Qualitative Spelling Inventory in *Words Their Way.*

For teachers who are not quite ready to jump into such detailed analyses of word knowledge, I recommend the Qualitative Inventory of Word Knowledge (QIWK) by Bob Schlagal (1982). Along with his students, he has recently developed a short form of this assessment that is excellent for screening all students and estimating their developmental spelling level (Palmer, 2004; Schlagal, in press). This short form is presented in Figure 7.7. The inventory is a reliable measure of students progress in word knowledge, and it can be helpful in analyzing students' errors to determine what spelling patterns students "use but confuse," providing you with a starting place for instruction.

Schlagal recommends using the following lists:

Grade 3: Give lists for levels 1, 2, and 3

Grade 4: Give lists for levels 2, 3, and 4

Grade 5: Give lists for levels 3, 4, and 5

Grade 6: Give lists for levels 4, 5, and 6

For scoring purposes, grade each of the students' spelling tests separately. To determine the students' accuracy score, use the table on the next page. For example, if a student makes four errors, we deduct 33 percent from 100 percent to arrive at an accuracy score of 67 percent. Scores below 33 percent are an indication of frustration.

QIWK (short form) Quantitative Scoring Guide						
Number of errors	1	2	3	4	5	6
% to subtract from 100	8	17	25	33	42	50
Number of errors	7	8	9	10	11	12
% to subtract from 100	58	67	75	83	92	100

In my experience, the pattern of students' errors reveals itself quickly, and it is quite easy to use the information for instruction. In Kaylie's case, for example, she made errors on most lists, but not enough to clearly indicate a problem with the concepts. On the other hand, when she got to the Level 5 list, she made nine errors (25 percent accuracy), missing all of the doubled consonants at the syllable junctures (*sufering, ofered*) and many endings (*nedel, luner*).

Qualitative Inventory of Word Knowledge (QIWK) (Short Form)

LEVEL 1	LEVEL 2	LEVEL 3	LEVEL 4	LEVEL 5	LEVEL 6
trap	train	scream	popped	explosion	mental
bed	thick	noise	plastic	justice	commotion
when	chase	stepping	cable	compare	declaration
wish	trapped	count	gazed	settlement	musician
sister	dress	careful	cozy	measure	dredge
girl	queen	chasing	scurry	suffering	violence
drop	cloud	batter	preparing	needle	wreckage
bump	short	caught	stared	preserve	decision
drive	year	thirsty	slammed	honorable	impolite
plane	shopping	trust	cabbage	lunar	acknowledge
ship	cool	knock	gravel	offered	conceive
bike	stuff	send	sudden	normal	introduction

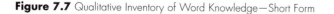

Figure 7.7 Qualitative Inventory of Word Knowledge—Short Form

Assessing Fluency

Most students in grades 3 to 6 are still consolidating their fluency abilities, especially in diverse texts. Among students who are struggling in grades 3 to 6, reading fluency is a major factor.

Fortunately, fluency can be assessed quite easily and as part of the normal daily routine. All it requires is a stopwatch (or watch with a second hand) and a quiet place for students to read aloud to the teacher. Rate is an important component of fluency. Students' rate of reading can be reported in terms of words read per minute (WPM) or in terms of the number of words *correct* per minute (WCPM). Although there is some controversy about what fluency rates are appropriate, the guidelines in Figure 7.8 are generally accepted and can be used to decide if a student's reading problems are related to fluency. Rates vary depending on the time of year.

Recommended Fluency Rates (in words read correctly per minute)						
	GRADE 1	GRADE 2	GRADE 3	GRADE 4	GRADE 5	GRADE 6
ORAL	50–80	80–100	90–120	115–140	125–150	135–160
SILENT	N/A	N/A	115–140	130–175	160–200	190–220

Figure 7.8 These are the rates recommended by the Northeast Consortium for Assessment (NECAP). Among the sources consulted to determine recommended fluency rates: Caldwell, 2002; Hasbrouck & Tindal, 1992, 2005; M. Y. Lipson & Wixson, 2003; NAEP, 2005.

Fluency consists of more than accuracy and rate, however. Oral fluency also involves readers' ability to group words into meaningful phrase units. Smoothness and the maintenance of comprehension are important as well (Harris & Hodges, 1995). As Louisa Moats has noted, "Fluent readers make their message understood. They read in phrases, respect the intonation patterns in syntax, and communicate with the listener. Speed must be adequate, but processing the meaning during reading and phrasing of the text are more important indicators of fluency" (2004).

An assessment procedure used by the National Assessment of Educational Progress (NAEP) evaluates fluency by providing an estimate of whether or not a student consistently reads sentences predominantly word by word or in larger groups and phrases. (See Figure 7.9.) Follow these steps to assess students' phrase-level fluency:

1. Select instructional level material that is no less than 250 words in length.

2. Listen to the student read aloud, marking the boundaries of his or her pauses or phrasing.

3. Use the scale in Figure 7.9 to evaluate fluency.

Adapted NAEP Fluency Scale

LEVEL 4	Reads in meaningful phrase groups that preserve the author's meaning; reads expressively
LEVEL 3	Majority of reading in three- or four-word phrases that maintain meaning and syntax
LEVEL 2	Reads mostly in two-word phrases with some word-by-word reading
LEVEL 1	Reads mostly word-by-word

Figure 7.9 Rubric adapted from Pinnell et al. (1995)

Many teachers find that it is helpful to assess fluency several times across the year to monitor students' progress. Among the most popular and easy-to-use tools is Tim Rasinski and Nancy Padak's *3-Minute Reading Assessments* (2005), which contains leveled passages that are good for assessing and monitoring fluency. A whole-class or small-group profile can be created quite easily. The sample in Figure 7.10 shows how useful this kind of informal tracking can be.

Sample Third-Grade Class Summary: Monitoring Fluency in the Classroom

STUDENT	FALL ACCURACY	FALL RATE & RATING	MIDYEAR ACCURACY	MIDYEAR RATE & RATING	SPRING ACCURACY	SPRING RATE & RATING
AMELIA	98%	100 wpm, above target	99%	110 wpm, above target	99%	135 wpm, above target
YASMIN	76%	60 wpm, below target	82%	65 wpm, below target	93%	90 wpm, below target
JARED	85%	65 wpm, below target	90%	90 wpm, nearing target	95%	110 wpm, on target
LIAM	94%	90 wpm, on target	93%	92 wpm, on target	94%	95 wpm, below target

Figure 7.10

Yasmin has clearly made progress in word-recognition accuracy and in fluency, but she is still below grade-level expectations. Amelia started the year in excellent shape and that trend continued throughout, whereas Jared really hit his stride at midyear. Liam, though reading on target at the beginning of the year, has made very little progress during the year. Although his rate remained the same, this actually places him below target by the end of the year.

Assessment in Action: Tyler's Fluency

Despite his good overall word-recognition accuracy, Tyler's oral reading rate on the QRI and the DRA indicated that fluency was an area of concern. (See Figure 7.11.) As I observed him reading, I could see other evidence that Tyler is not a fluent reader. He reads slowly, loses his place with some frequency, and often reads past phrase and sentence markers (periods, quotation marks, etc.).

	Tyler's Reading Rate		
READING RATE GUIDELINES BY GRADE LEVEL	THIRD-GRADE TEXTS QRI	FOURTH-GRADE TEXT QRI	LEVEL 40 BOOK DRA
WCPM 1 50–80 2 80–100 3 90–120 4 115–140 5 125–150	80 wcpm ("The Friend") 75 wcpm ("Trip to the Zoo") 68 wcpm ("Wool")	58 wcpm ("Johnny Appleseed")	66 wcpm ("A New School Experience")

Figure 7.11

In addition, on the NAEP scoring rubric, Tyler was consistently rated at Level 2. He read in phrases but often ignored sentence or phrase boundaries. In this respect, Tyler is like a great many of his age/grade peers. Of course, limited fluency affects both comprehension and stamina—and, consequently, motivation. Tyler does not really like to read, and at least part of the problem is related to his fluency. He complains about reading too slowly, and this problem makes reading assignments unpleasant and unsatisfying. He also complains that he has trouble concentrating, and it is likely that his fluency contributes to this problem, as well—he reads so slowly that it causes him to lose track of the main ideas and story events.

TEACHING READING BEYOND THE PRIMARY GRADES

Assessing Comprehension

Many students who were considered relatively good readers during the primary grades begin to struggle in grades 3 to 6. The source of this struggle is often comprehension. Diagnosing problems in comprehension can be very challenging since there are so many possible factors (see Chapter 8), including prior knowledge and/or vocabulary development, strategy use, ability to understand the task and respond appropriately, and/or ability to engage in higher-level reasoning.

The DRA does a good job of surveying these concerns. Students' literal, interpretive, and evaluative comprehension are all assessed. The DRA uses long stories and expository texts that take a long time to read, providing an insight into stamina. The QRI-4 provides multiple texts at each grade level that vary in terms of text type (both narrative and exposition) and also in terms of familiarity. As a result, it is possible to see how students comprehend under different conditions.

Comprehension is most often assessed using student responses to questions, but increasingly, students' ability to construct responses to open-ended prompts has provided additional and important information. These constructed responses are typically evaluated using a rubric. For one that I have used and found helpful, see Figure 7.12.

Other aspects of reading and comprehension are also captured on the DRA. For example, students' strategic abilities in the area of prediction and summarization are assessed, and students' metacognitive abilities are examined in relation to other strategies, such as using background knowledge, questioning, making connections, and visualizing. Students are asked to indicate which strategies they used as they read and then to write how they used them.

Response Rubric

	Getting Started	Almost There	On Target	Wow!
PERSONAL RESPONSE	Limited comprehension with no connections between reading and personal experience or knowledge	Some attempts made to connect reading to self; may be too general or confusing	Comprehension demonstrated using some personal experience and/or connection between text and self	Response reveals personally relevant and meaningful comprehension, with examples from prior experience
CRITICAL RESPONSE	Does not take a critical stance (may relate events, describe characters, etc.) and/or responses show mis-understanding	Uses little evidence from the text to support ideas and opinions, or uses that evidence inappropriately	Effectively identifies an element of author's craft or message and analyzes it—making connections to other text and/or evaluating the work	Analyzes the author's message, identifying big ideas, themes or style; specific examples provided as evidence to support opinions and judgments
ORGANIZA-TION AND DETAILS	Unfocused writing, random details with little coherence	Response occasionally focused, with some detail	Generates a reasonably focused, connected and coherent response with good use of details to support ideas	Excellent organization that enhances ideas, making extensive use of text details for support
OTHER (e.g., spelling, mechanics)				

Figure 7.12 Rubric for assessing students' responses to reading

In our reading clinic at the University of Vermont, almost all of the students in grades 3 to 6 need some work on building independence and self-regulation. One of the teachers in the clinic recently created a check sheet to monitor her students' progress over time. (See next page.)

TEACHING READING BEYOND THE PRIMARY GRADES

Strategies That Good Readers Use

Reader's Name _____

Title of Text _____

Directions: Check each strategy that the reader shows you he or she is using by talking out loud about his or her thinking.

Before Reading

❏ Thinking about what he or she already knows about the topic

❏ Predicting what the text will be about

❏ Predicting what will happen next

❏ Asking questions about the material to be read

During Reading

❏ Asking questions

❏ Predicting

❏ Inferring

❏ Making connections (relating what is read to previously read text, to self, to world)

❏ Checking for meaning and monitoring progress

❏ Visualizing

❏ Evaluating the content and own progress

❏ Stopping to think and to remedy any comprehension problems

After Reading

❏ Summarizing and/or synthesizing information

❏ Evaluating the text and own performance

❏ Using text information to make personal response

❏ Using text information for other purposes, as appropriate

Assessment in Action: Tyler's Comprehension

Tyler's comprehension results, summarized in Figure 7.13, reveal that his comprehension is not as strong as his accuracy. He was able to decode accurately right through fourth-grade-level materials, but he is not independent for comprehension even at grade 3. In the area of strategy use and metacognitive abilities, Tyler is not especially proficient either. He does use some metacognitive strategies during reading, but the quality of these efforts is not good, and he needs much more work in this area. His written responses are especially weak.

	Tyler's Comprehension Results		
	INDEPENDENT LEVEL	**INSTRUCTIONAL LEVEL**	**FRUSTRATION LEVEL**
OVERALL COMPREHENSION	None without support. Third-grade silent narrative when "look-backs" were allowed.	Third-grade narrative text ("*The Friend*") Fourth-grade familiar narrative text	Third-grade oral narrative ("*Trip to the Zoo*") and oral exposition ("*Wool*"). Third-grade silent narrative ("*Birthday for Rosa*")

	SKILLS/STRATEGIES RATINGS	**REFLECTION RATING**	**METACOGNITION RATING**
LEVEL 40 DRA NARRATIVE RATINGS 1 = Intervention 2 = Instructional 3 = Independent 4 = Advanced	2 Prediction and literal comprehension 1 Summary and interpretation	2 Reflections, and metacognitive awareness	2 Metacognitive

Figure 7.13

A closer examination is revealing. When Tyler was given a chance to look back in the text (one of the diagnostic procedures in the QRI-4), he was able to answer all questions correctly. In fact, he worked his way through the text, identifying responses to a whole group of missed questions without prompting. Also, I observed that he reads much better when he wears his glasses—and even he believes it helps him stay focused!

Assessing Vocabulary

We have seen how important vocabulary development is for reading comprehension. Evaluating students' vocabulary prior to reading can provide good insight into their readiness for understanding the materials and can be especially important if you are going to be spending quite a lot of time with the material. In Figure 7.14, you can see the self-assessment vocabulary chart that Amber Profitt's students completed at the beginning of a biography unit in fifth grade. Amber used it to assess students' readiness to read a biography of Graham Hawkes, a diver and pilot of underwater submersible exploration vehicles. While the topic was fascinating and the book's appearance was motivating, she was aware that some students might struggle with the meanings of the words. Since she planned to work on base

Vocabulary Chart

Directions: Read each word and think about what you know about it already. Put a checkmark in the column that tells what you know about the word.

Word	Know it well; can explain it and use it in a sentence	Know something about it; can relate it to a situation	Have seen or heard the word	Do not know the word; have never seen or heard it before
engineer				
horizontally				
submersibles				
tinkering				
vertical				
enveloping				
inaccessible				
launched				
simultaneously				

Figure 7.14 Self-assessment chart for vocabulary

words and affixes in the unit, she was especially interested in words that contained those elements. Of course, the chart can be used with any unit of text.

The QRI-4 provides an assessment of vocabulary concepts for each of its passages. In this way, you can get an idea about whether students have the necessary vocabulary for that passage. This is one of the great strengths of that test, and I find the information very helpful.

Because there are very few "standardized tests" of vocabulary for classroom use, assessment should be varied, with multiple measures. Students' written work, teacher-made tests, cloze passages, and anecdotal records can all be used. Among others, Dale Johnson (2001) suggests asking students to do the following:

- Read a word and circle a definition
- Read a word and circle a synonym
- Read a word and circle an antonym
- Read a sentence and write the missing word
- Read a passage and fill in the blanks (a cloze passage)
- Read a word and put it in a category
- Find the word that doesn't belong in a category

Sometimes it is important to evaluate students' overall vocabulary development to see how it might be contributing to reading problems—especially when, as is the case with Tyler, the problems lie in the area of comprehension. The most common measure for elementary grades is the Peabody Picture Vocabulary Test, currently in its fourth edition (PPVT-4). Results from this test indicate that Tyler's receptive vocabulary is well above average. He is the 90th percentile for children his age. Since Tyler also did well on the background knowledge items (Concept Questions) of the QRI-4, it would appear that neither background knowledge nor oral language skill is a problem.

Assessing Motivation and Interest

Although we may not be able to respond to every difference in interest or motivation among our students, we won't be able to do anything at all if we don't know the range in our classroom. I have found it useful over the years to administer some form of interest/preferences survey. (See page 219.)

Reading Survey

Name _____ Date _____

1. How much do you enjoy reading? (Check one box.)
   - ❑ Not at all
   - ❑ A little
   - ❑ A lot
   - ❑ It's my favorite thing

2. How good a reader are you? (Circle one choice.)

1	2	3	4	5
Not a good reader	So-so reader	Average reader	Good reader	Excellent reader

3. Who do you know who reads? (Check all that apply.)
   - ❑ Most of my friends read.
   - ❑ Some of my friends read.
   - ❑ None of my friends read.
   - ❑ My mom likes to read.
   - ❑ My dad likes to read.
   - ❑ No one in my family really likes to read.
   - ❑ I have a brother or sister who does not read very well.

4. How often do you read outside of school? (Check one box.)
   - ❑ Almost never
   - ❑ Several times a month
   - ❑ Several times a week
   - ❑ Every day

5. For how long do you read each day? (Check one box.)
   - ❑ I don't really read.
   - ❑ 5–10 minutes
   - ❑ 25–45 minutes
   - ❑ An hour or more

6. Estimate how many books there are in your house. (Check one box.)
   - ❑ 0–10
   - ❑ 11–50
   - ❑ 51–150
   - ❑ 151–500
   - ❑ More than 500

7. Check the types of reading you do outside of school.

- ❑ Newspapers
- ❑ Magazines
- ❑ E-mails
- ❑ Instant messages
- ❑ Text messages
- ❑ Fiction: chapter books
- ❑ Comics

- ❑ Information books
- ❑ Jokes
- ❑ Manuals/instructions
- ❑ Poetry
- ❑ Encyclopedia
- ❑ Song lyrics
- ❑ TV guides

- ❑ Web sites
- ❑ Catalogs
- ❑ Other:

_____

_____

_____

8. I think reading is important because... (Check as many as you want.)

- ❑ It will help me get a job.
- ❑ You need it for school.
- ❑ It's my favorite thing.
- ❑ It makes you smart.

- ❑ It's fun.
- ❑ It helps me understand the world.
- ❑ It gives me information.
- ❑ It helps me escape.

- ❑ Other:

_____

_____

_____

9. If I could choose, I would like to read... (Check all that apply.)

FICTION
- ❑ Fantasy
- ❑ Science fiction
- ❑ Realistic stories
- ❑ Fairy tales
- ❑ Historical fiction
- ❑ Mystery
- ❑ Poetry
- ❑ Scary stories
- ❑ Funny stories

NONFICTION
- ❑ Newspapers
- ❑ Newsmagazines
- ❑ Biography
- ❑ Autobiography
- ❑ Information books:
  - ❑ Animals
  - ❑ Sports
  - ❑ Science
  - ❑ History
  - ❑ Other

OTHER
- ❑ TV guides
- ❑ Web sites
- ❑ Catalogs
- ❑ Comics
- ❑ Jokes
- ❑ Manuals/instructions
- ❑ Other:

_____

_____

_____

10. Things my teacher could do that might make me more interested in reading:

_____

_____

_____

Not surprisingly, Tyler reports that he does not like to read and views himself as a "so-so reader." He says he does not read at all unless his mother makes him. What was surprising, though, was that when provided with choices for reading, he consistently chose realistic fiction over, for example, science-related informational books. When I asked him about this, he said he preferred stories to information because it was easier to follow them.

Assessment in Action: Summarizing the Information About Tyler

The information from these multiple assessments provides an exceptionally good picture of Tyler's strengths and areas of need. Here is my summary:

Tyler's reading performance was quite consistent. He regularly performed better on word recognition than comprehension. His instructional level for word-recognition accuracy is generally at grade 4, but his comprehension level is much lower. Despite very good oral vocabulary, he struggled with comprehension questions and his retellings were sparse and focused primarily on material from the first third of the text. He definitely has a difficult time comprehending many types of text. On the other hand, when given the opportunity to revisit the text, he was able to answer all questions correctly. In fact, he worked his way through the text, identifying responses to a group of questions without prompting.

Tyler is not a fluent reader. He reads slowly, loses his place with some frequency, and often reads past phrase and sentence markers (periods, quotation marks, etc.). This is frustrating to him because he does notice these problems. As I mentioned to him, the good news is that he *does* monitor his reading—he recognizes when he is confused and when things don't make sense. He is not always able to correct the difficulty, however.

Tyler's slow rate is a matter of some concern as he enters the more-demanding fourth grade in a competitive school environment. He does not have good control over his reading abilities and has only limited stamina for reading longer texts. It seems likely that his poor motivation for reading is more the result of fluency and comprehension difficulties than an overall poor attitude. Despite his limited interest in reading, he does need to engage in significant amounts of reading to increase both his speed and stamina.

An instructional plan for Tyler will need to take these things into account. I recommended the following:

- A great deal of practice reading relatively easy text (repeated readings, etc.)
- Prereading instructional supports such as graphic organizers
- Reading guides to help him maintain concentration during reading
- Instruction in comprehension strategies
- Additional work on recognizing syllable patterns in multisyllabic words—to increase his ability to decode quickly and fluently

In Chapter 8, I describe differentiated instruction and return to Tyler as an example. But before I leave the topic of assessment, I want to discuss one more question: how much assessment do we need?

Into the Classroom

Good teaching relies heavily on good assessment. In Figure 7.15, we see the type of cyclical activities that are present in successful schools. In the center are various purposes for assessing students; around the outer circle are the actions we must take to ensure high-quality reading instruction. Note that it's possible to start almost anywhere on the outer circle. Certainly, we may start with assessment, analyze the results, and then plan our teaching. On the other hand, we often start by teaching— perhaps using required standards or curriculum materials. As we monitor students' progress, we may find that several students are not making progress or that another doesn't seem to need this work at all. So, we make adjustments. After a bit of time, we assess our efforts to see if those adjustments are working. And so on.

In my work, I often find that teachers are spending too much time assessing. They may be testing more students than they need to and/or they may be collecting information that is never used. Of course, some assessments are mandated by the state. But schools and districts impose many assessments also. Don't get me wrong—I think assessment is essential. But some guidelines are important. In planning a comprehensive assessment system, here are some useful things to consider:

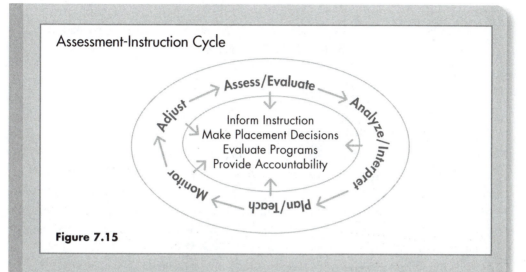

Assessment-Instruction Cycle

Assess/Evaluate

Adjust

Analyze/Interpret

Inform Instruction
Make Placement Decisions
Evaluate Programs
Provide Accountability

Monitor

Plan/Teach

Figure 7.15

- Assess as little as possible so that you can teach as much as possible.

- Assess things that matter. Assessment is no substitute for curriculum—so, identify what you want students to know and be able to do; then assess. Make decisions about what matters for different purposes and students.

- Use authentic materials and tasks whenever possible. Texts matter and so do tasks; they affect what readers do.

- Use multiple measures to capture the main facets of reading.

In recent years, I have worked with many schools that were doing too much testing. Frequently, these are schools that are requiring teachers to administer some type of informal reading inventory (IRI) to all students—often two or three times a year—as a way to determine, or report, students' reading levels. This is a good example of good intentions gone wrong.

Administrators often issue this mandate because they see that IRIs are generally a more authentic assessment. They have longer passages and more familiar administration procedures than many norm-referenced assessments, and many provide a good deal of flexibility and information, including information about rate, fluency, and comprehension on different types of text. There are two problems with this practice, however. First, although informal reading inventories are among the most useful literacy assessments available—especially in the hands of a highly trained teacher—they are also time-consuming. Second, most students don't need the extensive examination that IRIs involve.

When we spend time assessing students who are doing very well and who seem to be having success with the existing curriculum, we have too little time to *really* assess the students about whom we are worried. So, teachers collect information about students they aren't worried about in the first place and then don't have time to examine closely the struggling (or extremely capable) readers. The procedures described below provide a remedy for this situation.

Layered Assessment

We need assessment systems that (1) provide useful, trustworthy, and appropriate information about students but also (2) take as little time away from instruction as possible. The best solution to these challenges is to create a system of assessment that is "layered," so that not all assessments are designed to accomplish all purposes. By making use of the various types of assessment, it is possible to make decisions that can increase both the efficiency and the utility of assessment information.

A layered assessment system includes an effective screening assessment, which is followed by thoughtful and intentional assessment to meet specific purposes. (See Figure 7.16.) All students should be screened for major outcomes. At the screening level, we prefer to assess using the largest "unit of analysis." That is, we want to ask the biggest questions first. If students are capable of accomplishing these "big" tasks, then we generally do not need to assess the smaller ones—as long as the screening instrument is adequate and, especially, if it is accompanied by effective teacher insight.

This layered assessment system works very well in most schools. When the beginning-of-the-year screening test reveals that most students can read and

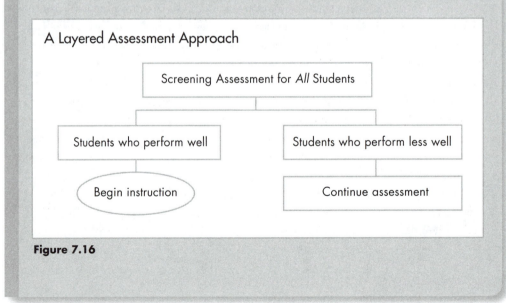

A Layered Assessment Approach

Screening Assessment for *All* Students

Students who perform well

Students who perform less well

Begin instruction

Continue assessment

Figure 7.16

comprehend grade-appropriate materials, teachers should move directly into instruction based on state standards and grade-level expectations, that is, proceed with the normal course of good, balanced teaching. High-quality and reasonably frequent monitoring with informal, classroom-based assessment (fluency checks, work samples, and discussion) may reveal that there are problems for several students. In that case, it is important to have powerful diagnostic assessments waiting in the wings.

When the screening assessment suggests that a student is not able to read with appropriate understanding, then we take a closer look—we move to diagnosis immediately. In most classrooms, there are three to five students whose performance is worrisome enough to trigger a closer look.

Layered Assessment in Action

SCREENING

A good screening tool assesses global aspects of reading and takes very little instructional time to administer. It does not need to capture all aspects of literacy, but it does need to merit our confidence. For norm-referenced assessments we ask whether a test is reliable—will it consistently result in the same scores if administered again or by someone else. For more informal assessments, we ask whether the assessment is trustworthy. The best way to enhance a test's reliability or trustworthiness is to make sure that there are standardized procedures for administering the test.

There are many possible screening tools. In the schools where I work, I often use the Gates-MacGinitie Reading Tests (4th edition). These are norm-referenced, timed tests of comprehension and vocabulary that result in standardized scores comparing each student with others in the same age/grade group. Other possible screening tools might include the Baseline Group Test (Houghton Mifflin, 1997) or the Degrees of Reading Power Test (Koslin, Koslin, Zeno, & Ivens, 1989). Of course, because states are currently required to administer tests of reading at every grade, these might be used as a screening device, as well. These tests of achievement are generally not specific enough to provide useful individual information, but they can definitely indicate which students need a closer look.

In Figure 7.17, you can see a partial listing of the results from the Gates-MacGinitie Reading Tests in one fifth-grade class. A few concepts are needed to interpret norm-referenced data like these:

- Scores are distributed between the 1st percentile and the 99th. The fiftieth percentile is considered average. A student whose score is in the 60th percentile is performing better than 59 percent of the norming sample.

- Stanine scores range from 1 to 9, with 1 representing the lowest and 9 the highest. Five is the most common stanine because it falls directly on the mean of the curve. If a student has a stanine of 5, she or he has performed better than half of the sample. Each stanine encompasses a range of percentile scores.

- The NCE (normal curve equivalent) is a standard score that has a fixed mean (average) score of 50. Students who have NCE scores above 50 are doing better than average.

Gates-MacGinitie Reading Tests (4th Edition) Class Summary Record

Test Level: 5   Test Form: T   Teacher: Janice MacIntosh

STUDENT'S NAME	VOCABULARY				COMPREHENSION				TOTAL			
	Raw Score	NCE	PR	S	Raw Score	NCE	PR	S	Raw Score	NCE	PR	S
Helena	29	59	67	6	22	41	34	4	51	49	48	5
Keira	18	37	27	4	17	32	19	3	35	34	22	3
Aaron	32	65	76	6	40	70	83	7	72	71	84	7
Maura	37	78	91	8	41	73	86	7	78	80	92	8
Angela	20	41	34	4	14	25	12	3	34	33	21	3
Zlatko	14	30	17	3	13	23	10	2	27	25	12	3
Tyler	12	25	12	3	12	22	9	2	24	22	9	2
Nicholai	26	52	54	5	16	27	16	3	42	41	33	4
Sasha	22	45	40	5	13	23	10	2	35	34	22	3
Weston	27	55	59	5	20	38	28	4	47	46	42	5
Harley	6	7	2	1	14	25	12	3	20	15	5	2
Mark	25	51	51	5	25	47	44	5	50	48	47	5
Amelia	34	70	83	7	43	78	91	8	77	77	90	8
Trevor	31	63	73	6	26	48	47	5	57	55	60	6
Alex	21	43	37	4	4	1	1	1	25	23	10	2
Nathaniel	16	34	22	3	20	38	28	4	36	35	24	4
Bethany	36	75	88	7	38	66	78	7	74	74	87	7
Rafer	25	51	51	5	27	50	50	5	52	50	50	5

Figure 7.17

When I look at the test results from Janice MacIntosh's room, I notice:

- For total reading scores, 9 of the 18 students are at or above average (stanine 5 or higher).

- Four of these nine students are well above average (stanines 7–9).

- Seven of the 18 students are performing below average (stanine 3 or lower).

There are other things to notice about these screening results. For example, students didn't always perform equally well on the vocabulary and the comprehension subtests. For these students, the total score sometimes masks important information.

- Consider Sasha, for example: She scored at the stanine 5 for vocabulary but the stanine 2 for comprehension! Her total score of 3 covers up this critical fact.

- Similarly, Alex scored at the stanine 4 for vocabulary but the stanine 1 for comprehension. In fact, the majority of students in this fifth-grade-class are performing less well on comprehension than they are on vocabulary (11 of the 18).

This is a pattern of performance that I see quite often. It usually means one of two things: 1) the students' poor rate and fluency may be keeping them from finishing the comprehension part or may be causing them to rush, and/or (2) the students' overall ability to comprehend (use strategies, think with print, etc.) is weak.

Janice MacIntosh has her hands full with such a range of students, but she is not alone. I will pick up on this theme in the next chapter in a discussion of differentiating instruction.

MAKING DECISIONS

Once the screening is completed, we have decisions to make. In Janice's classroom, the students who are at or above the norm can begin a balanced instructional program (although accommodations may be needed for the two students who are performing at the eighth stanine). Some students need a closer look immediately. In this fifth-grade class, we assessed all of the students at or below the fourth stanine using the DRA. Because there were so many, there are implications for both whole-group and small-group instruction. It quickly became apparent that many students had problems in two areas: fluency and the ability to summarize and employ other strategies for comprehension. Janice was able to implement classroom-based instructional strategies in these two areas with the help of the reading teacher. Several students were of particular concern to Janice. Tyler and Harley were both already receiving special services, so she and the special educator worked to intensify their programs. Zlatko is a relatively recent immigrant from Bosnia who is receiving some help from an ELL teacher. Alex's scores, however, were surprising to the staff. While he had never been an excellent student, no one had been worried about him until this screening. He was referred for closer examination.

ONGOING MONITORING

Once the instructional program is underway, effective teachers monitor students' performance—both their overall reading development and their acquisition of newly taught knowledge and skill. One of the best ways to monitor students' reading progress is to notice how they are reading day in and day out. This daily or weekly monitoring creates a picture of students' reading achievement that is invaluable—both for reporting to others and for planning instruction. As students read, we can notice:

- What students *can* read (text difficulty and text type)
- What students *do* read (motivation and range)
- How *well* students read grade-/age-appropriate texts (accuracy, fluency, comprehension)

To evaluate progress in reading this way, however, we really need a way to capture the difficulty of the material being read. This is one of the most challenging aspects of assessing reading in grades 3 to 6. Text leveling in the intermediate grades is much less precise than it is in the earlier grades. Tools for estimating word, or even sentence, difficulty provide incomplete results because they do not tell us much about the content or genre or text structure—all things that can make texts more or less difficult for readers.

For many years, teachers were advised (and many publishers used) various readability formulas to determine how difficult a text was (Fry, 1968; Klare, 1984). Among the most common formulas are ones developed many years ago by Edward Fry (1968) and by Edgar Dale and Jeanne Chall (1948). These, and other common formulas, rely on certain text features to determine difficulty: sentence and word length (number of words in a sentence, number of syllables in a word) and/or the "familiarity" or "rareness" of words in a text. Although they can provide a good general estimate of text difficulty, they have been criticized in recent years for not taking into account other factors such as the content difficulty or familiarity of the materials; the length of the text; and the denseness or "considerateness" of the writing.

As a result, alternative ways of estimating text difficulty have been generated. There are several good systems for estimating difficulty in primary-level texts. Irene Fountas and Gay Su Pinnell, for example, have provided guidelines for creating what they call a "text gradient" that can be used to classify selections or books "along a continuum based on the combination of variables that support and confirm readers' strategic actions and offer the problem-solving opportunities that build the reading process" (1996). The factors used to determine relative difficulty include:

- Length
- Size and layout of print
- Vocabulary and concepts
- Language structure
- Text structure and genre
- Predictability and patterns of language
- Illustration support

It's easy to see how helpful it would be to be able to designate text difficulty. If, for example, I knew that a book's difficulty was "fifth grade," then I could observe a student reading that book and determine whether she was able to read and comprehend "grade-appropriate text." I would be able to communicate more easily with my fellow teachers and track student achievement over time.

Unfortunately, text gradient systems for the intermediate grades are not quite as stable as they are for primary grades. In addition, they cannot be applied to the types of short text that would be easier to use for assessment purposes. However, the system devised by Irene Fountas and Gay Su Pinnell for determining the "text level" of books in grades 3 to 6 provides very useful guidelines. Their book *Leveled Books for Readers, Grades 3 to 6* (2001) is an important source of information. Some commercial basal programs have their own leveling system also. It is important to understand that these systems of determining difficulty may vary greatly in their results and that, especially at grades 3 to 6, there may be quite a range of difficulty even within a "text level" or "readability level." Fountas and Pinnell's system uses a letter gradient, while other systems use grade-level estimates (e.g., the Fry Readability graph), and still others use a Lexile system. The Lexile measure, like other readability formulas, uses word length and syntax to estimate text difficulty. (You can download the Lexile Map at http://teacher.scholastic.com/products/sri/pdfs/Lexile_Map.pdf.) Scores range from BR (beginning reading) to Level 1500 (high school). The chart in Figure 7.18 provides a comparison of several different leveling systems. Any system of estimating text difficulty has pros and cons. It is especially important to remember that a Level M book might be harder or easier to read depending on the content and depending on the reader's prior knowledge and experience with the content and genre.

Comparison Chart of Text Levels

GUIDED READING LEVEL (Fountas & Pinnell)	DRA LEVEL	LEXILE READING LEVEL	ESTIMATED GRADE LEVEL
L	24	300–500	2
M	28	300–500	2
N	30	500–700	3
O	34	500–700	3
P	38	500–700	3
Q	40	650–850	4
R		650–850	4
S		650–850	4
T	50	750–950	5
U		750–950	5
V		750–950	5
W	60	800–1300	6
X			6
Y			6

Figure 7.18 Comparison of systems for leveling text difficulty

I have found it useful to refer to a set of "anchor" texts: lists of highly familiar and widely used books that have been leveled by using one or another system. For example, I used the Fountas and Pinnell (2001) system to create a list of anchor books that are meaningful for me:

Grade 3
Freckle Juice by Judy Blume (1971) at the beginning of the year (Level M)
Ramona Quimby, Age 8 by Beverly Cleary (1962) later in the year (Level O)

Grade 4
Charlotte's Web by E. B. White (1956) at beginning of the year (Level Q)
Stuart Little by E. B. White (1945) later in the year (Level R)

Grade 5

Mississippi Bridge by Mildred Taylor (1992) at the beginning of the year (Level S)
Bridge to Terabithia by Katherine Paterson (1972), or *Sign of the Beaver* by Elizabeth George Speare (1983) for later (Level U)

Grade 6

Holes by Louis Sachar (1998) or *The Westing Game* by Ellen Raskin (1978) at the beginning of the year (Level V)
The Giver by Lois Lowry (1993) later in the year (Level Y)

Because most teachers are familiar with these texts, the books serve as an anchor for other books that we may use or children may read. I compare other books with these—using a compare/contrast set of criteria. I find that most teachers can do this very easily using their well-developed professional sense—although your anchor books might differ.

CONDUCTING QUICK TEXT LEVEL CHECK-INS

Once we have a way to determine the relative difficulty of texts, it is quite easy to keep track of students' progress. To simplify this process, Sue Biggam and Ellen Thompson (2005) created the Quick Text Level Check-In (QT). A student reads only a 100-word segment of a book, and then the teacher assesses his or her performance in terms of accuracy, fluency, and comprehension. These check-ins can take place as often as needed and can be used (in conjunction with text-difficulty information) to plan instruction and/or discuss progress. Of course, students' reading performance on a small sample cannot tell everything that may be important about students' reading ability, but it is a good *snapshot* that can be combined with other snapshots to get the whole picture and/or to alert teachers to the need for a closer examination. To administer the QT assessment, follow these steps:

1. Select an appropriate 100-word segment of the text. If possible, choose one that is relatively coherent and self-contained. Avoid choosing portions that have too many new or unusual names and/or dates.

2. Make two copies of this portion of the text.

3. Introduce the portion and, if necessary, provide a bit of background. For example, when I selected the book *Anastasia Krupnik* for use in QT (Level Q, grade 4), I introduced it by saying, "You are going to read a part of a story about a girl named Anastasia. She is ten years old and is having a difficult

year. First, her teacher doesn't like her work, and now she finds out that she is about to have a baby brother."

4. As the student reads aloud, keep track of his or her errors on your copy.

5. Also try to keep track of the student's phrasing (fluency) while reading.

6. Stop the student after he or she has read 100 words. Ask the student to read the rest of the text silently (choose a place to stop that will keep the storyline intact).

7. Ask the student to summarize or retell this part of the text. To get a good picture of comprehension, use probes such as "Tell me more" or "I'm not sure I understand. Can you clarify that?"

8. Complete the form on page 233 to determine whether this book appears to be a good match for the student.

Of course, daily work samples such as response journals and discussion preparations are very good indications of students' comprehension, as are their contributions to class or small-group discussions. I have noted elsewhere (M. Y. Lipson, 1995) that conversation is really a terrific way to assess many aspects of students' reading ability—especially, comprehension. The types of work samples and journals displayed throughout this book show how careful "noticing" can lead to excellent assessment information. Rubrics are an excellent way to systematize this ongoing informal assessment. An "all-purpose" rubric (page 234) can be kept handy and then filled in with the specific criteria you intend to assess.

One of the reasons that rubrics make such good assessment tools is that they can promote student self-assessment. The Reading Notebook Student Rubric (page 235), designed by Sue Biggam, is intended to be used by students to guide their work and evaluate its success.

QT: Quick Text Level Check-In, Adapted

Student _____ Text _____

Date _____ Teacher _____ Grade _____ Level of text_____

PART 1: ORAL READING ACCURACY: 100 words sampled, from page no.: _____
Tally errors:

PATTERNS OBSERVED (Note: Self-corrections do not count as errors.):

Check accuracy level below:

❑ 11 or more errors (<90%) (frustration) ❑ 8–10 errors (90–92%) (marginal instructional) ❑ 6–7 errors (93–94%) (instructional) ❑ 0–5 errors (95–100%) (independent)

Check fluency level:

❑ Mostly word-by-word reading ❑ Some phrases (two or three words that make sense together) read together ❑ Mostly read in phrases (two or three words that make sense together) ❑ Smooth, meaningful reading, with phrasing and emphasis that makes sense and generally shows understanding

---

PART 2: EVIDENCE OF SURFACE COMPREHENSION:

Ask the student to read the next section of text silently, saying, "When you are finished, I will ask you to tell me about the part you read." After reading, say, "Now, tell me about the part you just read."

Student's response:

❑ Limited comprehension ❑ Some comprehension ❑ Acceptable comprehension ❑ Excellent comprehension

SUMMARY COMMENTS:

Overall Evaluation:

❑ Easy

❑ Okay

❑ Marginal

❑ Too hard

Level: _____

All-Purpose Rubric

Name _____ Teacher _____ Date _____

ELEMENT TO BE ASSESSED	CRITERIA			
	1 Beginning	2 Developing	3 Accomplished	4 Expert
Name the skill, aspect of work, etc.	Description of this level of performance	Description of this level of performance	Description of this level of performance	Description of this level of performance

Reading Notebook Student Rubric

Name _____ Text read _____

CRITERION	1	2	3	4
Understanding of Text and Evidence of Deep Thinking	My response shows that I wrote about what I read.	My response provides some evidence that I understood what I read and thought about what it meant.	My response shows that I understood what I read. If there were questions to respond to, I did. I explained my deep thinking and supported it by using evidence from the text.	My response shows that I understand what I read. If there were questions to respond to, I did. I explained my deep thinking and supported it by using evidence from the text, including well-chosen quotes.
Organization and Clarity	It might be hard for a reader to follow what I wrote.	My response can be followed, but there are parts that are confusing.	It's easy to follow what I wrote, and my response has a clear beginning, middle, and end.	I wrote a well-organized response; it reads smoothly and I have a strong lead, good transitions, and a clear conclusion.
GUM (Grammar, Usage, Mechanics)	Many errors (in spelling, punctuation, or grammar) make my response hard to read.	Mostly okay spelling, punctuation and grammar for my grade level and classroom expectations.	A-okay for my grade level and classroom expectations.	A-okay, and I took some risks to write complex sentences and/or challenging words as well.

Concluding Thoughts

Without good assessment it is difficult to accomplish good instruction. The best assessment is always responsive to specific student needs. Of course, a good, balanced, and comprehensive program will be all that many students require. Even then, however, it is important to monitor progress and make sure that we, and our students, are on the right track. Ongoing, classroom-based assessment is mostly a matter of noticing—and knowing what to notice—about students and their performance.

Students who are not making good progress and students who are ready for much more than the regular classroom program can provide need a closer look. For these students, a repertoire of assessment tools and strategies, as well as a good working relationship with other professionals in the building, are necessary. We don't expect classroom teachers to work in a vacuum. Reading coaches, Title I teachers, special educators, and even administrators can be invaluable sources of information and support. Catherine Snow and her colleagues (1991) have demonstrated how much our most vulnerable students need a concerted approach involving the whole school. Of course, a school-wide commitment to all students is also essential. Good assessment that improves communication and enhances the picture we have of each student is one of the best ways to demonstrate that commitment.

Discussion and Reflection

- Which types of assessment do you already use?

- Review the assessments suggested in this chapter and decide which have the most utility for you. Try one or more.

- Are there gaps in the assessment system used in your school/classroom? Discuss with others in your grade/school.

- Work with your colleagues to identify the types of student work that can be used to assess student progress.

Digging Deeper

If you are interested in knowing more about assessment—especially classroom-based assessment—check out these resources:

- *Assessment and Instruction of Reading and Writing Difficulties: An Interactive Perspective,* 3rd ed., by Marjorie Y. Lipson and Karen K. Wixson. New York: Allyn & Bacon/Pearson, 2003.

- *Reading Assessment: Principles and Practices for Elementary Teachers,* 2nd ed., edited by Shelby Barrentine and Sandra Stokes. Newark, DE: International Reading Association, 2005.

- *A Teacher's Guide to Standardized Reading Tests* by Lucy Calkins, Kate Montgomery, and Donna Santman. Portsmouth, NH: Heinemann, 1998.

- *3-Minute Reading Assessments: Word Recognition, Fluency, and Comprehension: Grades 5–8,* by Timothy Rasinski and Nancy Padak. New York: Scholastic, 2005.

- *Words Their Way: Word Study for Phonics, Spelling, and Vocabulary Development,* 3rd ed., by Donald Bear, Marcia Invernizzi, Shane Templeton, and Francine. Johnston. Upper Saddle River, NJ: Merrill/Prentice Hall, 2003.

CHAPTER 8

Differentiate Instruction to Reach All Students

In a diverse classroom, differentiation is an absolute necessity. That statement is as true as it is difficult to accomplish. In this chapter, I attempt to make it easier for you by describing how an interactive model of reading can provide direction in meeting the needs of diverse students and provide specific tools and ideas for implementing that model. The chapter is divided into four major sections: an interactive model of reading, differentiation, using assessment information to inform instruction, and differentiating instruction for particular student populations.

I took my very first teaching job in a large Midwestern city. It was a fourth- and fifth-grade split class. Because of budget cuts, I was expected to teach both the fourth- and the fifth-grade curriculum. The fourth-grade students were all struggling, and several were repeating the grade. In a misguided attempt to "balance" the class, the administration had made sure that the fifth-grade students were all "accelerated." Among the 27 students, there were 19 whose families had arrived in the U.S. over the past ten years and whose first (for some, only) language was Spanish—roughly half from Puerto Rico and half from Mexico, and one, Elena, who had just arrived from Costa Rica. Four of the other students were Native Americans who had recently left their tribal reservation in the northern part of the state. They, too, spoke English as a second language, although the language of school had always been English for them. The final four students were English-language-only Caucasians. Although I did not know the term "differentiate" at that time, I certainly understood the need.

Remember, this was my first year of teaching. Understand also that my teacher preparation had been quite limited. Although thankfully, I'd had an excellent student teaching semester in a diverse school that was almost as challenging, I really struggled during this first year. There were no special services for English-language learners; the special education services were limited to those who were profoundly impaired, which my students clearly were not, and the one reading teacher for the building had a heavy load.

My teaching that year was uneven and marked by some significant successes and some dismal failures. Nevertheless, I learned a great deal. The most important lesson I learned was that I had to look at the students, and that my instruction had to follow what I knew about them. The fifth-grade curriculum might say that they should have already learned to "interpret information on a map, table, or graph," but if they could not, I had to be prepared to teach it. Maybe the fourth-grade curriculum said my students should be able to "demonstrate oral reading fluency of at least 140 words per minute in fourth-grade text with appropriate pacing, intonation, and expression," but if they could not, then I had better roll up my sleeves. For some of my students that meant starting at second-grade-level text, reading 40 words per minute! Of course, a few could read nothing in English at all.

Acquiring a student-centered perspective took time, though. During my second year of teaching, I had a self-contained classroom of fourth graders, but I quickly realized that the differences were almost as great as they had been in my mixed class the year before. I flirted with completely individualized programs (all the rage at the time) and employed one of the mammoth management systems that was designed to keep track of each student. But, really, it became clear that complete "individualization" was silly. First, it is difficult to establish a powerful sense of community when everyone is always doing their own thing. Second, teaching a skill today to one group and doing it again a week later for a different group when it was "ready" didn't result in very powerful changes, nor did it seem to be a good use of my time.

One of the most important insights I acquired along the way was that while most advocates of individualizing spoke of altering only the pace of instruction, pace was clearly not the only dimension that needed consideration.

Lessons From Research and Practice: What We Know About Differentiating Instruction

Our own experiences and the findings of research converge toward the inevitable conclusion that *students are different from each other*. In addition, becoming literate requires the orchestration of a number of complex skills and abilities. Throughout this book, I have made references to student differences, but up until now the book has been largely about creating a good structure for classroom-based reading instruction. Inside the structure, there needs to be room for variation. No one teaching tactic addresses all the components of reading/writing nor all the strategies and skills students need. Students have different strengths and weaknesses, and they require an instructional program that is flexible and responsive.

The Interactive Model of Reading

To promote success among all students, we need to understand where our leverage is. In the early 1980s, my colleagues, Karen Wixson and Charlie Peters, and I set out to write a definition of reading that could provide direction for both assessment and instruction in the state of Michigan.

> Reading is the process of constructing meaning through the dynamic interaction among the reader's existing knowledge, the information suggested by the text, and the context of the reading situation. (Michigan Department of Education, Michigan Reading Association, 1985/2005)

We went on to describe how this meant that reading was *constructive, dynamic*, and *variable*. We have been using this interactive model to work with teachers and students ever since (see Figure 8.1), and it has been especially helpful when thinking about the needs of individual students (Wixson & M. Y. Lipson, 1985; 2003). Summary principles that grow out of this model include:

- Students' performance varies as a result of the specific texts they are reading and/or tasks they are doing. Depending on the text or task, a reader may be very successful or not. Changing the text or the task or the type of instruction can make a big difference.

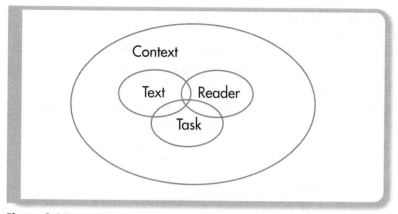

Figure 8.1 An interactive model of reading. Students' performance and motivation is viewed as the result of the dynamic interaction among the reader, the text, and the task within a specific context.

- Students' performance is an indication of what they can and/or will do at this time and with these materials, tasks, and so forth. Because different conditions have an impact on students, motivation as well as skill must be considered.

- The goal of instruction should be to specify the conditions under which students can/will learn. Simply identifying a "reading level" isn't helpful because the reading level may fluctuate depending on readers' interest, background knowledge, experience, and motivation.

In 2002, in its comprehensive review of comprehension research, the RAND Reading Study Group adopted a very similar definition, concluding, as we had, that the three-way interaction between reader, text, and task occurs within a larger sociocultural context. This model provides an extremely useful framework for thinking about differentiation. This interactive, dynamic model is descriptive of all students, not just struggling readers. *All* readers function within this complex, interactive environment. All of us read some things better than others, complete some tasks more effectively than others. The model has great instructional value because it does not locate problems entirely within the learner. Instead, it tells us that students' performance might improve if we modified the instructional context, the texts, or the tasks.

Differentiation

The interactive model of reading invites us to think about our teaching differently. Not all students are alike, and these interactions make for complicated learning environments. Traditional methods of "one size fits all" don't seem appropriate. At the same time, state and local standards and, more recently, grade-level-expectations (GLEs) demand that we have common outcomes for all students, so we need instruction that can address this challenge.

What Is Differentiation?

> To differentiate instruction is to recognize students' varying background knowledge, readiness, language, preferences in learning, and interests, and to react responsively. (T. Hall, 2002, p. 2)

According to Carol Ann Tomlinson (2001), differentiated learning is an approach to teaching in which students have multiple options for learning information and gaining meaning. It starts with student assessment information, but it includes an awareness of curricular goals (the standards and GLEs). Once we are clear about the outcomes, we identify places that can be varied to enhance learning for a diverse group of students. Figure 8.2 shows how this

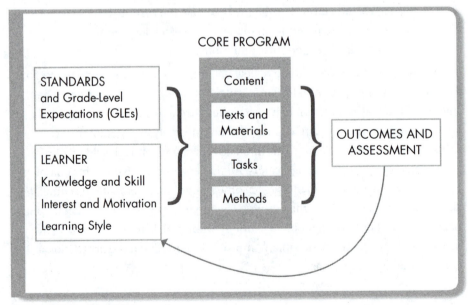

Figure 8.2 Model of differentiated instruction

works. Differentiated instruction starts with a strong core program. The first seven chapters of this book lay out the basis for this core program, describing the overall instruction-assessment framework and detailing what *everyone* needs. Within that framework, we place specific content, instructional support, texts, and tasks.

Differentiation is not a different program for every student. Instead, it is a core program that identifies major ideas, concepts, and skills that all students need to learn. Further, it does *not* require creating different assignments for individual students, although you might sometimes use them. Instead, it requires responsive teaching—with modifications to ensure that each student is successful. Differentiation involves intentional planning to modify content, methods, and materials. The idea is to think about how instruction can be differentiated within the regular classroom and to look for as many ways as possible to accommodate individual students' strengths and needs.

What Should We Differentiate?

All differentiation starts with assessment. Without a clear understanding of the student(s), there would be no direction for our modifications. Once we have a better understanding of a student's strengths and needs, we can begin to think about the types of alterations we might make to the core program to address these needs. Instructional differentiation is planned according to the content, the text and materials, and/or the reading and writing tasks.

Content

For reading, the content of instruction consists of skills, strategies, and knowledge of text structure that students need to master in order to learn how to read and comprehend. As a reminder, the components of reading include:

- Phonological awareness
- Phonics/decoding
- Fluency
- Vocabulary
- Comprehension

In addition, we must consider issues of motivation, stamina, strategic reading ability, and self-regulation.

The content of reading instruction changes over time. Developmentally, for example, very few students in grades 3 and beyond need instruction in phonological awareness. Those few who do require the services of a special educator. Similarly, while fluency is likely to be an important concern in grade 3, it should be less so in grade 6. Consequently, the focus for instruction is different in third grade than in sixth.

Despite these developmental trends, we know that some students in grade 6 are more like third graders in terms of their knowledge and skill and some students in grade 3 are more like sixth graders. So, the content must be differentiated for those students. What we teach can and should be responsive to their needs. To complicate matters even further, students vary in terms of their specific component needs. Some students, for example, need instruction that has a fluency component, while others need instruction on constructing themes or reading different text structures.

Texts and Materials

Of course, the varied nature of the texts and other materials that students encounter can also affect their reading—both in terms of comprehension and fluency. The good news about the impact of text on comprehension is that we can differentiate instruction by choosing appropriate texts that students read. The following are factors we might consider for specific students/small groups:

- **Difficulty:** the grade, age, and/or reading level of the books
- **Text features:** genre, structure, topic
- **Text type:** fiction or nonfiction (informational texts, biographies, how-to books, and so forth)
- **Student interest:** the topic should be appealing

The tools for determining text difficulty that I described in Chapter 7 are useful for making decisions about text difficulty for specific students. In classroom teaching, however, we need a way to weave differentiated texts into our overall plan. To do that successfully, it's a good idea to allow students some choice within the program and to design instruction that uses text sets.

Allowing Students Choice

Choice was discussed in Chapters 3 and 4, but it is an extremely important tool when implementing differentiation. If we make choice a part of our program, then students have a better chance of reading material that interests them and that is within their reach.

Choice is important precisely because students are different. A few years ago I was stunned when I entered a second-grade classroom and found two boys working diligently on their self-published book entitled *The Wilderness Battle of the Civil War*. At the time, I was completely unaware of this well-studied battle of 1864. And, of course, no sensible teacher would ever assign the study of this battle to 7-year-olds. Nevertheless, that is what these two were interested in. Their heightened motivation led them to find resources, read about and discuss this battle with others, and write their own book. Not many—perhaps no other—children this age want to read and think about the Civil War in this ways, and so our core program doesn't include this material.

A fairly typical sixth-grade classroom contains students with wide-ranging reading preferences, as in this example:

> Melissa is hooked on the Sammy Keyes mysteries by Van Draanen, Corey likes only sports biographies, Scott has already discovered adult novels by John Grisham, while Nora can't get enough of fantasy—especially Patricia Wrede's wry series Dealing With Dragons. Then there is Dillon who reads nothing at all if he can help it, and Sarina, who likes magazines but not much else. Other students in the room are reading hefty tomes—including Michael Crichton's *Jurassic Park*. Leila carries Harry Potter around but is really not able to read it. She'd rather be reading animal stories like *Carlotta's Kittens* by Phyllis Naylor, but she doesn't know how to find them, and they might "look" too easy anyway.

Of course, there is a similar range in grades 3, 4, and 5. Their varied interests and motivations for reading are a challenge, since we know that practice is essential if students are going to become really adept at reading. In addition, it is becoming increasingly clear that motivation to read texts and do tasks influences achievement in other ways. If students are not engaged in their studies, they are much less likely to learn what is required, and the cumulative effect can be devastating. (See Chapter 4.)

Although we may not be able to respond to every difference in interest or motivation, I enlist the support of the school librarian, scrounge in my own collection, and try to make sure that there is something for everyone in the classroom library. Brief talks about new books I have added increase students' interest. As the year goes along, students talk about the books they are reading, and these peer appraisals become much more important than the ones I give. Students get referrals from others who enjoy the same types of reading, but they also branch out and expand their reading lists.

Completely free choice is useful during sustained-silent-reading periods, but constrained choice based on text difficulty, genre type, or thematic content is also a powerful tool—one that is used widely in readers' workshop. Of course, it is important to teach students how to make good choices. Most teachers are familiar with the "Five-Finger Rule":

1. Choose a book that you are interested in reading.

2. Open the book and begin to read the first page.

3. Each time you come to a word that you don't know, put up one finger.

4. If all five fingers are up before the end of the page, this book is too difficult.

5. If you are not sure about the book, turn to another page (somewhere in the middle) and repeat.

6. If you have fewer than five fingers up, the book may be a "just right" book.

For students in grades 3 to 6, the Five-Finger Rule can be helpful, but students in these grades may find a book difficult for other reasons, and they need to develop more-comprehensive means for making choices. Students can be taught the "Goldilock's Rule"— a check to decide if a book is "too easy," "too hard," or "just right" (adapted from Ohlhausen & Jepsen, 1992). Goldilock's Rule for grades 3 to 6 might look like this:

Too Easy: This book may be too easy for you if you answer "yes" to most of these questions:

• Have I read this book before?

• Am I able to read this book easily and fluently at a good rate?

• Are the words and ideas easy for me to understand?

Too Hard: This book may be too hard for you if you answer "yes" to most of these questions:

- Are there more than five words per page that I don't recognize or understand?

- Am I having a hard time understanding the ideas?

- Am I finding that I am not interested in this book?

- Am I reading more slowly than usual?

Just Right: This book may be just right for you if you answer "yes" to most of these questions:

- Is this a new book for me?

- Am I interested in reading this book?

- Are the words and ideas challenging for me, but not too difficult?

- Am I reading the book with someone else who can help me if I get into trouble?

Using Text Sets

A text set is a group of books of varying levels of difficulty organized around a common feature, such as a topic, concept, standard, or theme. There are a numbers of reasons why text sets are effective in differentiation:

- All students can be engaged in the same overall experience— for example, reading mysteries or studying the solar system.

- All students can be involved in the same tasks—for example, creating a summary of the text or writing a response.

- All students can read material that is the appropriate difficulty level for them.

Topic text sets: Teachers most commonly base text sets on a topic—creating a collection of books about the Civil War, for example. Carol Hurst's children's literature Web site has online resources for dozens of topics, from the Civil War to geology to quilts, along with extensive book reviews. This resource can be accessed at http://www.carolhurst.com/subjects.curriculum.html. Visitors can search the site by subject, title, author, and grade level. Other sites that suggest text sets include these:

- Lesley University: http://www.lesley.edu/crr/content/lfa/ handouts/if_text_sets.pdf. Text sets are based on topics such as animals, friendship, and the environment.

- Walloon Institute: http://www.walloon.com/conference_ handouts/ALAN/AmericanHistoryLitCircleTextSets.doc. Text sets are based on topics such as the Civil War, westward expansion, and the 1920s.

Author text sets: Over the years, I have been exploring a variety of text sets with undergraduate students and experienced teachers. The most common ones involve author, genre, and theme. Author text sets require little effort to compile. However, because most authors write for a specific audience, there may not be many opportunities to manage reading levels. On the other hand, these sets allow us to really see author's craft in action. A few favorite authors worth studying in grades 3 to 6 are listed in the box below.

Sample Author Text Sets

Betsy Byars	**Easy Reading:** *The Golly Sisters Go West* • *The Golly Sisters Ride Again* • **Novels:** *The Pinballs* • *After the Goat Man* • *The Midnight Fox* (and others)
Andrew Clements	**Short Chapter Books:** *Frindle* • *Lunch Money* • Jake Drake series **Picture Books:** *Big Al* • *Big Al and Shrimpy* • *Double Trouble in Walla Walla*
Sharon Creech	**Novels:** *Love That Dog* • *Granny Torrelli Makes Soup* • *Walk Two Moons* • *Heartbeat* • **Picture Books:** *Who's That Baby?* • *Fishing in the Air* • *A Fine, Fine School*
Roald Dahl	**Novels:** *The BFG* • *James and the Giant Peach* • *Matilda* • *The Twits* • *Danny the Champion of the World* • *Fantastic Mr. Fox* (Dahl has also written many short stories; some are in *The Roald Dahl Treasury*.)
Sid Fleischman	**Novels:** *The Whipping Boy* • *Disappearing Act* • *The Midnight Horse* • *The Scarebird* • *Bo and Mzzz Mad* • *Here Comes McBroom* (and other books in the McBroom series)
Patricia Reilly Giff	**Easy Series:** *The Beast in Ms. Rooney's Room* • **Novels:** *Lily's Crossing* • *Pictures of Hollis Woods* • *Nory Ryan's Song*
Karen Hesse	**Novels:** *Just Juice* • *Letters From Rifka* • *Out of the Dust* • *Stowaway* • *Witness*

Ursula Le Guin	Novels: *Gifts • The Telling • A Wizard of Earthsea • The Left Hand of Darkness • The Tombs of Atuan • The Lathe of Heaven* (Le Guin also writes short stories and poetry)
Lois Lowry	Novels: *The Giver • Gathering Blue • Messenger • Number the Stars • Anastasia Krupnik* (and other books in this series) • All About Sam series, following from *Anastasia Krupnik • Autumn Street* (and others)
Nicholassa Mohr	Novels: *All for the Better • El Bronx Remembered: A Novella and Stories • Felita • Going Home*
Walter Dean Myers	Novels: *Fast Sam, Cool Clyde, and Stuff • Me, Mop, and the Moondance Kid • Mop, Moondance, and the Nagasaki Knights • 145th Street: Short Stories • Hoops • The Legend of Tarik* (and others)
Katherine Paterson	Novels: *The Great Gilly Hopkins • Jacob Have I Loved • Bridge to Terabithia • Come Sing, Jimmy Jo • The Flip Flop Girl* (and others)
Louis Sachar	**Easy reading:** Marvin Redpost series • **Novels:** *Wayside School* series • *Holes • There's a Boy in the Girl's Bathroom* (and others)
Gary Soto	**Short novels:** *The Cat's Meow • Marisol • The Skirt •* **Novels:** *Taking Sides • Pacific Crossing •* **Short story collections:** *Baseball in April • Help Wanted • Local News •* **Picture books:** *Chato's Kitchen • Too Many Tamales • If the Shoe Fits •* **Poetry:** *Neighborhood Odes • Canto Familiar* (and others)
Jerry Spinelli	**Easy reading:** *The Bathwater Gang • Do the Funky Pickle* (and more School Daze series books) • *Blue Ribbon Blues: A Tooter Tale* (Stepping Stone) • **Novels:** *Loser • Maniac Magee • There's a Girl in My Hammerlock • Fourth Grade Rats* (and others)
Mildred D. Taylor	Novels: *The Friendship • The Gold Cadillac • Let the Circle Be Unbroken • Mississippi Bridge • Roll of Thunder Hear My Cry • Song of the Trees*

Genre text sets: Genre text sets offer the greatest freedom of choice. Because they are drawn from many authors and many reading levels, these can be exciting units to teach. In addition, genre text sets offer an excellent way to expand students' reading experience. Of course, some students may dislike the chosen genre, and a lengthy unit can pose motivation problems for them. An example of a genre text set is provided in the box below.

Sample Genre Text Set: Mystery

James Lawrence	*Binky Brothers, Detectives (An I Can Read Mystery)* *Binky Brothers and the Fearless Four*	Below Grade 3
Elizabeth Levy	Invisible Inc. series • *The Schoolyard Mystery* *The Snack Attack Mystery* • *Parents' Night Fright* *Creepy Computer Mystery*	Very Easy
David Adler	Cam Jansen series: *Cam Jansen and the Triceratops Pops Mystery* *Cam Jansen and the Ghostly Mystery* *Cam Jansen and the Chocolate Fudge Mystery*	Easy
Patricia Reilly Giff	Polka Dot Private Eye series: *The Clue at the Zoo* • *Powder Puff Puzzle* *The Riddle of the Red Purse* (and others)	Easy
Donald J. Sobol	Encyclopedia Brown series: *Encyclopedia Brown, Boy Detective* *Encyclopedia Brown Gets His Man* *Encyclopedia Brown and the Case of the Disgusting Sneakers* (and others)	Easy– Moderate
Gertrude Warner	Boxcar Children series: *The Chocolate Sundae Mystery* *The Hockey Mystery* • *The Pizza Mystery* (and others)	Easy– Moderate
Patricia Reilly Giff	*Kidnap at the Catfish Café*	Moderate
Wendelin Van Draanen	Sammy Keyes series: *Sammy Keyes and the Sisters of Mercy* *Sammy Keyes and the Hollywood Mummy* *Sammy Keyes and the Hotel Thief* (and others)	Moderate
Jean Van Leeuwen	*The Great Googlestein Museum Mystery*	Moderate

E. L. Konigsburg	*From the Mixed-Up Files of Mrs. Basil E. Frankweiler*	Moderate–Challenging
Ellen Raskin	*The Westing Game* *The Mysterious Disappearance of Leon (I Mean Noel)*	Challenging
Zilpha Snyder	*The Egypt Game • The Gypsy Game* *The Headless Cupid*	Challenging

Theme text sets: Theme text sets are typically mixed genre sets that are selected for their potential to explore a significant issue from multiple perspectives—they invite students to think about complex ideas expressed in a variety of forms. Unlike topic sets, these are unified by the type of "big ideas" described in Chapter 4. With text sets, even if there is not a cross-disciplinary theme in place, all students can be reading texts that share a common theme but are written at different levels of difficulty. Although they vary considerably in quality, some commercial core programs are very helpful in providing leveled resources and also leveled bibliographies organized around themes. For example, Houghton Mifflin has a thematic set for fifth graders called "Voices of the Revolution" (2000), which includes these texts:

> *And Then What Happened, Paul Revere?* by Jean Fritz (historical fiction, point of view: Patriot)
>
> *Katie's Trunk* by Ann Turner (historical fiction, point of view: Tory)
>
> "James Forten" from *Now Is Your Time* by Walter Dean Myers (biography and historical narrative)
>
> *Voices of the Revolution* (an anthology of constructed, easy-to-read nonfiction that parallels each of the texts above, to be used with below-grade level readers)

Multi-leveled theme books accompany this unit:

> Easy: *Daughter of Liberty* by Robert Quackenbush (historical fiction based on true events)
>
> Average/on-level: *Phoebe the Spy* by Judith Berry Griffin (historical fiction)

Challenging: *Guns for General Washington* by Seymore Reit
(historical fiction based on true events)

This program also provides a bibliography listing related books for very easy, easy, on-level, and challenging reading.

Reading and Writing Tasks

The types of texts that people read affect their comprehension, but so do the particular tasks or purposes that accompany the reading. Research makes clear that even small alterations in a task can influence the outcome. For example, telling students before they read that they are going to have to discuss the "main idea" afterward dramatically improves their ability to do so. Similarly, asking students to "tell me what you remember" produces different outcomes than asking them to "summarize the story," and, both of these are different from the prompt "Now *you* tell *me* that story." We also know that the location of questions can affect students' comprehension (Cotton, 1989). Questions asked before reading, for example, focus

Students plan a reading response for their challenging literature book.

students' attention but also cause them to ignore some information. Questions asked after reading often cause students to synthesize or reconstruct their ideas.

Over time, a steady diet of one type of task can have even more significant effects. Jane Hansen demonstrated many years ago that when students were asked only rote questions about detail, they were not very successful at answering higher-order inferencing questions (1981). Even more interesting was the fact that when students practiced answering inferencing questions, they got better at answering them. What all this means is that even when the reader and the text stay the same, tasks can affect reading achievement.

Much of the reading students do in school is not self-selected and often involves complex or specified tasks that are new and difficult. Although students in these grades may choose to read for many purposes—for pleasure, to gather information for their own interests, to communicate with others—they are most often reading and writing in response to the requirements of their teachers. In other words, their purpose is intertwined with the tasks they need to accomplish—they are reading or writing to demonstrate knowledge or complete assignments like these:

- Writing summaries of informational materials
- Obtaining information to answer questions
- Analyzing and interpreting elements of author's craft
- Generating a personal response to reading
- Using multiple sources of information to write a report
- Supporting opinions with evidence
- Discussing text—orally and in writing

There are ways to differentiate instructional tasks and, in the process, to help students learn to read better *and* acquire more content knowledge, such as:

- Inviting open-ended responses
- Task slicing and compacting
- Question shaping
- Activity shaping

Thoughtful adjustments at the level of expectations for performance can keep some students from feeling overwhelmed and others from feeling complacent. In fact, good teaching always involves knowing who needs a bit of a push and who needs support. Some tasks are easy to differentiate in this way.

Inviting Open-Ended Responses

Inviting open-ended responses is an excellent way to differentiate. When we ask for written responses to reading, for example, we always call forth varying levels of response because students will write only what they can. In earlier chapters, I discussed how response journals and literature logs can provide open-ended vehicles for student participation. In Figure 8.3, you see two journal responses

1/67

Dear MS. Murnane I
am reading Sarah Plane and
tall. It is a really rally go
book. It is Just Right a
a littal hard but not m
But it is a really good b

①

I oue
Amar

December

Dear Amanda,
   ☺ Hey now... peachy. Thanks for the letter
appreciate that you included the title of the
reading, it's helpful information for m
like you are enjoying this book but
hard to tell what you like about it
little about that. Do you like one
characters? If so, what do you li
making any connections to the text?
think will happen? Do you think
stay with her new family? I loo
your next letter. Please remember
in your reading log.
yours in ☮. MS. Murnane

9/19

Willy

Dear MS Murnane

   I am reading Theodorium sequence. the main
characteri's Rialle. She is being taken to silver town to
Calm the merlee. The merlee are like Fisl people or merl-
let Rialle sail across the sea safely.
   This book reminds me of the Harry potter series. Why?
Because it takes place at a large school type facilit
similar to Hogwarts. Rialle reminds m   r potter
hea...   th her
                                                  erlee and
                                                  dicated

                                                  lce a
                                                  it

September 20,

Dear Willy,
   ☺ Hey now... thanks for the letter. It sounds as
though you are enjoying your book thus far. I love
when I get a good book recommendation. Did our
librarian, Mrs. Binalski, recommend it or at the public
library? Have you read the City of Ember? If so,
what did you think?
   I thought it was interesting the parallel you found
between this and the Harry Potter books. I'm a fan
of mermaids so that in itself peaked my interest.
I'm assuming Rialle is not a mermaid because
you said you were surprised that they let her
cross the sea. Is she human? I liked your
choice of words, "chosen one" to discribe both her
and Harry. I recently read, Gregor the Overlander
and I think that the main character Gregor
is the "chosen one".
   In your next letter, try to write a little neater
it was a little difficult to follow near the end.
Nice job! Have a great week!
                          ☮ MS. Murnane

   P.S. Is the book you are reading part of a series?

Figure 8.3 Willy and Amanda's journal entries and Andrea's responses

from Andrea Murnane's sixth-grade class early in the year. Andrea accepts the responses and differentiates the feedback and instruction she offers. Amanda receives a great deal of scaffolding to help her in writing her next entry in the dialogue journal. Willy receives a different type of feedback. Andrea engages him in a more literary discussion, commenting on his ideas and choice of words. Andrea also suggests he write more neatly—a really important thing when you have to read a lot of journals!

Task Slicing and Compacting

Another way to differentiate tasks is to vary assignments and/or amounts of reading/writing according to students' needs. Struggling readers may read fewer pages—the task will be "sliced off" for them. Alternatively, capable students may be assigned *less* practice in some areas because they do not need it ("compacting"). They are assigned to move quickly through material in order to complete more challenging work afterward.

Student choice can be built into the tasks as well as the texts. In the classrooms I have described, students are often expected to decide what they will do to demonstrate or facilitate their comprehension. The discussion sheet in Figure 8.4 was designed by three students who were reading the book *Flipped* (Van Draanen, 2003). These students selected from several different types of activities the ones they thought they'd like and that would be helpful. Not everyone likes to draw in response to reading, but these students did. Note, that the "unknown words" category was a good choice since Amanda has identified many words. Importantly, one of Amanda's partners in the group had identified only two words

Figure 8.4 Amanda's literature circle discussion sheet

(*majestic* and *humble*). On the other hand, she recorded four really nice "confusing/connecting" entries:

1. What, exactly, does "Flipped" mean?

2. A connection I made is that Juli climbs on a favorite tree and when I was really little I used to climb on a favorite tree.

3. I'm confused! How can it smell like sunshine and wild grass?

4. When Juli lost the tree, it reminded me of losing my Grandma and Grandpa.

When these students get together, their discussion will be enriched by one another's work, yet each was able to select (compact or slice) the aspects that seemed appropriate.

Question Shaping

Some tasks are more complex than others, requiring higher-order thinking and/or multiple steps to complete. Of course, there are elaborate ways to differentiate task complexity—by creating different projects and assignments for different students, for example. However, for reading I find the easiest way to differentiate is to adjust my questions. I simply vary the types of questions according to students' ability to comprehend. To do this well, I find that I have to plan ahead since it is not always easy to think of different types of questions on the spot. However, the payoff is great because all students participate and are challenged at an appropriate level.

Overall ability is not the only thing that distinguishes students, however. Some are inclined to do certain types of thinking—their natural talents lead them to consider the ideas in texts in different ways. Robert Sternberg (2002) describes three types of knowledge and skill that underlie intelligence, noting that only some of these are valued in traditional school settings:

Analytic learning and thinking involves the ability to analyze, evaluate, explain, and judge. This type of thinking is the most widely used in school.

Creative learning and thinking involves creating new things, inventing, exploring, and imagining.

Practical learning and thinking involves learning by putting ideas into practice; using and applying knowledge and/or implementing a plan.

Some students tend to be analytic thinkers, some creative, and some practical. Shaping your questions to take advantage of these differences can benefit the entire class by offering them opportunities to hear different points of view or different ways to think about content. On the other hand, everybody needs to be able to do each of these to some extent, and Sternberg remarks that "one of the most useful things a teacher can do is to help a student figure out how to make the most of what he or she does well and to find ways around what he or she does not do so well" (p. 385).

Activity Shaping

Good differentiated instruction takes into account the relative strengths that students have in their ways of thinking and provides options for them. Certainly, there are different methods or approaches that can be used for different preferences. (Some students may want to discuss and discover the meaning of a text, while others may want to analyze the text on their own). On the other hand, different students may need different types of support depending on the text or the task.

Type of Learning and Thinking	Differentiated Assignments Based on Learning Preferences
Analytic	• Write a summary or report. • Make a chart comparing and contrasting the two settings. • Engage in a debate with partner. • Analyze the themes in music that are similar to themes in your book.
Creative	• Write a short story in the style of the author we have been studying. • Imagine how this character would behave if he lived today. • Think of another way to solve this problem.
Practical	• Use the information from your reading to advertise the work we have been doing in class. • Create a plan for getting more people to participate in _____. Use the information in our chapter to help you.

Using Assessment Information to Inform Instruction

In the schools I work with, we examine assessment data—both formal and informal—for evidence of varying needs. In the last chapter, we looked at screening data from Janice MacIntosh's class. (See Figure 7.17.) To help her make sense of the assessment information, I asked her to complete the reproducible summarizing sheet on page 259. Janice noticed the following patterns:

- Many students in her class did better on the vocabulary than on the comprehension assessment.
- Girls and boys are doing about equally well (and poorly).
- She has more students at the high or the low end than she does in the middle.

Janice listed the following students as doing well and not well:

Who is performing well?		Who is not performing well?	
Aaron	Maura	Keira	Angela
Amelia	Trevor	Zlatko	Tyler
Bethany		*Sasha	Harley
		*Alex	Nicolai

She decided she would take a closer look at all the students who are struggling, but she was especially concerned about Alex and Sasha, who seem bright and capable but who, despite good vocabulary, are performing poorly on the comprehension portion of the test. Janice made four immediate instructional decisions on the data:

1. Start a whole-class focus on comprehension immediately.

2. Differentiate reading materials based on overall (or comprehension) ability.

3. Form a flexible group focused on vocabulary for:

Harley	Nathaniel
Tyler	Zlatko

4. Provide additional comprehension support for:

Keira	Angela
Nicholai	Sasha

Summarizing Assessment Information

What patterns do you observe?

1. _____

2. _____

3. _____

Who is performing well?	Who is not performing well?

The most common level(s) of performance in my class is:

_____

Students who need a CLOSER LOOK:

Student   Question

_____

_____

_____

_____

_____

_____

So, instructionally, I will:

Based on further assessment, she formed a fluency group for:

Alex	Tyler
Helena	Weston

In clustering students together by specific reading need, we often find that students of differing *overall* abilities nevertheless have similar specific needs. In the example in Figure 8.5, Alex and Tyler are reading at a lower level than Weston and Helena but they can all benefit from the same instruction in the specific area of fluency.

Instructional Planning Sheet

Needs:

Needs work in
reading fluency

Students:

Alex

Tyler

Helena

Weston

Instructional Strategies:

1. Repeated readings (see Talking Dictionary below)

2. Additional practice in easy books

3. Rapid-recognition practice for sight vocabulary

Figure 8.5

Although these flexible groups will help Janice's students, she knows that she must also provide differentiated materials. Her initial decisions have placed the following students together in groups for guided reading and/or literature discussion:

Challenge Readers	On-level	Struggling
Aaron	Helena	Keira
Maura	Weston	Angela
Amelia	Mark	Zlatko
Trevor	Alex	Tyler
Bethany	Nathaniel	Nicholai
	Rafer	Sasha
		Harley

The range in overall reading levels is so great that she needs to have books at different levels of difficulty. Later she can plan to support some students in more challenging material (notice that she has already placed Alex in the on-level group, even though his comprehension and fluency are weaker). For now, however, she wants to have choices that are appropriately difficult for her students. Perhaps the best way to provide multilevel materials but still keep an overall coherence in the classroom instructional program is through text sets.

Differentiating Methods

Relatively small alterations in content, materials, or tasks are often enough to address student needs in the classroom. However, sometimes we need to differentiate for particular student populations: students who need to be challenged, students who need extra support, and students who are culturally diverse. In such cases, we often need to add or change our approach in a more significant way by introducing:

- Different methods for different outcomes
- Different amounts and types of instruction for different students
- Culturally responsive methods, when appropriate

In Janice's classroom, there are probably seven students who would benefit from these alterations:

- Maura, Amelia, and Bethany require significantly more challenging texts and tasks than their peers.

- Tyler and Harley are struggling and need an intervention program in addition to classroom reading.

- Zlatko and Nicholai are both immigrants. Zlatko is from Bosnia, and his family speaks little English. Nicholai is from Poland; he has been in the U.S. much much longer, and arrived here under much better circumstances.

Students Who Need to Be Challenged

Let's start with the three really capable readers: Maura, Amelia, and Bethany. It is tempting to just "let them read." They are obviously doing well and are likely to be successful no matter what we do. However, students like these may not reach their potential if we do not push their thinking about and response to literature. A recent experience with another fifth-grade class illustrates that even very bright students can "let things slide."

Here, too, there was a trio of very capable girls who had been in the same literature group for several months—reading sophisticated books (most recently, *Bud Not Buddy*). Despite their excellent reading skills, two of the three are not really digging deeper for meaning. Helena and her good friend Hilary seemed content to "just read." Only Caroline was pushing for more. The day I was there, they were creating the categories for their own literature log. They had already decided that they would have a category to "find a favorite part." I thought that was too easy for them.

MARJORIE: Why don't you think of a category that fits *this* book—maybe finding a part that is realistic, that makes you think about the characters as real people.

HELENA, *sitting at the keyboard*: Oh, I like "favorite part."

CAROLINE: How about the most humorous part?

MARJORIE: Oh, that's good—there is some good humor in this book.

HILARY: We'll make it "favorite *or* humorous part."

CAROLINE: That doesn't really work. Anything could be your favorite part—it's your opinion. But, for humor, it has to be funny—you have to tell what the author does that makes it funny.

(*Helena ignores Caroline's remark and continues typing "favorite or humorous."*)

For students like these, it is not enough to put them in the "right text." Their instruction should help them improve their reading and thinking abilities, too. In this case, the teacher decided that she would need to do a bit of guided reading with these girls to stretch their thinking and create a more demanding environment. She also decided that they needed new models for their literature logs; although others in the room were not ready for them, these girls certainly were.

In Janice's room, Maura, Amelia, and Bethany need to be placed in challenging material, but they also need to be working on different outcomes: focusing on extended responses, being attentive to author's craft, and creating more sophisticated conversation during literature circles. This is important for the three girls, but it is also good for the whole class. Once they become more adept at these more mature discussion modes, they can be planted in other groups to raise the level of *their* discussions.

Students Who Need Extra Support

Tyler and Harley are a different matter. They need support during reading in Janice's room, as well as additional support from other personnel, such as the Title I reading teacher, the speech and language pathologist, or the special educator. These students need three things:

Different outcomes: Tyler and Harley have not acquired grade-appropriate knowledge and skill in reading. They need word-level work in phonics/decoding, but they also need vocabulary and comprehension development.

More instruction to begin to close the gap: Their program should include "double doses" of reading.

Culturally responsive instruction: Both boys are from high-poverty homes. Their families live in rural isolation and have limited educational backgrounds themselves. Both boys' interests lie in "doing"—they like snowmobiling, fishing, dirt biking, and working on their families' farms—and they're likely to be more engaged by books and assignments that deal with such topics.

In consultation, the special educator, the Title I reading teacher, and Janice decide on a plan of action for these two boys.

Classroom	Reading Teacher	Special Educator (With Para-educator)
Provide vocabulary and concept development through read-alouds.	Provide guided reading group three times a week in reading-level appropriate materials.	Provide pull-out support for word recognition and spelling.
Provide access to classroom literature text for discussion (listening station and partner reading).	Coordinate and support word-level work with special educator.	Para-educator: help provide access to grade-level literature in the classroom.
Provide flexible group work in fluency.		

In my experience, this type of coordinated approach is needed to create enough "power" to address the difficulties of students like Tyler and Harley. Students like these need the best efforts of all professional personnel.

The first thing we can do is place these students in multiple groups—one for literature discussion of grade-appropriate text, one for guided reading of ability-leveled text, and one to address word recognition directly. These students need experience with several types of text. The whole-group read-aloud will provide age-appropriate vocabulary exposure and can be used to help students think about cognitively complex ideas. It can be used for small-group discussions of literature and/or as the basis for comprehension mini-lessons. These can be applied in the leveled-text that students should be reading during guided reading. Finally, struggling readers need some controlled-vocabulary texts to practice the phonics/decoding they are learning.

Students Who Are Culturally Diverse

Some students require a different method or approach because there is a mismatch between the cultural communication patterns of home and school that undermines successful learning (Bowers & Flinders, 1990). Rebecca Novick provides an example:

> While many classrooms emphasize individual responsibility and achievement, competition, and teacher controlled learning, other cultural groups, such as Native Americans and Native Alaskans, may be unaccustomed to this style of learning, valuing group work that fosters shared responsibility, instead. A curriculum that emphasizes projects and joint inquiry can help children who share this cultural value feel comfortable in the school setting. (1996, p. 98)

This type of adjustment is called *culturally responsive teaching*. Geneva Gay (2000) defines culturally responsive teaching as using the cultural knowledge, prior experiences, and performance styles of diverse students to make learning more appropriate and effective for them; it teaches to and through the strengths of these students.

Many of the methods suggested by various scholars for responsive teaching are at the core of the instruction I have already been describing in this book. In the box on page 267, you will find a listing of the principles for culturally responsive teaching that have been summarized by the Knowledge Loom, an online resource from the Northeast and Islands Regional Educational Laboratory. The idea of creating teaching bridges between home and school cultures is a compelling one. Because so many of our struggling readers come from high-poverty, diverse communities and speak English as a second language, we absolutely must be attentive to the ways that we can differentiate using culturally responsive teaching. The Knowledge Loom also contains examples of how this looks in classroom practice.

These principles are obviously extremely important in highly diverse urban environments. However, I have already noted that even in Janice McIntosh's classroom, where all of the students are Caucasian, cultural differences have implications for Tyler and Harley as well as for Zlatko and Nicholai.

Tyler and Harley can benefit from a curriculum that communicates high expectations for their success and more actively engages them. They also need a teacher who recognizes and values their prior knowledge and experiences. While they do not have many of the experiences of middle-class urban and suburban

Flexible groups for extra
support or a focused need

children, they actually know a great deal. In my experience, these students may not be able to retell or summarize a literary story, but they are often excellent storytellers themselves. These can become the basis for writing and personal response and they can also help us decide what books to select.

For boys like these, I might choose Robert Newton Peck's Soup series:

Soup and Me	*Soup for President*
Soup's Drum	*Soup on Wheels*
Soup in the Saddle	*Soup on Fire*
Soup on Ice	*Soup's Hoop*

These stories take place in rural Vermont, and they feature two boys who find trouble wherever they go. They are funny, and the scenarios would be easy for Tyler and Harley to connect with. Even better, this is a series of books—once you've read one, you know the characters and also how the books "work." The first book can and should be read to students, but after that, they may be able to manage with less help.

Of course, these books won't work for all students. Students in different contexts with different concerns need other stories to pique their interest and convince them to read. For some this may be realistic fiction, for others it is science fiction. Many like informational texts, and, of course, silly, gross-out humour keeps many students reading (Captain Underpants thrives for a reason!).

Nicholai appears to be doing well in Janice's room, and little in the way of instruction needs to be done for him. His well-educated parents emigrated to

Principles of Culturally Responsive Teaching

Culturally responsive education recognizes, respects, and uses students' identities and backgrounds as meaningful sources (Nieto, 2000) for creating optimal learning environments.

1. **Communication of high expectations:** There are consistent messages, from both the teacher and the whole school, that students will succeed, based upon genuine respect for students and belief in their capabilities.

2. **Active teaching methods:** Instruction is designed to promote student engagement by requiring that students play an active role in crafting curriculum and developing learning activities.

3. **Teacher as facilitator:** Within an active teaching environment, the teacher's role is one of guide, mediator, and knowledgeable consultant, as well as instructor.

4. **Positive perspectives on parents and families of culturally and linguistically diverse students:** There is an ongoing dialogue with students, parents, and community members on issues important to them, and these individuals and issues are included in classroom curriculum and activities.

5. **Cultural sensitivity:** To maximize learning opportunities, teachers gain knowledge of the cultures represented in their classrooms and translate this knowledge into instructional practice.

6. **Reshaping the curriculum:** The curriculum is reshaped to be culturally responsive to the background of students.

7. **Culturally mediated instruction:** Instruction is characterized by the use of culturally mediated cognition, culturally appropriate social situations for learning, and culturally valued knowledge in curriculum content.

8. **Student-controlled classroom discourse:** Students are given the opportunity to control some portion of the lesson, providing teachers with insight into the ways that speech and negotiation are used in the home and community.

9. **Small-group instruction and academically related discourse:** Instruction is organized around low-pressure, student-controlled learning groups that can assist in the development of academic language.

the U.S. voluntarily, and they have conventional middle-class aspirations for him. Zlatko's Muslim family, on the other hand, fled Bosnia during a terrible civil war. Like many such immigrants, his family has struggled to adjust. The larger Bosnian community has significant mental health issues, and there is a fair amount of aggressive behavior on Zlatko's part. His parents are not comfortable coming into the school, and Zlatko serves as interpreter when they do. Yet in many ways, Zlatko is like any other boy his age—he's a soccer player, a budding musician, and a good friend.

Janice realizes that she needs to do more to develop Zltako's vocabulary and to get him more engaged in reading for comprehension. She locates a small handful of books on Bosnia and about the war:

> *Gleam and Glow* by Eve Bunting (2001)
>
> *Bosnia and Herzegovina* (Enchantment of the World, Second Series) by Joann Milivojevic (2004)
>
> *I Remember Bosnia* by Anita Ganeri (1995)

These she intends to use in a theme-based, mixed-ability discussion group because she realizes that some of her more capable readers may be interested in the topic. This will bring Zltako's experiences into the room. As Donna Ogle and Camille Blachowicz (2002) note, discussion groups work well with nonfiction texts also. In addition, Janice begins to look for ways to broaden Zlatko's reading and heighten the intensity of his instruction. Although there is no ELL teacher in this school, the speech and language pathologist agrees to see Zltako several times a week to work on more sophisticated vocabulary.

Into the Classroom

Bringing all of these elements into the classroom can be challenging. Remember to start with the core program—the program designed to be comprehensive and balanced. Then, you can begin to differentiate, using assessment information to determine which adaptations and modifications make the most sense. (See the reproducible on page 269.) Effective differentiating works better when there are some organizational patterns in place. Two that work well are flexible grouping and literacy centers.

Planning to Use Assessment Information

WHAT DO I KNOW ABOUT...?	HOW DO I KNOW IT?	WHAT WILL I DO ABOUT IT? More assessment? Different instruction? More support? More challenge?
Student's Knowledge and Skill in: Phonics/decoding		
Fluency		
Vocabulary		
Comprehension		
• Strategies		
• Text structure		
• Genre		
• Author's craft		
Student's Self-regulation and/or Metacognition		
Student's Stamina		
Student's Motivation		
Student's Instructional Program: • What works		
• What doesn't work		

Flexible Grouping

Flexible grouping was discussed in Chapter 2. However, it is in the context of differentiated instruction that flexible grouping makes the most sense. After the core program is up and running, we need to think about what types of small groups may be needed. In our project schools, we suggest teachers use a work sheet like the one on page 271 to plan for flexible groups.

Different configurations of groupings are used at different times during the year. These are formed, disbanded and reformed depending on your objectives and the students' progress. The key to flexible grouping is that the groups are formed for *specific purposes*. As a result, some students may be members of more than one group. I was recently visiting in Cathy Smith's fifth-grade classroom. During a portion of the day most of her students were meeting in literature groups. These groups were self-selected by the students based on a "book walk" they had taken before the unit began. Students were reading one of four texts:

Flipped by Wendelin Van Draanen (2003)
This group was meeting for a discussion using a discussion sheet they themselves had designed. The sheet asked students to list new and interesting vocabulary, to draw a response, and to raise questions.

The Watsons Go to Birmingham—1963 by Christopher Paul Curtis (1995)
This group had read about a quarter of the book and had now been asked to generate a literature discussion sheet to guide their work for the rest of the book.

A Taste of Blackberries by Doris Buchanan Smith (1973)
This group wasn't meeting for literature discussion that day since they needed more time to read, and the teacher wanted to guide their discussion. Instead, they worked on a guided fact find in an informational text.

The School Story by Andrew Clements (2001)
This group prepared for discussion with a graffiti board—students use markers to write or draw their thoughts, feelings, and responses to the previous night's reading.

These books are at different levels of difficulty, and Cathy's student teacher had differentiated the students' assignments as well, based on need and text.

The planning sheet on page 271 is used for all aspects of the reading program, especially for short-term instructional goals for different students. For example, one of these groups might involve an aspect of decoding and another may be focused on a comprehension strategy (summarizing is quite difficult for some students). Sometimes the flexible group meets before a whole-class reading event (perhaps a read-aloud or

Instructional Planning Sheet

NEEDS

NEEDS

NEEDS

STUDENTS:

STUDENTS:

STUDENTS:

INSTRUCTIONAL RESPONSE:

INSTRUCTIONAL RESPONSE:

INSTRUCTIONAL RESPONSE:

A flexible book group with student-selected reading materials

a social studies text). Then, this planner might identify students who need extra support for the vocabulary and concepts in that material.

Even a little bit of additional background knowledge, provided before reading, improves students' comprehension (Dole, Valencia, Greer, & Wardrop, 1991; McKeown, Beck, Sinatra, & Loxterman, 1992). Building background knowledge not only helps students answer questions better, it also helps them summarize. In my classroom and clinic work, I have found that if we anticipate which students are going to struggle, we can prepare them ahead of time by using a flexible group. Mary Ellen Vogt (1997) calls this "support in advance" or "jump-starting."

The jump start should focus on the specific text to be read and provide information or support about selection vocabulary and concepts. According to Vogt:

> This "support in advance" enables the students who struggle to fully participate in class discussions, writing, sharing, and reading. Instead of being excluded, they are now class members who have a chance to succeed. . . . Following the brief support in advance activity, the small group and the teacher rejoin the rest of the class for a discussion of what the students know about (e.g.) forest fires. Because the small group has received a "jump start," they are ready to participate fully with the rest of the class and can add their newly learned information to the discussion (p. 3).

Jump-start activities are designed to be quick and, if possible, active. They include a picture or text walk, structured preview, list-group-label activities, brief introductions of key vocabulary, listing predictions, and/or beginning a graphic organizer.

Any temporary type of support can benefit from flexible grouping. A group might meet for a day, a week, or for the duration of an entire unit. Once its purpose has been fulfilled, it is disbanded and new groups are formed.

Literacy Centers

Another way to differentiate is through literacy centers. They can provide a rich way to introduce variety and active engagement into the classroom.

I found centers invaluable in my own classroom—especially once I realized that it was better to have "big idea" centers than ones that housed specific tasks or worksheets that needed to be changed frequently. These are among the most useful types of centers:

Listening Center
- Listening to taped books and articles
- Creating tapes for other students to listen to

Word-Work Center
- Word sorts
- Word building
- Games
- Word-study journals

Writing Center
- Journal writing
- Process writing
- Poetry
- Reading interesting writing snippets

Reading Center
- Readers notebook
- Readers Theater scripts

"Wondrous Words" Center
- Personal dictionaries and thesaurus
- Word wall for interesting words
- Word challenge

Computer/Technology Center
- CD-ROM and/or DVD storybooks
- Literacy games
- Publishing-support software (e.g., Writing and Writers, Inspiration Software)
- Audiotape support
  - Chapter/selection summaries
  - Fluency recording

These stations are rotated around a teacher-led guided reading and/or literature circle.

Debbie Diller's helpful book *Practice with Purpose* places literacy workstations right at the heart of the instructional program. The title points to the way in which she uses literacy workstations to "reinforce and/or extend learning" in the classroom. "Materials are taught with and used for instruction first. Then they are placed in the work station for independent use" (2005, p. 5). This type of organization can be helpful for differentiation because students can be "assigned" to different stations and for different amounts of time. Thus, for example, a student with poor vocabulary would be assigned daily to the word-study station, while another child may not go there at all.

Adjusting instructional support is most effective when we think it through carefully. Here are some questions I ask:

- What can this child do independently?

- How much support must this student have to be successful with this assignment/text?

- Will I provide (or arrange for) this support before, during, or after the assignment?

- If I provide this support, how will I reduce it over time?

This last point is especially important because we do not want to lose sight of the primary reason for differentiating—as a way to help all students achieve very high levels of reading ability and motivation.

Literacy Center Goals

1. Provide a variety of activities to address diverse abilities and interests.

2. Allow students to make their own choices.

3. Encourage student independence.

4. Create a manageable classroom.

Concluding Thoughts

I started teaching because I wanted to make a difference for all students. My first teaching job sorely tested that commitment but it also taught me what rewards accompany the attempt. Contemporary concepts of differentiation represent a positive development in our ongoing efforts to meet the needs of all students in diverse classrooms. A problem-solving attitude, a tolerance for ambiguity, and a sense of humor are especially helpful in this work. As Michael Fullan (1997) has noted,

> Productive educational change roams somewhere between over-control and chaos. . . . You cannot mandate what matters, because what really matters for complex goals of change are skills, creative thinking, and committed action. (pp. 33–35)

I hope that you have found in this book something to help you in your own classroom.

Discussion and Reflection

- Identify a type of text or task that seems especially difficult for some of your students. Why do you think it poses such a challenge? How could you improve their performance?

- Think about the students in your own classroom. Use the reproducible charts on pages 269 and 271 to summarize the information you have about them.

- How does differentiation differ from individualizing?

- Identify 2 or 3 aspects of your reading program that you could differentiate. Think of both "easy-to-do" adjustments and more major ones.

Digging Deeper

If you are interested in reading more about differentiating instruction, check out:

- *The Differentiated Classroom* by Carol Ann Tomlinson. Alexandria, VA: Association for Supervision and Curriculum Development, 1999.

- *How to Differentiate Instruction in Mixed-Ability Classrooms* by Carol Ann Tomlinson. Alexandria, VA: Association for Supervision and Curriculum Development, 2001.

- *What Really Matters for Struggling Readers: Designing Research-Based Programs* by Richard Allington. Boston: Allyn & Bacon, 2000.

Professional References Cited

Adams, M. (1990). *Beginning to read: Thinking and learning about print.* Cambridge, MA: MIT Press.

Addison, P. A., & Hutcheson, V. K. (2001). The importance of prior knowledge to new learning. In A. Herrmann & M. M. Kulski (Eds.), *Expanding horizons in teaching and learning.* Proceedings of the 10th Annual Teaching and Learning Forum, 7/9 February 2001. Perth: Curtin University of Technology. Retrieved April 9, 2006, from http://Isn.curtin.edu.au/tif/tlf2001/addison.html

Adler, M., & Rougle, E. (2005). *Building literacy through classroom discussion.* NY: Scholastic.

Alexander, P. A. (Ed.). (1996). The role of knowledge in learning and instruction [Special issue]. *Educational Psychologist, 31*(2), 89–92.

Alexander, P. A., & Jetton, T. L. (2000). Learning from text: A multidimensional and developmental perspective. In M. L. Kamil, P. B. Mosenthal, P. D. Pearson, & R. Barr (Eds.), *Handbook of reading research* (Vol. 3, pp. 285–310). Mahwah, NJ: Erlbaum.

Allington, R. L., Johnston, P. H., & Day, J. P. (2002). Exemplary fourth-grade teachers. *Language Arts, 79,* 462–466.

Almasi, J. F. (1994). The effects of peer-led and teacher-led discussions of literature on fourth graders' sociocognitive conflicts. In C.K. Kinzer & D.J. Leu, Jr. (Eds.), *Multidimensional aspects of literacy research, theory, and practice: Forty-third yearbook of the National Reading Conference* (pp. 40–59). Chicago: National Reading Conference.

Almasi, J. F. (1995). The nature of fourth graders' sociocognitive conflicts in peer-led and teacher-led discussion of literature. *Reading Research Quarterly, 30,* 314–351.

Alvermann, D. E. (December, 2003). *Literacy research on student learning: What counts and who's counting.* Keynote address at the annual meeting of the American Reading Forum, Sanibel Island, FL.

Alvermann, D. E., Dillon, D. R., & O'Brien, D. G. (Eds.). (1987). *Using discussion to promote reading comprehension.* Newark, DE: International Reading Association.

Anderson, R. C., Hiebert, E. H., Scott, J. A., & Wilkinson, I. (1985). *Becoming a nation of readers.* Washington, DC: U.S. Department of Education.

Anderson, R. C., Wilson, P. T., & Fielding, L. G. (1988). Growth in reading and how children spend their time outside school. *Reading Research Quarterly, 23,* 285–303.

Armbruster, B. B. (1984). The problems of inconsiderate text. In G. G. Duffy, L. R. Roehler, & J. Mason, (Eds.). *Comprehension Instruction* (pp. 202–217). NY: Longman.

Armbruster, B. B, Anderson, T. H., & Ostertag, J. (1989). Teaching text structure to improve reading and writing. *The Reading Teacher, 43,* 130–137.

Armbruster, B. B., Lehr, F., & Osborn, J. (2001). *Put reading first.* Ann Arbor, MI: CIERA.

Au, K. H. (2003). Literacy research and students of diverse backgrounds: What does it take to improve achievement? In C. M. Fairbanks, J. Worthy, B. Maloch, J. V. Hoffman, & D. L. Shallert (Eds.), *Fifty-second yearbook of the National Reading Conference* (pp. 85–91). Oak Creek, WI: National Reading Conference.

Au, K. H., Hirata, S.Y., & Raphael, T.E. (December, 2004). Improving achievement through standards. Paper presented at the annual meeting of the National Reading Conference, San Antonio, Texas.

Baker, L. (2002). Metacognition in comprehension instruction. In C. C. Block & M. Pressley (Eds.), *Comprehension instruction: Research-based best practices* (pp. 77–95). NY: Guilford Press.

Baker, S., Gersten, R., & Scanlon, D. (2002). Procedural facilitators and cognitive strategies: Tools for unraveling the mysteries of comprehension and the writing process, and for providing meaningful access to the general curriculum. *Learning Disabilities Research and Practice, 17,* 65–77.

Barker, T. A., Torgesen, J. K., & Wagner, R. K. (1992). The role of orthographic processing skills on five different reading tasks. *Reading Research Quarterly, 27,* 334-345.

Bear, D. R., Invernizzi, M., Templeton, S., & Johnston, F. (2003). *Words their way: Word study for phonics, vocabulary, and spelling instruction* (3rd ed.). Upper Saddle River, NJ: Prentice-Hall.

Beaver, J., & Carter, M. (2004*).* *Developmental reading assessment, 4–8.* NY: Pearson (Celebration Press).

Beck, I. L., McKeown, M. G., Hamilton, R. L., & Kucan, L. (1997). *Questioning the author.* Newark, DE: International Reading Association.

Beck, I. L., McKeown, M., & Kucan, L. (2002). *Bringing words to life.* NY: Guilford Press.

Beck, I. L., Perfetti, C. A., & McKeown, M. G. (1982). Effects of long-term vocabulary instruction on lexical access and reading comprehension. *Journal of Educational Psychology, 74,* 506–521.

Biemiller, A. (2003). Oral comprehension sets the ceiling on reading comprehension. *American Educator, 27*(1), 23.

Biemiller, A. (2005, November). *Vocabulary issues in measurement and effects across ages.* In *Vocabulary and reading: crucial issues for measurement and instruction.* Symposium conducted at the meeting of the International Dyslexia Association, Denver, Colorado. Retrieved April 13, 2006, from http://www.interdys.org/56handouts/t29.doc.

Biggam, S. C., & Thompson, E. A. (2005). The "QT" quick text-level check-in: A practical tool for classroom-based reading assessment in the intermediate grades. *New England Reading Association Journal, 41*(1), 35–39.

Blachowicz, C. L. Z., & Fisher, P. (2000). Vocabulary instruction. In M. L. Kamil, P. B. Mosenthal, P. D. Pearson, & R. Barr (Eds.), *Handbook of reading research* (Vol. 3, pp. 503–523). Mahwah, NJ: Erlbaum.

Block, C., & Pressley, M. (Eds.). (2001). *Comprehension instruction: Research-based best practices.* NY: Guilford Press.

Bloodgood, J., & Pacifici, L. (2004). Bringing word study to intermediate classrooms. *The Reading Teacher, 58,* 250–263

Boekaerts, M. (1999). Motivated learning: The study of student * situation transactional units. *European Journal of Psychology of Education,* 14, 41–55.

Bowers, C. A., & Flinders, D. (1990). *An ecological approach to classroom patterns of language, thought, and culture.* New York: Teachers College Press

Brand, M. (2004). *Word savvy.* Portland, ME: Stenhouse.

Bransford, J., Brown, A., & Cocking, R. (Eds.). (2000). *How people learn:*

Brain, mind, experience, and school. Washington, DC.: National Academy Press.

Brookover, W., & Lezotte, L. (1979). *Changes in school characteristics coincident with changes in student achievement.* East Lansing, MI: The Institute for Research on Teaching.

Brophy, J. (Ed.). (1998). *Teachers' and students' expectations. Advances in research on teaching* (Vol. 7). St. Louis, MO: Elsevier.

Brophy, J., & Good, T. L. (1970). Teachers' communication of differential expectations for children's classroom performance: Some behavioral data. *Journal of Educational Psychology, 61,* 365–374.

Brown, J. S., Collins, A., & Duguid, P. (1989). Situated cognition and the culture of learning. *Educational Researcher, 18*(1), 32–42.

Brown, J. S., Collins, A. & Duguid, P. (1989). Situated cognition and the culture of learning. *Educational Researcher, 18,* 32-42.

Bryk, A. S., Nagaoka, J. K., & Newmann, F. M. (January, 2001). *Authentic intellectual work and standardized tests: Conflict or coexistence?* Chicago: Consortium on Chicago School Research.

Buehl, D. (2001). *Classroom strategies for interactive learning.* Newark, DE: International Reading Association.

Caldwell, J. S. (2002). *Reading assessment.* NY: Guilford Press.

Cazden, C. B. (1988). *Classroom discourse: The language of teaching and learning.* Portsmouth, NH: Heinemann.

Chall, J. S., & Jacobs, V. A. (2003). The classic study on poor children's fourth-grade slump. *American Educator, 27*(1), 14–15, 44.

Clinton, P. (2002, September–October). Literacy in America: The crisis you don't know about, and what we can do about it. *Book, 24,* 4–9.

Collins, K. (2004). *Growing readers.* Portland, ME: Stenhouse.

Corden, R. (1998). Talking into literacy. *Reading, 32*(3), 27–31.

Corno, L., & Mandinach, E. B. (1983). The role of cognitive engagement in classroom learning and motivation. *Educational Psychologist, 18,* 88–108.

Cotton, K. (1989). *Classroom questioning* (School Improvement Reading Series). Retrieved August 2003, from the Northwest Regional Educational Laboratory Web site: http://www.nwrel.org/scpd/sirs/3/cu5.html.

Cunningham. P. M., (1975–76). Investigating a synthesized theory of mediated word identification. *Reading Research Quarterly, 11,* 127–143.

Cunningham. P. M., (1979). A compare-contrast theory of mediated word identification. *The Reading Teacher, 32,* 774–778.

Cunningham. P. M. (2000). *Phonics they use* (3rd ed.). NY: Longman.

Cunningham. P. M., & Allington, R. L. (2007). *Classrooms that work* (4th ed.). NY: Pearson.

Cunningham. P. M., Hall, D., & Cunningham, J. (2000). *Guided reading the 4-blocks way.* Greensboro, NC: Carson-Dellosa.

Dale, E., & Chall, J. (1948). A formula for predicting readability. *Educational Research Bulletin, 27,* 11–20, 37–54.

Dewey, J. (1938). *Experience and education.* NY: Macmillan.

Dickson, S. V., Simmons, D. C., & Kameenui, E. J. (1995a). *Text organization and its relation to reading comprehension: A synthesis of the research* (Tech. Rep. No. 17). Eugene, OR: National Center to Improve the Tools of Educators.

Dickson, S. V., Simmons, D. C., & Kameenui, E. J. (1995b). *Text organization: Curricular and instructional implications for diverse learners* (Tech. Rep. No. 19). Eugene, OR: National Center to Improve the Tools of Educators.

Diller, D. (2005). *Practice with purpose: Literacy workstations for grades 3–6.* Portland, ME: Stenhouse.

Dole, J. A., Duffy, G. G., Roehler, L. R., & Pearson, P. D. (1991). Moving from the old to the new: Research on reading comprehension instruction. *Review of Educational Research, 61,* 239–264.

Dole, J. A., Valencia, S. W., Greer, E. A., & Wardrop, J.L. (1991). Effects of two types of prereading instruction on the comprehension of narrative and expository text. *Reading Research Quarterly, 26,* 142–159.

Dowhower, S. L. (1987). Effects of repeated reading on second-grade transitional readers' fluency and comprehension. *Reading Research Quarterly, 22,* 389–406.

Dreher, M. J (2003). Motivating struggling readers by tapping the potential of information books. *Reading and Writing Quarterly, 19,* 25–38.

Dubin, L. (2003). *Discussion and how it supports the acquisition of literacy skills.* Retrieved January 23, 2006, from Bridgewater State College Web site: http://www.bridgew.edu/Library/CAGS_Projects/LDUBIN/review%20of%20the%20literature.htm

Duffy, G. (1993). Teachers' progress toward becoming expert strategy teachers. *Elementary School Journal, 94,* 109–120.

Duffy, G. G., Roehler, L. R., Meloth, M. S., Vavrus, L. G., Book, C., Putnam, J., et al. (1986). The relationship between explicit verbal explanations during reading skill instruction and student awareness and achievement: A study of reading teacher effects. *Reading Research Quarterly, 21,* 237–252.

Duffy, G. G., Roehler, L. R., Sivan, E., Racklifee, G., Book, C., Meloth, M., et al. (1987). Effects of explaining the reasoning associated with using reading strategies. *Reading Research Quarterly, 23,* 347–368.

Duke, N. K. (2000a). 3.6 minutes per day: The scarcity of informational texts in first grade. *Reading Research Quarterly, 35,* 202–224.

Duke, N. K. (2000b). For the rich it's richer: Print experiences and environments offered to children in very low- and very high-SES first-grade classrooms. *American Educational Research Journal, 37,* 441-478.

Duke, N. K., & Bennett-Armistead, V. S. (2003). *Reading and writing informational text in the primary grades: Research-based practices.* NY: Scholastic.

Duncan, D., & Lockhart, L. (2000). *I-search, you search, we all learn to research.* NY: Neal-Schuman.

Dunn, L. M., & Dunn, D. M. (2007). *Peabody picture vocabulary test* (4th ed.) (PPVT-4). NY: Pearson.

Dweck, C. S. (1975). The role of expectations and attributions in the alleviation of learned helplessness. *Journal of Personality and Social Psychology, 31,* 674–685.

Edmonds, R. R. (1979). Effective schools for the urban poor. *Educational Leadership, 37*(1), 15–23.

Ehrlich, I. (2005). *Instant vocabulary.* NY: Simon & Schuster.

Elbaum, B. E., Schumm, J. S., & Vaughn, S. (1997). Urban middle-elementary students' perceptions of grouping formats for reading instruction. *Elementary School Journal, 97,* 475–500.

Elbaum, B. E., Vaughn, S., Hughes, M. T., Moody, S. W., & Schumm, J. S. (2000). A meta-analytic review of the effect of instructional grouping format on the reading outcomes of students with disabilities. In R. Gersten, E. Schiller, J. S. Schumm, & S. Vaughn (Eds.), *Issues and research in special education* (pp.105–135). Mahwah, NJ: Erlbaum.

Englert, C. S.& Mariage, T. V. (1991). Making students partners in the comprehension process: Organizing for reading "posse." *Learning Disability Quarterly, 14*, 123–138.

Fall, R., Webb, N. M., & Chudowsky, N. (2000). Group discussion and large scale language arts assessment: Effects on students' comprehension. *American Educational Research Journal, 37*, 911–941.

Fielding, L. G., & Pearson, P. D. (1994). Reading comprehension: What works. *Educational Leadership, 51*, 62–68

Forgione, P. D. (1998). *Hanging on: Are our children ready to learn?* Washington, DC: National Center for Education Statistics. Retrieved November 18, 2006 from http://nces.ed.gov/Pressrelease/senhrtest.asp

Fountas, I. C., & Pinnell, G. S. (1996). *Guided reading: Good first teaching for all children.* Portsmouth, NH: Heinemann.

Fountas, I. C., & Pinnell, G. S. (2000). *Guiding readers and writers, grades 3-6.* Portsmouth, NH: Heinemann.

Fountas, I. C., & Pinnell, G. S. (2001). *Leveled books for readers, grades 3-6.* Portsmouth, NH: Heinemann.

Fowler, G. (1982). Developing comprehension skills in primary students through the use of story frames. *The Reading Teacher, 36*, 176–184.

Fry, E. (1968). A readability formula that saves time. *Journal of Reading, 11*, 513–516, 578.

Fuentes v. Shevin, 407 U. S. 67 (Supreme Court, 1972). Cited by Lipson, M. H., & Katz, R. S. (1988) *Materials on the process of federal civil litigation.* NY: Matthew Bender, p. 89.

Fullan, M. (1997). The complexity of the change process. In M. Fullan (Ed.), *The challenge of school change* (pp. 33–56). Arlington Heights, IL: Skylight.

Fullan, M. (April, 2000). The three stories of education reform. *Phi Delta Kappan, 81*, 581–584.

Gambrell, L. B. (1996). Creating classroom cultures that foster reading motivation. *The Reading Teacher, 50*, 14–25.

Gambrell, L. B., & Almasi, J. F. (1993). Fostering comprehension through discussion. In L. M. Morrow, J. K. Smith, & L. C. Wilkinson (Eds.), *Integrated language arts: Controversy to consensus* (pp. 71–90). Boston: Allyn & Bacon.

Ganske, K. (2000). *Word journeys.* NY: Guilford Press.

Gaskins, I. W., (2000). *Benchmark's Word Detectives Intermediate Program, Program A.* Media, PA: Benchmark.

Gaskins, I. W., (2002). *Benchmark's Word Detectives Intermediate Program, Program B.* Media, PA: Benchmark.

Gaskins, R. W., Gaskins, J. C., Gaskins, I. W. (1992). Using what you know to figure out what you don't know: An analogy approach to decoding. *Reading and Writing Quarterly, 8*, 197–221.

Gay, G. (2000). *Culturally responsive teaching: Theory, research, and practice.* NY: Teachers College Press.

Gillett, J., & Kita, M. J. (1979). Words, kids, and categories! *The Reading Teacher, 32*, 538–542.

Goldenberg, C. (1993). Instructional conversations: Promoting comprehension through discussion. *The Reading Teacher, 46*, 316–326.

Goldman, S. R., & Rakestraw, J. A. (2000). Structural aspects of constructing meaning from text. In M. L. Kamil, P. B. Mosenthal, P. D. Pearson, & R. Barr (Eds.), *Handbook of reading research* (Vol. 3, pp. 311–335). Mahwah, NJ: Erlbaum.

Gore, J. (2002). Student achievement and teacher expectations. New South Wales, Australia: Department of Education and Training. Retrieved January 9, 2006, from http://www.curriculumsupport.education.nsw.gov.au/primary/hsie/assets/pdf/csarticles/studachiev.pdf

Graham, S., Harris, K. R., & Loynachan, C. (1993). The basic spelling vocabulary. *Journal of Educational Research, 86*, 363–368.

Graham, S., Harris, K. R., & Loynachan, C. (1994). The spelling for writing list. *Journal of Learning Disabilities, 27*, 210–214.

Guthrie, J. T. (2001, March). Contexts for engagement and motivation in reading. *Reading Online, 4*(8). Retrieved February 15, 2006, from http://www.readingonline.org/articles/art_index.asp?HREF=/articles/handbook/guthrie/index.html

Guthrie, J. T., & Anderson, E. (1998). Engagement in reading: Processes of motivational, strategic, knowledgeable, social readers. In J. T. Guthrie & D. A. Alvermann (Eds.), *Engaged reading: Processes, practices and policy implications* (pp. 17–45). NY: Teachers College Press.

Guthrie, J., & Wigfield, A. (2000). Engagement and motivation in reading. In M. Kamil, P. Mosenthal, & R. Barr (Eds.), *Handbook of reading research* (Vol. 3, pp. 403–422). NY: Longman.

Guthrie, J. T., Wigfield, A., & Perencevich, K. C. (Eds.). (2004). *Motivating reading comprehension: Concept-oriented reading instruction.* Mahwah, NJ: Erlbaum.

Hall, T. (2002). *Differentiated instruction.* Wakefield, MA: National Center on Accessing the General Curriculum. Retrieved June 11, 2005, from http://www.cast.org/publications/ncac/ncac_diffinstruc.html.

Hansen, J. (1981). The effects of inference training and practice on young children's reading comprehension. *Reading Research Quarterly, 16*, 391–417.

Harris, T. L., and Hodges, R. E. (1995). *The literacy dictionary: The vocabulary of reading and writing.* Newark, DE: International Reading Association.

Hartman, H. (1994). From reciprocal teaching to reciprocal education, *Journal of Developmental Education, 18*(1), 2–4, 6, 8, 29.

Harvey, S., & Goudvis, A. (2000). *Strategies that work.* Portland, ME: Stenhouse.

Hasbrouck, J. E., & Tindal, G. (1992, Spring). Curriculum-based oral reading fluency norms for students in grades 2 through 5. *Teaching Exceptional Children, 24*, 41–44.

Hasbrouck, J. E., & Tindal, G. (2005). *Oral reading fluency: 90 years of measurement* (Tech. Rep. No. 33). Eugene, OR: University of Oregon, College of Education, Behavioral Research and Teaching.

Haycock, K. (1998). Good teaching matters a lot. *Thinking K–16, 3*, 1–14.

Haycock, K. (2001). Closing the achievement gap. *Educational Leadership, 58*(6), 6–11.

Herrell, A. L., & Jordan, M. (2006). *50 strategies for improving vocabulary, comprehension, and fluency.* NY: Pearson.

Hiebert, E. H. (1983). An examination of ability grouping for reading instruction. *Reading Research Quarterly, 18*, 231–255.

Hirsch, E. D. (2003). Reading comprehension requires knowledge—of words and the world: Scientific insights into the fourth-grade slump and the nation's stagnant comprehension scores. *American Educator, 27*(1), 11–29.

Howard, J. (1995). You can't get there from here: The need for a new logic in education reform. *Daedalus, 124*(4), 85–92.

Huitt, W. (2004). Bloom et al.'s taxonomy of the cognitive domain. *Educational Psychology Interactive*. Valdosta, GA: Valdosta State University. Retrieved August 9, 2005, from http://chiron.valdosta.edu/whuitt/col/cogsys/bloom.html

Israel, S. E., Block, C. C., Bauserman, K. L., & Kinnucan-Welsch, K. (Eds). (2005). *Metacognition in literacy learning: Theory, assessment, instruction, and professional development.* Mahwah, NJ: Erlbaum.

Ivey, G., & Fisher, D. (2006). *Creating literacy-rich schools for adolescents.* Washington, DC: Association for Supervision and Curriculum Development.

Jacobs, H. H. (1997). *Mapping the big picture: Integrating curriculum and assessment.* Alexandria, VA: Association for Supervision and Curriculum Development.

Jacobs, J. S., Morrison, T. G., & Swinyard, W. R. (2000). Reading aloud to students: A national probability study of classroom reading practices of elementary school teachers. *Reading Psychology, 21,* 171–193.

Jitendra, A. K., Edwards, L. L., Sacks, G., & Jacobson, L. A. (2004). What research says about vocabulary instruction for students with learning disabilities. *Exceptional Children, 70,* 299–322.

Johnson, D. (2001). *Vocabulary in the elementary and middle school.* Boston, MA: Allyn & Bacon.

Juel, C. (1988). Learning to read and write: A longitudinal study of fifty-four children from first through fourth grade. *Journal of Educational Psychology, 80,* 437–447.

Kamil, M. L., Mosenthal, P. B., Pearson, P. D., & Barr, R. (Eds.). (2000). *Handbook of reading research* (Vol. 3). Mahwah, NJ: Erlbaum.

Kaufman, D. (2001). Organizing and managing the language arts workshop: A matter of motion. *Language Arts, 79,* 114–123.

Keene, E. O., & Zimmerman, S. (1997). *Mosaic of thought.* Portsmouth, NH: Heinemann.

Kershaw, S. (August, 2005). The relationship between oral comprehension and reading fluency as it relates to reading comprehension. *Florida State University D-Scholarship Repository, Article #133.* Retrieved September 10, 2006, from http://fdscholarship.lib.fsu.edu/undergrad/133.

Klare, G. (1984). Readability. In P. D. Pearson (Ed.), *Handbook of reading research* (Vol. 1, pp. 681–744). NY: Longman.

Knapp, M. S. (1995). *Teaching for meaning in high-poverty classrooms.* NY: Teachers College Press.

Koskinen, P. S., & Blum, I. H. (1986). Paired repeated reading: A classroom strategy for developing fluent reading. *The Reading Teacher, 40,* 70–75.

Koslin, B. L., Koslin, S., Zeno, S., & Ivens, S. (1989). *The degrees of reading power test: Primary and standard forms.* Brewster, NY: TASA DRP Services.

Kurtz, B. E., & Weinert, F. E. (1989). Metamemory, metaperformance, and causal attributions in gifted and average children. *Journal of Experimental Child Psychology, 48,* 45}61.

Langer, J. A. (1998). Beating the odds: Critical components boost student performance. *English Update, A newsletter from the Center on English Learning & Achievement.* SUNY, Albany: CELA.

Langer, J. A. (2001). Beating the odds: Teaching middle and high school students to read and write well. *American Education Research Journal, 38,* 837–880.

Langer. J. A. (2002). *Effective literacy instruction: Building successful reading and writing programs.* Urbana, IL: National Council of Teachers of English.

Langer J. A. (2004). *Getting to excellent: How to create better schools.* NY: Teachers College Press.

Leslie, L., & Caldwell, J. (2005). *Qualitative reading inventory—4.* Boston: Allyn & Bacon.

Lipson, M. H., & Katz, R. S. (1988). *Materials on the process of federal civil litigation.* NY: Matthew Bender.

Lipson, M. Y. (1982). Learning new information from text: The role of prior knowledge and reading ability. *Journal of Reading Behavior, 14*(3), 243–261.

Lipson, M. Y. (1983). The influence of religious affiliation on children's memory for text information. *Reading Research Quarterly, 18,* 448–457.

Lipson, M. Y. (1995). Conversations with children—and other classroom-based assessment strategies. In L. Putnam (Ed.), *How to become a better reading teacher: Strategies for diagnosis and remediation* (pp. 167–179). Columbus, OH: Merrill/Macmillan.

Lipson, M. Y. (2003). The challenge of comprehension instruction. *New England Reading Association Journal, 39*(2), 1–6.

Lipson, M. Y., & Cooper, J. D. (2002). *Understanding and supporting comprehension development in the elementary and middle grades.* Boston: Houghton Mifflin.

Lipson, M. Y., Mosenthal, J. H., & Mekkelsen, J. (1999). The nature of comprehension among grade 2 children: Variability in retelling as a function of development, text, and task. In T. Shanahan & F. V. Rodriguez-Brown (Eds.), *Forty-eighth yearbook of the National Reading Conference* (pp. 104–119). Chicago: National Reading Conference.

Lipson, M. Y., Mosenthal, J. H., Mekkelsen, J., & Russ, B. (2004). Building knowledge and fashioning success one school at a time. *The Reading Teacher, 57,* 534–542.

Lipson, M. Y., Valencia, S. W., Wixson, K. K., & Peters, C. (1993). Integration and thematic teaching—integration to improve teaching and learning. *Language Arts, 70,* 252–263.

Lipson, M. Y., & Wickizer, E. A. (1989). Promoting self-control and active reading through dialogues. *Teaching Exceptional Children, 21*(2), 28–32.

Lipson, M. Y., & Wixson, K. K. (2003). *Assessment and instruction of reading and writing difficulties: An interactive perspective.* Boston: Allyn & Bacon.

Lou, Y., Abrami, P. C., Spence, J. C., Poulsen, C., Chambers, B., & d'Appolonia, S. (1996). Within-class grouping: A meta-analysis. *Review of Educational Research, 66,* 423–458.

Lovett, M., & Steinbach, K. (1997). The effectiveness of remedial programs for reading disabled children of different ages: Does the benefit decrease for older children? *Learning Disability Quarterly, 20,* 189–210.

Lundberg, M. (1987). Metacognitive aspects of reading comprehension: Studying understanding in legal case analysis. *Reading Research Quarterly, 22,* 407–432.

Macrorie, K. (1988). *The I-Search Paper.* Portsmouth, NH: Heinemann.

McConaughy, S. H. (1982). Developmental changes in story comprehension and levels of questioning. *Language Arts, 59,* 580–589, 600.

McIntosh, R., Vaughn, S., Schumm, J., Haager, D., & Lee, O. (1993). Observations of students with learning disabilities in general education classrooms. *Exceptional Children, 60*, 249–261.

McKeown, M. G., Beck, I. L., Sinatra, G. M., & Loxterman, J. A. (1992). The contribution of prior knowledge and coherent text to comprehension. *Reading Research Quarterly, 27*, 79–93.

McNamara, D., Kintsch, E., Songer, N., & Kintsch, W. (1996). Are good texts always better? Interactions of text, coherence, background knowledge, and levels of understanding in learning from text. *Cognition and Instruction, 14*, 1–43.

Meara, P. (1997). Models of vocabulary acquisition. In N. Schmitt & M. McCarthy (Eds.), *Vocabulary: Description, acquisition and pedagogy* (pp. 109–121). Cambridge: Cambridge University Press.

Memory, D. M. (1992). Guiding students to independent decoding in content area classes. In E. K. Disner, R. W. Beam, J. E. Readence, & D. W. Moore (Eds.), *Reading in content areas* (3rd ed., pp. 210–218). Dubuque, IA: Kendall/Hunt.

Michigan Department of Education (1985/2005). Michigan definition of reading. Lansing, MI. Retrieved August 20, 2006, from http://www.michiganreading.org/MI%20DEFINITION%20OF%20READING0505.pdf

Mikulincer, M. (1994). *Human learned helplessness: A coping perception.* PB Plenum Press: New York.

Moats, L. C. (2004). *LETRS: Language essentials for teachers of reading and spelling.* Longmont, CO: Sopris West Educational Services.

Moll, L. (1992). Bilingual classroom studies and community analysis. *Educational Researcher, 21*(2), 20–24.

Moore, D. W. (1996). Contexts for literacy in secondary schools. In D. J. Leu, C. K. Kinzer, & K. A. Hinchman (Eds.), *Literacies for the 21st century: Research and practice: Forty-fifth yearbook of the National Reading Conference* (pp. 15–16). Chicago: National Reading Conference.

Mosenthal, J. H., Lipson, M. Y., Torncello, S., Russ, B., & Mekkelsen, J., (2004). Contexts and practices in six schools successful in obtaining reading achievement. *Elementary School Journal, 104*, 361–385.

Moss, B. (2005). Making a case and a place for effective content area literacy instruction in the elementary grades. *The Reading Teacher, 59*, 46–55.

Nagy, W. E. (1988). *Teaching vocabulary to improve reading comprehension.* Urbana, IL: ERIC Clearinghouse on Reading and Communication Skills and the National Council of Teachers of English.

Nagy, W. E., & Herman, P. (1987). Breadth and depth of vocabulary knowledge: Implications for acquisition and instruction. In M. G. McKeown & M. E. Curtis (Eds.), *The nature of vocabulary acquisition* (pp. 19–36). Hillsdale, NJ: Erlbaum.

Nagy, W. E., Herman, P. A., & Anderson, R. C. (1985). Learning words from context. *Reading Research Quarterly, 20*, 233–253.

Nagy, W. E., & Scott, J. A. (2000). Vocabulary processes. In M. L. Kamil, P. B. Mosenthal, P. D. Pearson, & R. Barr (Eds.), *Handbook of reading research* (Vol. 3, pp. 269–284). Mahwah, NJ: Erlbaum.

National Assessment of Educational Progress (NAEP). (2005a). *Fourth grade students reading aloud: NAEP 2002 special study of oral reading.* Retrieved January 15, 2006, from http://nces.ed.gov/nationsreportcard/pubs/studies/2006469.asp#Section3

National Assessment of Educational Progress (NAEP). (2005b). *The nation's report card.* Washington, DC: National Assessment of Educational Progress, National Center for Education Statistics, U.S. Department of Education.

Nation, I. S. P. (1990). *Teaching and learning vocabulary.* New York: Heinle and Heinle.

National Reading Panel (NRP). (2000). *Teaching children to read: Summary Report.* Washington, DC: U.S. Government Printing Office.

Newmann, F. M., & Associates (1996). *Authentic achievement: Restructuring schools for intellectual quality.* San Francisco: Jossey-Bass.

Newmann, F. M., Lopez, G., & Bryk, A. (1998, October). *The quality of intellectual work in Chicago schools: A baseline report.* Chicago: Consortium on Chicago School Research.

Nieto, S. (2000). *Affirming diversity: A sociopolitical context of multicultural education* (3rd ed.). White Plains, NY: Longman.

Novick, R. (1996). *Developmentally appropriate and culturally responsive education: Theory in practice* (ED397985). Portland, OR: Northwest Regional Educational Laboratory.

Oczkus, L. D. (2003). *Reciprocal teaching at work: Strategies for improving comprehension.* Newark, DE: International Reading Association.

Ogle, D., & Blachowicz, C. L. Z. (2002). Beyond literature circles: Helping students comprehend informational texts. In C. C. Block & M. Pressley (Eds.), *Comprehension instruction: Research-based best practice* (pp. 259–274). NY: Guilford Press.

Ohlhausen, M., & Jepsen, M. (1992). Lessons from Goldilocks: Somebody's been choosing my books but I can make my own choice now! *The New Advocate, 5*(1), 36.

Opitz, M. (1999). *Flexible grouping in reading.* NY: Scholastic.

Ozburn, M. S. (1995). A successful high school sustained silent reading program. *English in Texas, 26*(3), 4–5.

Palincsar, A. S. (1986). The role of dialogue in providing scaffolded instruction. *Educational Psychologist, 21*, 73–98.

Palinscar, A. S., & Brown, A. L. (1984). Reciprocal teaching of comprehension-fostering and comprehension-monitoring activities. *Cognition and Instruction, 1*, 117–175.

Palmer, L. F. (2004). *Acquisition of English orthography by ESL students and its relationship to their reading performance.* Unpublished doctoral dissertation. Appalachian State University, Boone, North Carolina.

Paratore, J., & Indrisano, L. (2003). Grouping for instruction in literacy. In J. Flood, D. Lapp, J. R. Squire, & J. M. Jensen (Eds.), *Handbook of research on teaching the English language arts* (2nd ed., pp. 566–572). Mahwah, NJ: Erlbaum.

Paris, S. G. (1985). Using classroom dialogues and guided practice to teach comprehension strategies. In E. Cooper & T. Harris (Eds.), *Reading, thinking, and concept development: Interactive strategies for the classroom* (pp. 133–146). New York: The College Board.

Paris, S. G., Cross, D. R., & Lipson, M. Y. (1984). Informed strategies for learning: A program to improve children's reading awareness and comprehension. *Journal of Educational Psychology, 76*, 1239–1252.

Paris, S. G., Lipson, M. Y., & Wixson, K. K. (1983). Becoming a strategic reader. *Contemporary Educational Psychology, 8*, 293–316.

Paris, S. G., & Paris, A. H. (2001). Classroom applications of research on self-regulated learning. *Educational Psychologist, 36*, 89–101.

Paris, S. G., Wasik, B. A., and Turner, J. C. (1991). The development of reading strategies. In J. Flood, J. M. Jensen, D. Lapp, & J. Squire (Eds.), *Handbook of research in the English language arts* (pp. 609–635). NY: Macmillan.

Paris, S. G., & Winograd, P. (1999). *The role of self-regulated learning in contextual teaching: Principles and practices for teacher preparation* (Tech. Rep. No. 01-03). Ann Arbor, MI: Center for the Improvement of Early Reading Achievement.

Parsons, L. (2001). *Response journals revisited.* Portland, ME: Stenhouse.

Pearson, P. D., & Gallagher, M. (1983). The instruction of reading comprehension. *Contemporary Educational Psychology, 8,* 317–344.

Peterson, C., Maier, S. F., & Seligman, M. E. P. (1993). *Learned helplessness.* Oxford University Press: Oxford England.

Pikulski, J. J, & Chard, D. J. (2005). Fluency: Bridge between decoding and reading comprehension. *The Reading Teacher, 58,* 510–519.

Pikulski, J. J., & Templeton, S. (2004). *Teaching and developing vocabulary: Key to long-term reading success.* Current Research in Reading/Language Arts. Boston: Houghton Mifflin.

Pilgreen, J. (2000). *The SSR handbook: How to organize and manage a sustained silent reading program.* Portsmouth, NH: Heinemann Boynton/Cook.

Pinell, G. S. (1991). Interactive assessment: Teachers and children as learners. In J. A. Roderick (Ed.), *Context-responsive approaches to assessing children's language* (pp. 79–96). Urbana, IL: National Conference on Research in English.

Pinell, G. S., Pikulski, J. J., Wixson, K. K., Campbell, J. R., Gough, P. B., & Beatty, A. S. (1995). *Listening to children read aloud: Data from NAEP's integrated reading performance record (IRPR) at Grade 4.* Washington, DC: Office of Educational Research and Improvement, U.S. Department of Education; Princeton, NJ: Educational Testing Service.

Puma, M. J., Karweit, N., Price, C., Ricciuiti, A., Thompson, W., & Vaden-Kiernan, M. (1997). *Prospects: Final report on student outcomes.* Washington, DC.: Department of Education, Planning and Evaluation Service.

RAND Reading Study Group (2002). *Reading for understanding* (Catherine Snow, Chair). Santa Monica, CA: RAND.

Raphael, T. E. (1982). Question-answering strategies for children. *The Reading Teacher, 36,* 186–190.

Raphael, T. E. (1986). Teaching question-answer-relationships, revisited. *The Reading Teacher, 39,* 516–522.

Raphael, T. E., & Au, K. H. (2005). QAR: Enhancing comprehension and test taking across grades and content areas. *The Reading Teacher, 59,* 206–221.

Raphael, T. E., Florio-Ruane, S., George, M., Hasty, N. L., & Highfield, K., (2004). *Book club plus! A literacy framework for the primary grades.* Lawrence, MA: Small Planet.

Raphael, T. E., Kehus, M., & Damphousse, K. (2001). *Book club for middle school.* Lawrence, MA: Small Planet.

Raphael, T. E., Pardo, L., Highfield, K., & McMahon, S. I. (2002). *Book club: A literature-based curriculum* (2nd ed.). Lawrence, MA: Small Planet.

Rasinski, T. V. (1990). Effects of repeated reading and listening-while-reading on fluency. *Journal of Educational Research,* 83, 147–150.

Rasinski, T. V. (2003). *The fluent reader.* NY: Scholastic.

Rasinski, T. V., & Padak, N. (2005). *3-minute Reading Assessments: Word recognition, fluency, & comprehension: Grades 5–8.* NY: Scholastic.

Resnick, L. (1987). *Education and learning to think.* Washington, DC: National Academy Press.

Reyes, P., Scribner, J. D., & Scribner, A. P. (1999). *Creating learning communities: Lessons from high-poverty high-performance schools.* NY: Teachers College Press.

Rief, L. (1992). *Seeking diversity: Language arts with adolescents.* Portsmouth, NH: Heinemann.

Rosenshine, B. (1971). *Teaching behaviors and student achievement.* Slough, England: National Federation for Educational Research.

Rosenshine, B. (1983). Teaching functions in instructional programs. *Elementary School Journal, 83,* 335–351.

Rosenshine, B., Meister, C., & Chapman, S. (1996). Teaching students to generate questions: A review of the intervention studies. *Review of Educational Research, 66,* 181–221.

Rosenthal, R., & Jacobson, L. (1968). *Pygmalion in the classroom: Teacher expectations and pupils' intellectual development.* NY: Holt, Rinehart and Winston.

Ryder, R. J., & Graves, M. F. (1980). Secondary students' internalization of letter-sound correspondence. *Journal of Educational Research, 73,* 172–178.

Sadowski, M. (1980). Ten years of uninterrupted sustained silent reading. *Reading Improvement, 17,* 153–156.

Sanders, W., & Rivers, J. C. (1996). *Cumulative and residual effects of teachers on future student academic achievement.* Knoxville, TN: University of Tennessee Value-added Research and Assessment Center.

Schlagal, R. (1982). A qualitative inventory of word knowledge: A developmental study of spelling, grades one through six. *Dissertation Abstracts International,* 47 (03), 915A. (UMI No. 86-il, 798)

Schlagal, B. (Forthcoming). Best practices in the teaching of spelling and handwriting. In S. Graham, C. MacArthur, & J. Fitzgerald (Eds.), *Best practices in writing.* NY: Guilford Press.

Schwartz, R. M. (1988). Learning to read vocabulary in content area textbooks. *Journal of Reading, 32,* 108–118.

Schwartz, R. M., & Raphael, T. E. (1985). Concept of definition: A key to improving students' vocabulary. *The Reading Teacher, 39,* 198–205.

Sewall, G. T. (2000). Lost in action. *American Educator, 24*(2), 4–9, 42.

Shefelbine, J. (1990). A syllabic-unit approach to teaching decoding of polysyllabic words to fourth and sixth-grade disabled readers. In J. Zutell, S. McCormick, M. Connolly, & P. O'Keefe (Eds.), *Literacy theory and research* (pp. 223–229). Chicago: National Reading Conference.

Shefelbine, J., & Newman, K. K. (2001). *SIPPS: Systematic instruction in phoneme awareness, phonics, and sight words.* Oakland, CA: Developmental Studies Center; NY: Scholastic.

Smith, J. K. (2000). *Wildland fire ecosystems: effects of fire on fauna* (Gen. Tech. Rep. RMRS-GTR-42-vol. 1). Ogden, UT: Department of Agriculture Forest Services.

Snow, C. E., Barnes, W. S., Chandler, J., Goodman, I. R., & Hemphill, L., (1991). *Unfulfilled expectations: Home and school influences on literacy.* Cambridge, MA: Harvard University Press.

Snow, C. E., & Biancarosa, G. (2003). *Adolescent literacy and the achievement gap: What do we know and where do we go from here?* NY: Carnegie Corporation of New York.

Snow, C. E., & Biancarosa, G. (2004). *Reading next: A vision for action and research in middle and high school literacy.* NY: Carnegie Corporation of New York.

Snow, C. E., Burns, M. S., & Griffin, P. (Eds.). (1998). *Preventing reading difficulties in young children.* Washington, DC.: National Academy Press.

Snow, C., Griffin, P., & Burns, M. S. (2005). *Knowledge to support the teaching of reading: Preparing teachers for a changing world.* San Francisco: Jossey-Bass.

Solomon, M., & Hendren, R. L. (2003). A critical look at brain-based education. *Middle Matters, 12*(1), 1–3.

Stanovich, K. E. (1992). Are we overselling literacy? In C. Temple & P. Collins (Eds.), *Stories and readers: New perspectives on literature in the elementary classroom* (pp. 209–232). Norwood, MA: Christopher Gordon.

Stein, N. L., & Glenn, C. G. (1979). An analysis of story comprehension in elementary school children. In R. O. Freedle (Ed.), *New directions in discourse processing.* Hillsdale, NJ: Erlbaum.

Sternberg, R. (2002). Raising the achievement of all students: Teaching for successful intelligence. *Educational Psychology Review, 14,* 383–393.

Strickland, D. Balanced literacy: Teaching the skills and thrills of reading. *Scholastic Instructor.* Retrieved January 22, 2006, from, http://teacher.scholastic.com/professional/teachstrat/balanced.htm#effective

Taylor, B. M., Frye, B. J., & Maruyama, G. M. (1990). Time spent reading and reading growth. *American Educational Research Journal, 27,* 351–362.

Taylor, B. M., Pearson, P. D., Clark, K., & Walpole, S. (2000). Effective schools and accomplished teachers: Lessons about primary-grade reading instruction in low-income schools. *Elementary School Journal, 101,* 121–165.

Taylor, B. M., Pearson, P. D., Peterson, D. S., & Rodriguez, M. C. (2003). Reading growth in high-poverty classrooms: The influence of teacher practices that encourage cognitive engagement in literacy learning. *Elementary School Journal, 104,* 3–28.

Templeton, S. (1991). Teaching and learning the English spelling system: Reconceptualizing method and purpose. *Elementary School Journal, 92,* 183–199.

Templeton, S., & Bear, D. R. (Eds.). (1992). *Development of orthographic knowledge and the foundations of literacy: A memorial festschrift for Edmund H. Henderson.* Hillsdale, NJ: Erlbaum.

Templeton, S., & Morris, D. (2000). Spelling. In M. L. Kamil, P. B. Mosenthal, P. D. Pearson, & R. Barr (Eds.), *Handbook of Reading Research* (Vol. 3, pp. 525–543). Mahwah, NJ: Erlbaum

Tomlinson, C. A. (2001). *How to differentiate in mixed-ability classrooms.* Alexandria, VA: Association for Supervision and Curriculum Development.

Torgesen, J. K. (2002). The prevention of reading difficulties. *Journal of School Psychology,* 40, 7–26.

Torgesen, J. K. (2004). *Struggling readers: What works for intermediate-level students.* Invited presentation to the Pennsylvania Summer Reading Conference, State College, PA. Retrieved August 22, 2005, from the Florida Center for Reading Research Web site: http://www.fcrr.org/science/pdf/torgesen/penn_special_ed.pdf

Valencia, S. W. (1990). Portfolio assessment: Separating the wheat from the chaff. *The Reading Teacher, 44,* 60–61.

Valencia, S. W., & Lipson, M. Y. (1998). Thematic instruction: A quest for challenging ideas and meaningful learning. In T. Raphael & K. Au (Eds.), *Literature-based instruction: Reshaping the curriculum.* Norwood, MA: Christopher Gordon.

Valencia, S. W., & Pearson, P. D. (1987). Reading assessment: Time for a change. *The Reading Teacher, 40,* 726–733.

Valeri-Gold, M. (1995). Uninterrupted sustained silent reading is an effective authentic method for college developmental learners. *Journal of Reading, 38,* 385–386.

Vaughn, S., Hughes, M. T., Moody, M. W., & Elbaum, B. (2001). Instructional grouping for reading for students with LD: Implications for practice. *Interventions in School and Clinic, 36,* 131–137.

Vaughn, S., Schumm, J. S., Niarhos, F. J., & Gordon, J. (1993). Students' perceptions of two hypothetical teachers' instructional adaptations for low achievers. *Elementary School Journal, 94,* 87–103.

Vermont Department of Education (2006). Education School Report. http://crs.uvm.edu/schlrpt/cfusion/schlrpt06/vermont.cfm

Villaume, S. K., & Brabham, E. G. (2002). Comprehension instruction: Beyond strategies. *The Reading Teacher, 55,* 672–675.

Villaume, S. K., & Hopkins, L. (1995). A transactional and sociocultural view of response in a fourth-grade literature discussion group. *Reading Research and Instruction, 34,* 190–203.

Villaume, S. K., Worden, T., Williams, S., Hopkins, L., & Rosenblatt, C. (1994). Five teachers in search of a discussion. *The Reading Teacher, 47,* 480–487.

Vogt, M. E. (1997). *Cross-curricular thematic instruction. Current research in reading/language arts.* Boston: Houghton Mifflin Reading.

Vygotsky, L. (1978). *Mind and society: The development of higher psychological process.* Cambridge, MA: Harvard University Press.

Walsh, K. (2003). Lost opportunity. *American Educator, 27*(1), 24–27.

Weber, G. (1971). *Inner-city children can be taught to read: Four successful schools.* Washington, DC: Council for Basic Education.

Weinstein, R. S. (2002). *Reaching higher: The power of expectations in schooling.* Cambridge, MA: Harvard University Press.

Wiggins, G., & McTighe, J. (1998). *Understanding by design.* Alexandria, VA: Association for Supervision and Curriculum Development.

Wilkinson, L. C., & E. R. Silliman (2000). Classroom language and literacy learning. In M. L. Kamil, P. B. Mosenthal, P. D. Pearson, & R. Barr (Eds.), *Handbook of reading research* (Vol. 3, pp. 337–360). Mahwah, NJ: Erlbaum.

Wixson, K. K. (1979). Miscue analysis: A critical review. *Journal of Reading Behavior, 11,* 163–175.

Wixson, K. K. (1983). Questions about a text: What you ask about is what children learn. *The Reading Teacher, 37,* 287–293.

Wixson, K. K. & Lipson, M.Y. (1985). Reading (dis)ability: An interactionist perspective. In T. E. Raphael & R. Reynolds (Eds.), *Contexts of school-based literacy.* (pp. 131-148). NY: Random House.

Wixson, K. K., Valencia, S., & Lipson, M. Y. (1994). Critical issues in literacy assessment: Confronting the realities of external and internal assessment. *Journal of Reading Behavior, 26,* 315–337.

Wolf, M. (Ed.). (2001). *Time, fluency, and dyslexia.* Timonium, MD: York Press.

Wolf, M., & Bowers, P. (1999). The "Double-Deficit Hypothesis" for the developmental dyslexias. *Journal of Educational Psychology, 91*(3), 1–24.

Wood, D. J., Bruner, J. S., & Ross, G. (1976). The role of tutoring in problem solving. *Journal of Child Psychology and Psychiatry, 17,* 89–99.

Wood, K. D., & Robinson, N. (1983). Vocabulary, language, and prediction: A prereading strategy. *The Reading Teacher, 36,* 392–395.

Zigmond, N., & Baker, J. (1990). Mainstream experiences for learning disabled students (Project MELD): Preliminary report. *Exceptional Children, 57,* 176–185.

Children's Books Cited

Adler, D. *Cam Jansen Adventure* (Series). NY: Puffin.
• *Cam Jansen and the Triceratops Pops Mystery* (1998)
• *Cam Jansen and the Ghostly Mystery* (1996)
• *Cam Jansen and the Chocolate Fudge Mystery* (1993)

Aliki. 1979/1987. *The Two of Them.* NY: Harper Trophy.

Bauer, M. D. 1994. *A Question of Trust.* NY: Scholastic.

Beatty, K. 2004. *Graham Hawkes: Underwater Pilot.* Boston: Houghton Mifflin.

Blume, J. 1971. *Freckle Juice.* NY: Dell Yearling.

Bunting, E. (2001). *Gleam and Glow.* Orlando, FL: Harcourt.

Byars, B. 1974. *After the Goat Man.* NY: Puffin.
• 1985. *The Golly Sisters Go West.* NY: HarperCollins.
• 1994. *The Golly Sisters Ride Again* NY: HarperCollins.
• 1968. *The Midnight Fox.* NY: Puffin.
• 1977. *The Pinballs.* NY: Harper Trophy.
• 1970. *The Summer of the Swans.* NY: Puffin.

Calvert, P. 1994. *Bigger.* NY: Aladdin Paperbacks/Simon & Schuster.

Cameron, A. 1981. *Stories Julian Tells.* NY: Dell Yearling.

Cheng, A. 2005. *Shanghai Messenger.* NY: Lee & Low.

Choldenko, G. 2004. *Al Capone Does My Shirts.* NY: Penguin.

Christopher, J. 1967. *The White Mountains.* NY: Aladdin.

Cleary, B. 1962. *Henry and the Clubhouse.* NY: Harper Collins.
• 1981. *Ramona Quimby, Age 8.* NY: Harper Trophy.

Clements, A. 1991. *Big Al.* NY: Simon & Schuster.
• 2002. *Big Al and Shrimpy.* NY: Simon & Schuster.
• 1997. *Double Trouble in Walla Walla.* Minneapolis, MN: Carolrhoda Books.
• 1996. *Frindle.* NY: Aladdin.
• Jake Drake (series of easy chapter books). NY: Aladdin.
• *Jake Drake, Class Clown (2002)*
• *Jake Drake, Know-It-All (2001)*
• *Jake Drake, Bully Buster (2001)*
• 2002. *The Jacket.* NY: Simon & Schuster.
• 2005. *Lunch Money.* NY: Simon & Schuster.
• 2001. *School Story.* NY: Aladdin.

Clinton, C. 2002. *Stone in My Hand.* Cambridge, MA: Candlewick Press.

Coles, R. 1995. *The Story of Ruby Bridges.* NY: Scholastic.

Cooper, M. L. 1995. *Bound for the Promised Land: The Great Black Migration.* NY: Dutton.
• 2004. *Dust to Eat: Drought and Depression in the 1930s.* NY: Clarion.
• 2002. *Remembering Manzanar: Life in a Japanese American Relocation Camp.* NY: Clarion.

Cottonwood, J. 1995. *Quake.* NY: Scholastic.

Creech, S. 2001. *A Fine, Fine School.* NY: HarperCollins.
• 2003. *Granny Torrelli Makes Soup.* NY: HarperCollins.
• 2000. *Fishing in the Air.* NY: HarperCollins.
• 2004. *Heartbeat.* NY: HarperCollins.
• 2001. *Love That Dog.* NY: HarperCollins.
• 1994. *Walk Two Moons.* NY: HarperCollins.
• 2005. *Who's That Baby.* NY: HarperCollins.

Curtis, C. P. 1999. *Bud, Not Buddy.* NY: Delacorte.
• 1995. *The Watsons Go to Birmingham—1963.* NY: Bantam.

Dahl, R. 1975. *Danny the Champion of the World.* NY: Puffin.
• 1970. *Fantastic Mr. Fox.* NY: Puffin.
• 1961. *James and the Giant Peach.* NY: Puffin.
• 1988/1998. *Matilda.* NY: Puffin.
• 1980. *The Twits.* NY: Puffin.

DiCamillo, D. 2000. *Because of Winn-Dixie.* Cambridge, MA: Candlewick Press.

Duffey, B. 1998. *Spotlight on Cody.* NY: Puffin.

DuPrau, J. 2003. *The City of Ember.* NY: Random House.

Everett, F., & Reid, S. 1991. *The Usborne Book of Explorers.* Tulsa, OK: EDC Publishing.

Fleischman. S. 2001. *Bo & Mzzz Mad.* NY: HarperCollins.
• 2003. *Disappearing Act.* NY: Greenwillow.
• 1999. *Here Comes McBroom* NY: Greenwillow.
• 1990. *The Midnight Horse.* NY: HarperCollins.
• 1987. *The Scarebird.* NY: Greenwillow.
• 1986. *The Whipping Boy.* NY: Greenwillow

Freedman, R. 1995. *Immigrant Kids.* NY: Puffin.

Fritz, J. 1973. *And Then What Happened, Paul Revere?* NY: Putnam.

Ganeri, A. 1995. *I Remember Bosnia.* Austin, TX: Steck-Vaughn.

Giff, P. R. 1997. *Lily's Crossing.* NY: Dell.
• 1999. *Kidnap at the Catfish Café.* NY: Puffin.
• 2000. *Nory Ryan's Song.* NY: Delacorte Press.
• 2002. *Pictures of Hollis Woods.* NY: Wendy Lamb/Random House.
• Polk Street Books series. NY: Yearling/ Random House:
• *The Beast in Ms. Rooney's Room* (1990)
• *B-E-S-T Friends* (1988)
• *The Candy Corn Contest* (2001)
• Polka Dot Private Eye series. NY: Bantam Doubleday Dell.
• *The Clue at the Zoo.* (1990)
• *Powder Puff Puzzle* (1987)
• *The Riddle of the Red Purse* (1987)

Golenbock, P. 1990. *Teammates.* Orlando, FL: Harcourt.
• 2001. *Hank Aaron: Brave in Every Way.* Orlando, FL: Harcourt.

Griffin, J. B. 1977. *Phoebe the Spy.* NY: Scholastic.

Grover, L. A. 2004. *On Pointe.* NY: Margaret McElderry Books.

Haas, J. 1998. *Keeping Barney.* NY: HarperTrophy.

Hamilton, V. 1993. *Many Thousand Gone.* NY: Random House.

Haskins, J. 1998. *African Beginnings.* NY: William Morrow.
• 1976. *The Story of Stevie Wonder.* NY: Lothrop.
• 1978. *Scott Joplin: The Man Who Made Ragtime.* NY: Doubleday.
• 1992. *Rosa Parks.* NY: Puffin.

Hesse, K. 1998. *Just Juice*. NY: Scholastic.
- 1993. *Letters from Rifka*. NY: Puffin.
- 1997. *Out of the Dust*. NY: Scholastic.
- 2000. *Stowaway*. NY: Margaret McElderry/Simon & Schuster.
- 2001. *Witness*. NY: Scholastic.

Hopkinson, D. 1993. *Sweet Clara and the Freedom Quilt*. NY: Alfred A. Knopf.

James, L. 1968. *Binky Brothers, Detectives* (An I Can Read Mystery). NY: Harper Row.
- 1970. *Binky Brothers, and the Fearless Four*. NY: Harper & Row.

Jiang, Ji-li. 1997. *Red Scarf Girl*. NY: HarperCollins.

Kadohata, C. 2004. *Kira-Kira*. NY: Atheneum.

Keller, L. 2003. *Arnie the Doughnut*. NY: Henry Holt.

Konigsburg, E. L. 1996. *The View From Saturday*. NY: Aladdin.
- 1967. *From the Mixed-Up Files of Mrs. Basil E. Frankweiler*. NY: Aladdin.

Kramer, S. 1997. *Eye of the Storm*. NY: Putnam.
- 1998. *The Dark Zone: Exploring the Secret World of Caves*. NY: McGraw Hill/Learning Triangle Press.
- 1992. *Tornado*. Minneapolis, MN: Carolrhoda Books.

Lauber, P. 1994. *The News About Dinosaurs*. NY: Aladdin.
- 1996. *Hurricanes: Earth's Mightiest Storms*. NY: Scholastic.
- 1986. *Volcano: Eruption and Healing of Mount St. Helens*. NY: Aladdin.
- 2003. *Who Came First? New Clues to Prehistoric Americans*. Washington, DC: National Geographic Children's Books.

Lawrence, J. 1968. *Binky Brothers, Detectives*. NY: Harper.
- 1970. *Binky Brothers and the Fearless Four*. NY: Harper.

Le Guin, U. 2004. *Gifts*. Orlando, FL: Harcourt.
- 1971. *The Lathe of Heaven*. NY: HarperCollins.
- 1969. *The Left Hand of Darkness*. NY: Berkley/Penguin.
- 2000. *The Telling*. Orlando, FL: Harcourt.
- The Earthsea series. NY: Bantam.
  - *The Farthest Shore* (1972)
  - *Tales from Earthsea* (2001)
  - *Tehanu* (1990)
  - *The Tombs of Atuan* (1971)
  - *A Wizard of Earthsea* (1968)

Levy, E. Invisible Inc. Hello Reader series. NY: Cartwheel Books/Scholastic.
- *Parents' Night Fright* (1998)

- *The Schoolyard Mystery* (1994)
- *The Snack Attack Mystery* (1995)
- *Creepy Computer Mystery* (1996)

Lowry, L. 1980. *Autumn Street*. NY: Bantam Doubleday Dell.
- 1979. *Anastasia Krupnik*. Bantam Doubleday Dell (and further books in the series).
- 2000. *Gathering Blue*. NY: Dell Laurel-Leaf.
- 1993. *The Giver*. NY: Houghton Mifflin.
- 2004. *Messenger*. NY: Houghton Mifflin.
- 1989. *Number the Stars*. NY: Bantam Doubleday Dell
- 1988. *All About Sam*. NY: Bantam Doubleday Dell.

Macaulay, D. 1982. *Castles*. NY: Houghton Mifflin.
- 1981. *Cathedral*. NY: Houghton Mifflin.
- 1988/2006. *The New Way Things Work*. NY: Houghton Mifflin.

MacLachan, P. 1985. *Sarah Plain and Tall*. NY: HarperCollins.

Milivojevic, J. (2004). *Bosnia and Herzegovina* (Enchantment of the Word, Second Series). CT: Children's Press.

Mochizuki, K. 1997. *Passage to Freedom: The Sugihara Story*. NY: Lee & Low Books.
- 1993. *Baseball Saved Us*. NY: Lee & Low Books.

Mohr, Nicholassa. 1992. *All for the Better*. NY: Steck-Vaughn.
- 1975. *El Bronx Remembered: A Novella and Stories*. NY: HarperCollins.
- 1979. *Felita*. NY: Puffin.
- 1986. *Going Home*. NY: Puffin.

MUSE magazine. Peru, IL: Carus Publishing Company/Cricket Books.

Myers, W. D. 2004. *Antarctica: Journeys to the South Pole*. NY: Scholastic.
- 1981. *At Her Majesty's Request*. NY: Scholastic.
- 1975. *Fast Sam, Cool Clyde and Stuff*. NY: Puffin.
- 2005. *The Harlem Hellfighters: When Pride Met Courage*, NY: Amistad.
- 1981. *Hoops*. NY: Bantam Doubleday Dell.
- 1982. *The Legend of Tarik*. NY: Scholastic.
- 2000. *Malcom X: A Fire Burning Brightly*, NY: HarperCollins.
- 1993. *Mop, Moondance and the Nagasaki Knights*. NY: Dell Yearling.
- 1988. *Me, Mop, and the Moondance Kid*. NY: Bantam Doubleday Dell.
- 1991. *Now Is Your Time*. NY: HarperCollins.
- 2000. *145th Street: Short Stories*, NY: Delacorte/Random House.

Namioka, L. 1992. *Yang the Youngest and His Terrible Ear*. NY: Bantam Doubleday Dell
- 1996. *Yang the Third and Her Impossible Family*. NY: Dell Yearling.
- 2004. *Half and Half*. NY: Dell Yearling.

Naylor, P. 2005. *Carlotta's Kittens*. NY: Aladdin.

Nolen, J. 1998. *Raising Dragons*. Orlando, FL: Harcourt.

Paterson, K. 1972. *Bridge to Terabithia*. NY: Harper Trophy.
- 1985. *Come Sing, Jimmy Jo*. NY: Dutton.
- 2001. *The Field of Dogs*. NY: Harper Trophy.
- 1994. *The Flip Flop Girl*. NY: Puffin.
- 1978. *The Great Gilly Hopkins*. NY: Harper Trophy.
- 1990. *Jacob Have I Loved*. NY: Harper Trophy.

Peck, R. 1998. *A Long Way from Chicago*. NY: Dial.

Peck, R. N. Soup Series. NY: Dell Yearling.
- *Soup* (1974)
- *Soup for President* (1978)
- *Soup and Me* (1975), Knopf
- *Soup's Hoop* (Rereleased 1992).
- *Soup in the Saddle* (1987)
- *Soup on Fire* (1987)
- *Soup on Ice* (1988)
- *Soup's Drum* (1988)
- *Soup on Wheels* (1986)

Pilkey, D. 1997. *Captain Underpants*. NY: Blue Sky Press/Scholastic.
- 1993. *Dogzilla*. Harcourt Brace.

Pinkey, A. D. 2002. *Ella Fitzgerald*. NY: Hyperion.
- 1998. *Duke Ellington*. NY: Hyperion.
- 2000. *Let It Shine: Stories of Black Women Freedom Fighters*. Orlando, FL: Harcourt.

Polacco, P. 1994. *Pink and Say*. NY: Penguin Putnam.

Quackenbush, R. 1999. *Daughter of Liberty*. NY: Hyperion Books.

Raskin, Ellen. 1978/1992. *The Westing Game*. NY: Dutton/Puffin.
- 1971/1989. *The Mysterious Disappearance of Leon (I Mean Noel)*. NY: Dutton/Puffin.

Reit, S. 1990. *Guns for General Washington*. Orlando, FL: Harcourt.

Rylant, C. 1995. *Van Gogh Café*. Orlando, FL: Harcourt.

Sachar, L. 2000. *Holes*. NY: Yearling/Random House.
- Marvin Redpost series (Stepping Stone books). NY: Random House
- *Marvin Redpost Alone in His Teacher's House* (1994)

- *Marvin Redpost Class President* (1999)
- *Marvin Redpost Is He a Girl?* (1993)
- *Marvin Redpost Kidnapped at Birth?* (1999)
- *Marvin Redpost Why Pick on Me?* (1993)
- 1987. *There's a Boy in the Girl's Bathroom*. NY: Dell Yearling.
- Wayside School series (more challenging) NY: Harper Trophy.
- *Sideways Stories from Wayside School* (1978)
- *Wayside School Gets a Little Stranger* (1996)
- *Wayside School Is Falling Down* (1989)

Dr. Seuss. 1971. *The Lorax*, NY: Random House.

Simon, S. 1991. *Earthquakes*. NY: William Morrow.
- 1998. *Destination Jupiter*. NY: HarperCollins.
- 1996. *Wildfires*. NY: William Morrow.
- 1993. *Wolves*. NY: HarperCollins.

Skarmeta, A. 2000. *The Composition*. Toronto, Canada: Groundwood Books.

Smith, D. B. 1973. *A Taste of Blackberries*. NY: Harper Trophy.

Snyder, Z. 1967. *The Egypt Game*. NY: Bantam Doubleday Dell.
- 1997. *The Gypsy Game*. NY: Dell Yearling.
- 1971. *The Headless Cupid*. NY: Bantam Doubleday Dell.

Sobol, D. J. Encyclopedia Brown. series. NY: William Morrow/Skylark Bantam Books.
- *Encyclopedia Brown and the Case of the Disgusting Sneakers* (1990)
- *Encyclopedia Brown, Boy Detective* (1985)
- *Encyclopedia Brown Gets His Man* (1967/1982)

Soto, G. 1990. *Baseball in April*. Orlando, FL: Harcourt.
- 1995. *Canto Familiar*. Orlando, FL: Harcourt.
- 1987. *The Cat's Meow*. NY: Scholastic.
- 1995. *Chato's Kitchen*. NY: Putnam.
- 2005. *Help Wanted*. Orlando, FL: Harcourt.
- 2002. *If the Shoe Fits*. NY: Penguin Putnam.
- 1993/2003. *Local News*. NY: Harcourt.
- 2005. *Marisol*. Madison, WI: Pleasant.
- 1992. *Neighborhood Odes*. Orlando, FL: Harcourt.
- 1992. *Pacific Crossing*. Orlando, FL: Harcourt.
- 1992. *The Skirt*. NY: Bantam Doubleday Dell.

- 1992. *Taking Sides*. Orlando, FL: Harcourt.
- 1993. *Too Many Tamales*. NY: Putnam.

Speare, E. G. 1983. *Sign of the Beaver*. NY: Bantam Doubleday Dell.

Spinelli, J. 1990. *The Bathwater Gang*. NY: Little Brown.
- 1998. *Blue Ribbon Blues: A Tooter Tale* (Stepping Stone)
- 1992. *Do the Funky Pickle* (and more School Daze series) NY: Scholastic.
- 1991. *Fourth Grade Rats*. NY: Scholastic.
- 2002. *Loser*. NY: Harper Collins.
- 1990. *Maniac Magee*. NY: Little Brown.
- 1991. *There's a Girl in My Hammerlock*. NY: Aladdin.

Stanley, D. 1992. *Bard of Avon: The Story of William Shakespeare*. NY: William Morrow.
- 1990. *Good Queen Bess*. NY: HarperCollins.
- 2000. *Michelangelo*. NY: HarperCollins.
- 2002. *Saladin: Noble Prince of Islam*. NY: HarperCollins.
- 1988. *Shaka: King of the Zulus* NY: William Morrow.

Taylor, M. D. 1998. *The Friendship*. NY: Puffin.
- 1987. *The Gold Cadillac*. NY: Puffin.
- 1981. *Let the Circle Be Unbroken*. NY: Puffin.
- 1992. *Mississippi Bridge*. NY: Dell Skylark.
- 1991. *Roll of Thunder Hear My Cry*. NY: Puffin.
- 1975. *Song of the Trees*. NY: Bantam Doubleday Dell.

TIME for Kids (TFK). NY: Time Inc.

Turner, A. 1992. *Katie's Trunk*. NY: Aladdin.

Van Allsburg, C. 1981. *Jumanji*. NY: Houghton Mifflin.

VanCleave, J. 1989. *Chemistry for Every Kid*, NY: John Wiley & Son.

Van Draanen, W. 2003. *Flipped*. NY: Alfred Knopf.
- Sammy Keyes series. NY: Dell Yearling.
- *Sammy Keyes and the Hotel Thief* (1998)
- *Sammy Keyes and the Hollywood Mummy* (2001)
- *Sammy Keyes and the Sisters of Mercy* (1999)
- *Sammy Keyes and the Skeleton Man* (1998)

Van Leeuwen, J. 2003. *The Great Googlestein Museum Mystery*. NY: Phyllis Fogelman Books/Penguin.

Warner, G. Boxcar Kids series. Morton Grove, IL: Albert Whitman.
- *The Chocolate Sundae Mystery* (1995)
- *The Hockey Mystery* (2001)
- *The Pizza Mystery* (1993)

Westrige Young Writers Workshop. 1997. *Kids Explore Kids Who Make a Difference*. Mexico: Jon Muir Publications.

White, E. B. 1952. *Charlotte's Web*. NY: HarperCollins.
- 1945. *Stuart Little*. NY: HarperCollins.

Wilson, J. 1985. *Mosaic and Tessellated Patterns*, NY: Dover.

Wilcox, C. 1993. *Mummies and Their Mysteries*. Minneapolis, MN: Carolrhoda Books.

Wrede, P. 1990/2002. The Enchanted Forest Chronicles series.
- 1990/2002. *Dealing With Dragons*. NY: Magic Carpet Books.

Woodson, J. 2000. *Miracle's Boys*. Penguin Putnam.

Zalben, J. B. 1996. *Unfinished Dreams*. NY: Simon & Schuster.

Index

phonics, 169–171
Pikulski, J. J., & Chard, D. J., 89, 182
Pikulski, J. J., & Templeton, S., 175, 178, 186
Pilgreen, J., *SSR Handbook, The: How to Organize and Manage a Sustained Silent Reading Program*, 56
Pilkey, D., *Dogzilla*, 142–145
Pinell, G. S., 200
poetry, 190
practical learning and thinking, 256–257
progress-monitoring measure, 199. *see also* assessment
Puma, M. J., Karweit, N., Price, C., Ricciutti, A., Thompson, W., & Vaden-Kiernan, M., 108

Q

Qualitative Inventory of Word Knowledge (QWIK), 208, 209
Qualitative Reading Inquiry (QRI), 202, 213, 218
Qualitative Spelling Inventory, 208
Question Answer Relationships (QAR), 81–83
question shaping, 256–257
questioning
    for comprehension, 132
    to promote deep thinking about text, 108–111
    to promote thinking about reading process, 111–113
Questioning the Author (QtA), 112
Quick Text Level Check-In (QT), 231–233
"quickwrites," 59–62

R

RAND Reading Study Group, 8, 10, 11, 12, 86, 127, 146, 182, 241
Raphael, T. E., 6–7, 69, 76
Raphael, T. E., & Au, K. H., "QAR: Enhancing Comprehension and Test Taking Across Grades and Content Areas," 81
Raphael, T. E., Kehus, M., & Damphousse, K., 56, 57
Rasinski, T. V., 89, 107, 184
Rasinski, T. V., & Padak, N., *3-Minute Reading Assessments*, 211
read-alouds, 70–73
readers: below basic, basic, proficient, 10
readers theater, 184
reading
    before, during and after, 114
    repeated, 183
reading and writing, opportunities for large amounts of, 23–24
Reading Notebook Student Rubric, The, 232
reading survey, 219–220
reciprocal teaching, 155–156
recognition, assessing word, 203–205
regulating, for comprehension, 132

Resnick, L., 140
response journals, 58–62
responses, personal, critical and creative, 57
Reyes, P., Scribner, J. D., & Scribner, A. P., 52
Rivet, 101–102
"root of the day," 188
Rosenshine, B., 108
Rosenshine, B., Meister, C., & Chapman, S., 132
Rosenthal, R., & Jacobson, L., 33
rubrics
    all-purpose, 234
    Reading Notebook Student Rubric, The, 232, 235
    response, 214
Ryder, R. J., & Graves, M. F., 202

S

Sadowski, M., 56
San Francisco Unified School District, 120
Schlagal, R., 208
Schwartz, R. M., 100
Schwartz, R. M., & Raphael, T. E., 100
screening reading assessment, 199. *see also* assessment
self-regulated learning, providing opportunities for, 153–157
semantic map, 100
seven strategies capable readers use, 132
Sewall, G. T., 90
shared reading, 95
Shefelbine, J., 175
Shefelbine, J., & Newman, K. K., 178
Shefelbine, J., & Newman, K. K., *SIPPS: System Instruction in Phoneme Awareness, Phonics, and Sight Words*, 193, 207–208
silent reading, sustained, 56–58
slicing, task, 255–256
small groups, 29–32, 35
    guidelines for starting instruction, 37–40
Smith, D. B., *Taste of Blackberries, A*, 36, 270
Smith, J. K., "Wildland Fire in Ecosystems: Effects of Fire on Fauna," 98, 105, 106
Snow, C. E., & Biancarosa, G., 11, 13, 202
Snow, C. E., Barnes, W. S., Chandler, J., Goodman, I. R., & Hemphill, L., 236
Snow, C. E., Burns, M. S., & Griffin, P., 24, 96
Snow, C., Griffin, P., & Burns, M. S., 33
Snyder, Z., *Egypt Game, The*, 148
Solomon, M., & Hendren, R.L., 127
sorts, word, 189. *see also* words
Soto, G., *Chato's Kitchen*, 160–162
Soto, G., *Too Many Tamales*, 12

spelling
    developing skills in, 185–187
    patterns, 179–180
Stanovich, K. E., 24
Stein, N. L., & Glenn, C. G., 146
Sternberg, R., 256
strategies that good readers use, 132, 215
strategy journal, 138
Strickland, D., 30–31
structures in texts, 148–150
struggling readers, 202–203
    helping with first literature discussion, 36–37
    working with, 192–193
students
    challenged, who need to be, 262–263
    culturally diverse, who are, 265–268
    support, who need extra, 263–264
summarizing
    assessment information, 259–260
    for comprehension, 132
    reading, 137
"support in advance," 272–273
syllabication, 172–173
syllables, 179–180

T

taped read-alongs, 95
task slicing and compacting, 255–256
Taylor, B. M., Frye, B. J., & Maruyama, G. M., 24
Taylor, B. M., Pearson, P. D., Clark, K., & Walpole, S., 23, 24, 29, 35, 36, 196
Taylor, B. M., Pearson, P. D., Peterson, D. S., & Rodriguez, M. C., 23, 108
teaching comprehension, 126–129. *see also* comprehension
    good readers comprehending, 129–133
    helping students acquire and use strategies, 136–140
    providing explicit instruction in comprehension strategies, 133–136
    providing opportunities for self-regulated learning, 153–157
    providing opportunities to use comprehension strategies, 141–150
Templeton, S., 185
Templeton, S., & Bear, D. R., 186
Templeton, S., & Morris, D., 187
text-level concerns, 13
text sets, 247–252
themes, integrated, 116–123
think-alouds, 70, 73–75
Time for Kids, 31, 32, 67, 102
Tomlinson, C. A., 242
topic text sets, 247–248
topics and themes, enhancing comprehension of, 104–107
Torgesen, J. K., 24, 168, 192

U

universal literary concept, 119–123

V

Valeri-Gold, M., 56
Van Draanen, W., *Flipped*, 255–256, 270
Vaughn, S., Hughes, M. T., Moody, M. W., & Elbaum, B., 29
Vermont Department of Education, 8
Villaume, S. K., & Brabham, E. G., 53, 126
Villaume, S. K., & Hopkins, I., 69
Villaume, S. K., Worden, T., Williams, S., Hopkins, L., & Rosenblatt, C., 65
visualization, for comprehension, 132
vocabulary. *see also* words
    assessing, 217–222
    developing, 96–107
Vocabulary-Language-Prediction (VLP), 102–103
Vogt, M. E., 272
Voices of the Revolution, 251–252
Vygotsky, L., 70

W

Walsh, K., 73, 116
Weber, G., 23
weekly schedules, samples, 45–46
Weinstein, R. S., 33
Wiggins, G., & McTighe, J., 41
Wilcox, C., *Mummies and Their Mysteries*, 146–147
Wilkinson, L. C., & Silliman, E. R., 71
Wixson, K. K., 88, 183, 240
Wixson, K. K., & Lipson, 240
Wood, D. J., Bruner, J. S., & Ross, G., 71
Wood, K. D., & Robinson, N., 102
word-level concerns, 12-13
word recognition, assessing, 203–205
word study stations (word work), 188–193
words. *see also* vocabulary
    basic, sophisticated, low-frequency, 97–99
    developing skills in identification, 169–181
    identifying multisyllabic, 178-179
    recognizing meaning-based elements, 181
    selecting carefully, 104–107
    sort, bank, map, 100

Z

Zigmond, N., & Baker, J., 29